DAVEY HUGHES

UNTAMED

The Extraordinary
Adventures of the
Swazi Man

RANDOM HOUSE
NEW ZEALAND

This one's for you Maggie.
For your belief in a raggedy-arsed possum trapper.

A RANDOM HOUSE BOOK published by Random House New Zealand
18 Poland Road, Glenfield, Auckland, New Zealand

For more information about our titles go to www.randomhouse co.nz

A catalogue record for this book is available from the National Library of New Zealand

Random House New Zealand is part of the Random House Group
New York London Sydney Auckland Delhi Johannesburg

First published 2011. Reprinted 2011 (twice), 2012.

ISBN 978-1-86979-439-2

Design: Megan van Staden
Cover image: Tad Gilbert
Printed in China by Everbest Printing Co Ltd

ROB SUISTED

He Tangata
He Tangata
He Tangata

It is People
It is People
It is People

Contents

STEVE LAWRIE

Preface

My wife, Maggie, has often suggested that I keep a diary of my adventures. It's truly not in my nature to do so, and I would struggle to scratch down on paper my travels, thoughts and escapades. However, her perseverance paid off and although I would at times squirm as she handed me a travel diary at the departure lounge, I got better at writing down my experiences. At her bidding I also began to record more and more trips, at first on film, then on digital media. I love those digi-cameras!

Life really is a journey; it has a beginning and an end. The piece in the middle? Well, the piece in the middle is where adventure lies. What you do with it, how you choose to live it, is entirely up to you. What follows in these pages is a slice of how I have chosen to trek through my life thus far. I would not change any of it. I believe we are where we are, and that we do what we do, by choice. If it were not so, we'd change it.

There is nothing I love more than a good story, perhaps because I enjoy being taken somewhere I have yet to visit, or more often than not, simply because I relish the thought of being entertained. I am so incredibly lucky that in my lifetime I have met many talented storytellers; even more so, that many of these storytellers have invited me to sit by their fires and listen to their yarns. They would poke at the embers, lift their heads and then, with a crooked grin, sparkling eyes and much gesticulation, let the story roll!

This is my campfire and you are most welcome to sit.

Davey Hughes
Levin, New Zealand
July 2011

‘These recollections are based on collections. All the trouble begins when you try to recollect the things you failed to collect in your diary. Down with it and done with it is the good old lead-pencil rule.’

— Dan Crawford

ROB COATS

Foreword

For seven days we had been sneaking around wilderness streams, choked with spawning salmon, deep in the old-growth rainforest of south-east Alaska. Signs of the giant coastal brown bears were in evidence at every turn and twist in the river; their large feet had made deep tracks on the sandbar, wide claw marks left fresh scars down the trees that lay across the bear trails. Suddenly we froze in step. No words were needed as we stared in awe at the carnage. We were at the very end of the stream and all the salmon lay dead, half-eaten, strewn around the gravel bar. Huge tracks marked the sand under the log jam. Our neck hair bristled. He was close, very close! As one we quietly shrank back into the lush green bush to wait . . .

Years ago, far across the Pacific, Davey Hughes heard a story about hunting bear. Not long after that, he turned up at my remote lodge in Alaska to see for himself. The very next evening we almost got chewed on by a really mad mama grizzly bear protecting her young. Since that moment we have shared a rare and uncommonly strong bond: our mutual love and respect for true humans, wild places, wild things and the thrill of the chase.

Davey is truly a remarkable self-made man. Born a Scottish Highlander and kin to the wayward wind, he landed halfway around the world in New Zealand. What better place to grow into a true outdoorsman? Young and hungry, he found himself out in the bush trapping and hunting for a

living. The long, cold, wet nights were spent cultivating his ideas for the perfect clothing. Determined to find a better way to stay warm, dry and comfortable, he developed Swazi Outdoors. Since its conception, Swazi gear has swept around the globe, providing hunters, farmers and all outdoors-minded people with clothing that works! This is why he came to me, to the deep, dark rainforest of south-east Alaska. First, to ask me if my Swazi gear worked in the harsh, wet climate, and second, to walk with the giant coastal brown bears and see if the stories were, in fact, true.

For Davey, it's not about the destination but rather the journey. His determination to seek out and share his passion with others has taken him around the world. In this book you can follow this 'mad, keen hunter' on his journey down the trail.

My father once told me: 'In the end, you'll be able to count your true friends on one hand.' Davey Hughes would be my thumb!

James M. Boyce
Alaska Master Guide
US Navy Seal School
Sitka, Alaska
February 2011

ABOVE Lakota talking stick.

ROB COATS

Almost being killed in Alaska by the three bears and setting out my mantra.

1

'If you're going to be a bear, be a grizzly bear.'

— *Danny Ellis*

On the way home from hunting Dall sheep in the Chugach Mountains in Alaska, I decided to call into Baranof Island to visit my dear old friend Jimmy Boyce. Jimmy is an experienced bear-hunting guide, and the day I arrived he was taking a client hunting. Would I like to come? The answer was obvious. At Jim's request I also took my video camera to film the hunt. And my rifle. Having walked these tight streams before, I knew things can happen fast, plus, I guess, it always pays to have a back-up. Knowing I was bringing my rifle meant Jim decided to leave his behind — our first mistake of the day.

We headed up the coast aboard Jim's boat, the *Gunsmoke*, pulling into a small bay where we unloaded the skiff and motored to the shore. Off we went upstream, Jim's client in tow. A fair walk found us above a pool holding a large number of spawning

LEFT A sow relaxes with her two young cubs in Red Bluff Bay, Baranof Island.
RIGHT The bears became quite picky eaters, either nipping the head off the salmon to feast on the brains or just eating the skins.
OPPOSITE She was, to my mind, the most beautiful creature.

silver, or coho, salmon — a place where the bears had been recently feeding, judging by the large amount of fresh salmon carcasses lying upon the bank. Jim, his client and I got ourselves set up on a root wad (the protruding roots of a big tree that had fallen over), which provided an ideal vantage point. On one side was a decent drop down to the creek.

We'd been there less than two minutes when first one, then another, young adult bear came down to feed; the largest was a male, probably weighing 250kg. He casually circled the pool, watching the salmon, waiting for his chance to grab another fish. Gradually he made his way around until he was directly underneath our wad. Less than 3 metres below us he stopped, puzzled, unsure of what had set off his warning senses. All at once he caught our wind, woofed and took off across the face at a great rate of knots.

Unfortunately he ran bang smack into a huge female grizzly bear, causing a mammoth fight. The sow chewed him up real bad. The young bear, hind leg seriously mangled and dragging at an awkward angle, crawled into the bush as the big female slowly backed off, heading back up the hill.

She was, in my mind, the most beautiful creature. Just amazing. As the wind blew through her hair, standing it on end, you could see all her muscle tone defined. She was the matriarch, her demeanour leaving no doubt who was in charge. At that moment her two adult cubs came out from the scrub, both larger than the one she had recently ripped to shreds. No wonder she had acted so aggressively.

The young adult male fed on a freshly caught salmon just below our root wad, oblivious to the fact he would soon be in a fight for his life.

By now all three bears were probably 60–70 metres away, moving their heads from side to side, taking in the scene. Meanwhile, we sat below minding our own business — or so we thought. That's where the big female spotted us. Within seconds her tone of indifference became yet again one of aggression. She huffed, puffed and chomped on her teeth, woofing all the time.

Jim's client and I were blocking Jim's view of the events, so he asked what was happening.

'Well, Jim,' I said. 'It's like this, matey. We are in the shit.'

The female began pulling out logs, rolling forest debris and creating quite a spectacle. All the time she was moving that massive head of hers from side to side. She was pissed off, and wanted us to know it. Down the hill she advanced, her cubs following. As if this wasn't alarming enough, one of her cubs — possibly a male — seemed incredibly belligerent, salivating as he ground those large canine teeth.

In bear language, well . . . not good.

As they kept coming, I put away my video camera and took up the rifle, a weapon with bullets big enough to worry sheep, but not three charging grizzlies. The bears lumbered down the hill, not quickly but with deadly intent. My world slowed. The decisions I would make in the next few seconds would be pivotal. A week earlier I'd been talking with a great Alaskan hunter, Gary LaRose, who had once had his face badly chewed up by a bear. Gary's advice still rang in my ears: 'If grizzlies get within 50 metres, Davey, don't fire a warning shot, they're so darn quick you won't get the next one away.'

I said to myself, when they get to 20 metres I'm going to shoot. But which one? Nothing would be worse than wavering, as that would more than likely lead to missing all of them.

So I waited and waited, choosing alternatively between the Stroppy Young Male and Big Mama. But which one? All three were now within the range I'd set. I had to act. Maybe if I shot her, maybe, just maybe, I'd have time to get another round into the chamber. If the cub kept coming, then I'd have to shoot him as well, more than likely off the end of my barrel.

Then as the bears hit the 15-metre line a different thought entered my head. *It doesn't have to end this way. I really do not want to shoot any of these animals*. With that in mind, I steadied my rifle and in a strong yet stern voice, told the charging bears I was the meanest, darkest, most desperado son of a goddamned bitch ever to walk the face of the earth. I was also heavily armed and incredibly dangerous. If Big Mama knew what was best for her and her cubs, she'd get the hell out of Dodge.

An answer to the time-eternal question of whether bears do so in the woods.

And so they stopped. They turned and re-entered the forest. We breathed out in unison.

'Whoa! That was interesting.' Jim, a graduate of the US Navy Seal school, is one of the most laid-back bastards I know.

However, much like a movie, and a bad one at that, the baddie returned. The sow left her cubs in the scrub and was coming back for more. This time she meant business; you could see it in her small pig-like eyes. I realised now I'd have to do something. The adrenaline returned in a rush. Some days at the office you don't require an EpiPen shot to get the system going.

When she was within 15 metres I was ready to fire. Closer and closer. This was it. No turning back. It's her or us. Then, as if the gods of Alaska were looking out for us, her male cub came out from the undergrowth, right underneath her, and collided with her. No! This couldn't be happening! That cub got one hell of a hiding. We heard her laying into him in the low scrub as she chased him, caught him, then chased him again.

It didn't take the three of us long to decide it was for the best that *we* actually got the hell out of Dodge. We boulder-hopped out of that creek pretty damn quick. It was just on dark, not the best time to be walking out of a bear-laden creek.

You don't have to pull the trigger. You can talk.

The lesson I learnt? When your finger's on the trigger — or a decision has to be made, whether it's to do with an animal, an employee or a family member — you can sometimes just lower your rifle. You don't have to pull the trigger. You can talk.

Sometimes people shoot far too quickly. Go with your gut. Nine times out of 10 you'll find there's time to sit down and come to an arrangement, agreement or negotiation that benefits everyone. Something that surely beats hurting someone or making them upset. Or worse, having them sue your arse.

However, if you are going to pull the trigger, remember the mantra. If you don't know the mantra, don't worry too much, I'm going to tell you all about it.

ABOVE Blue Wildebeest. I don't know why, but they never appear so big on brainpower. Maybe that's just my perception of these strange-looking, good-tasting beasts. I do believe I'm right, but no doubt someone somewhere has a pet wildebeest which they have trained to perform all manner of party tricks. Tanzania.

LEFT They are just BIG. One wonders just how they can get enough food to sustain themselves each mid-winter day in the frozen north. That they do is testimony to how tough the old moose really is. Peace River, Canada.

BELINDA WALSHE

Learning how to hunt in the Wellington hills, dropping out of school and breaking my mother's heart.

2

PIGS AND POSSUMS

So where did all this madness begin? How did a boy from the sticks of little old New Zealand end up spending his days hollering at grumpy old grizzlies in Alaska? How could such a trip, one of the 14 times I've hunted Alaska, feel as familiar as driving from Levin to Paraparaumu?

That one of my first memories was the sound of wild bush pigs rubbing against the weatherboards of our house may explain a few things. My dad, Brian, had no idea how to stop them. Not that a plumber from the Isle of Man would. We lived in Wainuiomata, through the Hutt Valley and over the hill from Wellington. Back then, in the 1960s, Wainuiomata was known as Nappy Valley. It was chocka block full of first-generation Kiwis, a place out of the city where families could afford to buy their first homes. Saturday mornings we woke to the sound of concrete mixers. When it was your driveway's turn, half the neighbourhood would show

OPPOSITE To stand on a mountain, leaning on your musket, feeling the icy breeze on your legs? Why, you're a laird my friend.

up with wheelbarrows, shovels and empty beer flagons.

To most people, Wainuiomata was just a great big subdivision. But for me it was the most incredible place: the rivers full of trout and eels and the bush coming right down to the edge of our property. I found the presence of wild pigs, possums and deer exciting as hell. I dreamt they lived in my room. Under my bed actually. My father didn't share my enthusiasm. Eventually, when the little runts became a problem, he tried to take them out with a bread knife and a bastard file. Unsuccessfully. Not long after that episode, I befriended a hard-case Maori hunter named Tui, who lived across the road. He sorted them out and then taught me a few tricks about how to do it myself.

OPPOSITE The Hughes family growing up in Wainuiomata.

It was little wonder my father lacked bush skills. In the United Kingdom, hunting was a class thing. But here in New Zealand, British electricians and bricklayers were all of a sudden part of the land and able to do whatever they wanted. For many that included hunting — though not in my father's case. It just wasn't his scene; mainly, I guess, because he and Mum were busy raising five kids. In fact, I think Dad and I have only been in the bush together two or three times. The first was when we trapped possums for pocket money. One day, as primary-school kids, we'd snagged this huge dark-brown possum but couldn't kill it. It was making such a ruckus in the trap none of us wanted to go near it. I had to go all the way back home and ask if Dad could help us. So he came up the hill with his hammer and whacked the possum on the head. On ya, Dad.

Dad preferred having a beer and watching football (the round ball) over hunting, which is not to say he wasn't supportive. Any sport my brothers and sisters took up he followed religiously, often joining committees and helping run the club. Not a Saturday morning went by without Dad running up and down the sidelines, something by no means exclusive to our family. Wainuiomata is well known for its enthusiasm for sport, particularly rugby. Famous All Blacks from the area include Piri Weepu and Tana Umaga; the Waldrom brothers (Scott and Thomas) play for the Hurricanes and New Zealand Maori respectively. And what about the Australian NRL Grand Final in 2005? Each team contained a former member of the Wainuiomata Rugby League Club. It would be easy to put the town's sporting success down to something in the water, but a more truthful reason would be a community which trains and coaches young kids, and gives of its time so freely.

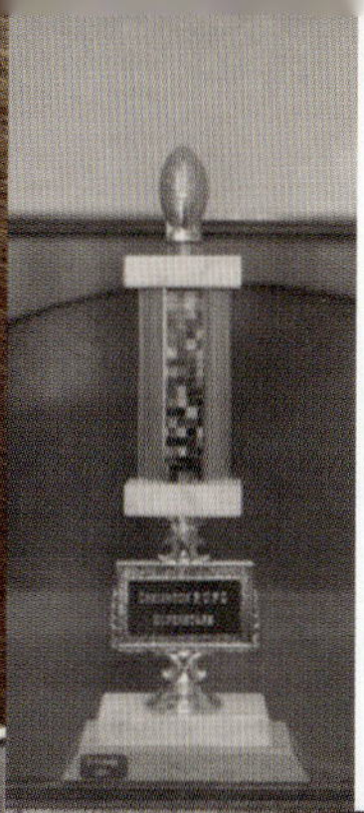

JAN • 62

113

Surrounded by hills and boasting warmer-than-average summers (and, less enviably, colder-than-average winters), Wainuiomata had been growing in popularity as a place for young families to settle since the end of the Second World War. My parents opted for this town in 1962, emigrating from Glasgow when I was 18 months old. My father was a Manxman, a nickname for someone from the Isle of Man. He wanted something better for his family and left his job as a plumber at the Clyde River shipworks to cross the world in search of that better life.

My mother, Jean, was Scottish and part of the Gunn clan, our heritage going right back to the Orkney Islands. The Clan Gunn claims direct descent from Gunni, grandson of Sweyn Asleifsson, the 'Ultimate Viking' and hero of the Orkneyinga Saga. *Ahhh!* The grand Orkneyinga Saga — loyalty to the clan, to one's family — is everything to all Scotsmen with bloodlines north of Perthshire. We are an incredibly tribal people. It defines who we are. To give you an example of the strength of those ties, we Gunns had a blood feud with those treacherous Keith sons of bitches that went back to 1478. A treaty of friendship was signed in 1978. 'Twas

Are milk boys made out of milk? Stephen and me doing the rounds for Trev Lahood, back in the days when your milk *and* your bread were delivered to the letterbox. I do believe those shoes are trendy again.

but a wee feud, lasting a mere 500 years. And those low-life tadpoles, those yellow-belly Keiths? Why, they are our friends!

My grandmother was Burmese, a short wee woman with skin as dark as mahogany. She met my maternal grandfather, a tall Scotsman, while he was in Burma (now Myanmar).

Stephen was the eldest in our clan, followed by me, John, Angela and

Diana. I looked up to Stephen, who owned a V8 by the time he was 16. By today's standards ours would have been a large family, but in those days five or six kids was the norm. While we always looked out for each other, we all had mates our own age. By the time I was nine my gang and I were heading up the Orongorongo River — the Rongas — in the Rimutaka Range, which came right down to the edge of the suburb and separated Wainui from the Wairarapa. Thrilled by such freedom, we would race home from school as soon as possible. We were always in the bush. Come dinner time you could hear the cacophony of bells and whistles as parents called their kids home. Everyone knew their own call. Certainly, much like sheepdogs, we knew Dad's whistle. Half an hour later, we would have sprinted through the bush, and a hot dinner would be served.

LEFT Dad at the start of the 'Gutbuster' track leading up and on to the Five Mile Track, Rimutakas.
RIGHT Seated, my grandfather, Thomas Hughes, with his brother, John, and sister, Nellie.

Wainuiomata's isolation may have taken some getting used to for my parents, but having access to the Rimutakas made it a magic place to grow up. When I was six I climbed over the ridge from Wainui and peered down at Wellington Harbour. Damn it all, if I didn't feel like Captain James Cook. I was discovering! That simple childhood act of climbing a tree and seeing Somes Island made me realise there was another world out there. That was all I would need: to climb every ridge and see what was on the other side. So for the past 45 years that's what I've been doing — climbing ridges.

We spent our days building tree forts and doing things that nowadays would be frowned upon, including chopping down an awful lot of native trees. We constructed dug-outs in the hillsides, digging shallow caves, and in the process chopping down manuka or small beech trees to fortify our new pa. We'd put a roof on each one, line it with tree ferns and pour sod back on top. The biggest challenge was making them look as natural as possible so they could be hidden from other kids. Nothing could top having a secret pa. I've gone back to these scenes of my boyhood and searched the hills around Wainui for those forts. Hard to tell 40 years on where exactly they were built. The country changes; a most powerful lesson even for an old bush hand. The bush mates' bounces back so quickly, and no damage is done in the long term plus the outcome is a bunch of independent kids in the meantime.

My buddies and I started hunting possums before moving on to pigs, hoping one day we'd be old enough to own our own guns and shoot deer. Every now and then — if you were lucky — there'd be an invitation to join one of your mates' fathers on a proper hunt. It was the stuff of our wildest imaginings, going on a real hunt. We'd bring home a couple of deer, maybe a pig or two, then distribute the meat throughout the hood. After swapping a few kilos of meat, the men would sit around the flagon, the talk focusing on the hunt. Then they'd roughly tousle your hair and say, 'And the boys helped us carry all the meat out.'

Yes, I know what it was like to have lived the life of a hunter 10,000 years ago, for the feelings are exactly the same. Exactly.

One of my nicknames at St Bernard's College in Lower Hutt was Schitz because people couldn't quite put a finger on me. You could have called me a maverick, but in saying that, I got on well with most of my teachers. Which isn't to say I didn't challenge them. I did, a lot. I wasn't great at studying and hated homework, but at that school if you avoided either, out came the cane. Some guys were caned virtually every day. That was the other thing I remember people asking when I went through school: 'How many times did you get caned, Hughesy?'

I never got caned once. Maybe I was good at hiding the fact I hadn't done my homework. Or just maybe some animals you don't want to beat.

In boys' schools — especially high schools — there is a class system, including nerds, brainy kids and sports jocks. Then there are the bullies, that group of people who love nothing better than picking on those who can't stand up for themselves. I never really fitted into any one particular group. And I wasn't one to want to hang out with bullies; they were arseholes then and they're arseholes now.

One of my teachers was an American dude who drove a great big V12 Jag. He was an accountant, and I firmly believed he was on the run from the FBI. My folks met up with him at school for a parent–teacher evening during my fifth form year, at the end of which my mother arrived home in tears having been told that the likelihood of her son getting School C would be the equivalent of the teacher pissing up a rope. Not great timing, as the national exams were to be sat the following week. My teacher's exact words were: 'He's going to be picking shit with the chickens for the rest of his life.' He was probably right. My aggregate book-keeping score for the year was 4 per cent. Not really top of the class . . . and definitely not enough to impress a guy on the run from the FBI, it would appear.

Definitely not enough to impress a guy on the run from the FBI, it would appear.

Despite being an incredibly strong woman, my mother, Jean, broke down, mainly because failing at a private school was not an option as far as she was concerned. She worked nights at the Griffin's biscuit factory just so I could go there. Youth, as they say, is wasted on the young. It wasn't until years later that I appreciated what my mother had done so I could get a decent education. All I remember is the free marshmallows she got from work!

But bugger that teacher. How dare he upset my mother in such a manner? I studied hard. A whole year's curriculum crammed into five days. I sailed through, and taught myself a good lesson about boys. About lighting a fire under their arse.

While St Bernard's was a strict school, that didn't mean there was any lack of disorder. We had a few fights. Arriving at a new school where I

Outside 113 Gartcraig Road, Glasgow, the house where I was born.

hardly knew a soul, mine was on my first day. It was very much Robin Hood and Little John. It involved a classmate called Chris Hawkey and a scuffle over a doorway. I was going one way and Chris the other.

He decided to put his hand out and say, 'Step aside.'

I decided I wasn't stepping aside for anyone, especially on my first day.

Then he said, 'I don't think so, mate.' And next thing there was a tremendous fight.

Neither of us was going to give an inch, though gradually we both realised we were running out of puff and nobody was going to win. So we jumped up, shook hands and became the best of mates.

Of all the guys at St Bernard's, it was Chris who shared my love of hunting. Nearly everyone else at school was in a rugby team. The college was run by Marist Brothers, and if you didn't play our national game you'd better have a bloody good excuse and a pretty darned comprehensive note from your mum and dad. Then maybe, just *maybe*, they'd let you play soccer. All I ever wanted to do was skive off into the bush and hunt. There's always one weirdo.

I guess I've always enjoyed being a bit different. Being different is good, and a love of hunting was never something I felt I should hide. There were a few teachers at school who were keen bushgoers, so school tramps were not uncommon, but more often than not Chris and I'd escape by ourselves. Chris's family owned farms out the back of Cheviot, in the South Island, and he had been on a few hunts. He'd shot his first deer at the age of 12 and he had a little bit of knowledge as a result.

I can still remember the first time we headed off hunting together, without adults showing us what to do. We were in the fourth form, 14 years old. We caught a train to Levin and a taxi to the Tararuas. Our plan was to head up the Ohau River valley, cross the main range, then drop down to Masterton. Once there we could catch a train back to the Hutt Valley. To get the train to Levin, however, we'd have to get to Wellington. So here we were, two 14-year-old kids — who really shouldn't own knives or guns — walking down Lambton Quay to get some money from the National Bank in Manners Street. It's hard to believe, but we walked in with guns hanging over our shoulders. I had a .303 and Chris carried a BSA Majestic .243 and no one said a thing. Were we as a nation more accepting and tolerant, or just naive and innocent? Nowadays you can't even walk into a bank wearing a motorcycle helmet.

Job done, it was then time to jump on the train bound north. We lay our rifles on the mesh racks above the seats, where civil servants' briefcases normally went. Despite the more relaxed attitude to guns in the 1970s, a firearms licence was still necessary. You had to be 16 before you were allowed to own or carry a rifle, but we always managed to find a spare one somewhere. I must have looked at least 16 because no one ever asked to see a licence.

Chris and I did this same hunting trip several times. On Monday mornings, when we were catching up with our schoolmates after the weekend, those in the first XV would say, 'Oh yeah, you know, we drew with St Pat's! What'd you guys get up to?'

'Oh man!' we'd reply. 'We saw three deer! We didn't shoot any, but we saw three. We're getting closer and closer!'

Finally one Monday morning we were able to say we had shot our first deer. Our first kill was at a place called Quoin, off Renata Ridge in the Tararuas. I guess you could say we were poaching in the water catchment area but at 14 we didn't know any better. Okay, we knew where we were, it's just we were so certain there'd be deer there. We snuck down to the 'waterworks', spied a mob, and next thing you know: Bang, boom, bang!

Much like your first love, you never forget that first animal. Or the smell of gun smoke and the immense sense of pride you get from bringing home your kill. How many shots? Unfortunately, I was firing shots for a long time — it took 13. I still remember pulling the trigger, thankful, despite using so much ammo, that the first bullet had mortally wounded the hind. We just thought we should keep on shooting. Thirteen rounds later, we were sitting on top of the deer hooting and hollering. Just about every piece of meat had a bullet hole in it, but we didn't care. We cut it up, dragged it out of the bush and went home on the train.

What a feeling being able to offer meat to your friends and family, a part of hunting which still attracts me today. The meat wasn't for us; the meat was for the community. To this day I give away three-quarters of what I shoot.

In 1976, halfway through sixth form, I'd had enough. Even though going to a private school was a luxury my siblings had been denied, I decided to call it quits. My mate Mike Gordon, who shared my love of adventure and a passion for the outdoors, and I hatched a plan: flag school, buy a couple of horses, travel around the North Island and find farm work wherever we could. It was decided. The next day I marched into the headmaster's office and told Brother Arnold my news. When he asked if I was sure — Yes! — he mused: 'Academically, Davey, you could further yourself — with a little effort — you're not a dullard, boy. So, the world beckons you now? Ah well, good luck, follow your dreams.'

Arnold was a good bastard. People talk about living their dreams, about following them. For me the best dreams are the ones I have while I'm still awake. Fact is, when I wake up in the morning I can't recall any dreams. Maybe that's why I dream so much during the day.

Relieved, I walked outside to find Mike eating his lunch.

'Did you do it?' he asked excitedly.

'Yep, sure did,' I replied. 'Your turn.'

'Davey,' he stammered. 'I've been thinking, mate . . . I can't do it!'

Sonnavabitch.

My decision to leave school must been a wrench for Mum, though she didn't appear to know about it until four or so days later. My first job as a fitter's mate at Feltex in Wainui required me to wear blue overalls and as I left the house one morning her confusion was clear.

'Where are you going?' she asked.

'Work,' I replied.

'You don't go to school anymore?'

'No, Mum, not for the last week!'

Six months later I got the sack. Feltex was in the process of moving its milling plant from Gracefield to Wainui, during which time we all worked pretty damn hard. There was always overtime and Saturday morning work. But I refused to clock in on Saturday afternoons. I'd taken up playing rugby and found I really loved the game. The manager at Feltex, a Pom who loved soccer, gave me an ultimatum: give up rugby and work Saturday arvos, or lose my job. The union (not the rugby union) got involved and Feltex paid me two weeks' wages. Despite having earned good money — and being slightly pissed off about my sacking —

I realised it was time to move on.

With my severance pay I bought one of the only suits I've ever owned and scored a job at Compton Advertising in Wellington. The next year taught me a lot about the advertising production game. I was a quick learner and Wellington was a small town. It wasn't long before an opportunity arose to work at the exotic-sounding Carlton Carruthers du Chateau in Ghuznee Street. I was hired as a production assistant, and not long afterwards the production manager was laid low with a long-term ailment. So, at the age of 17, I became the acting production manager. Determined not to make a mistake, I worked hard. Frickin' hard.

The Dude. Outside our house in Karaka Street, Wainui, aged 15 or 16.

My role was to deal with creatives (who dreamt up ads) and account managers (who sold the idea to clients) before taking those concepts and turning them into advertising. Production managers need to think on their feet and move quickly. Most campaigns were well thought out, but every so often one came out of left field and mistakes were not an option. In such a game as advertising, there were those in the wings who were jealous, pedantic or just straight A-grade arseholes. A 17-year-old kid running the production at a large agency? Clients such as adidas, Cadbury? . . . Downright preposterous! And so I worked harder.

It was a well-paid gig — and one that allowed me to hoof a ball about on Saturday afternoons — but I decided that if I wanted to travel it was now or never. When I turned 18 I bought a one-way ticket to London, where I would live on Mars bars, become engaged to be married, and be very nearly killed by a mad Dutchman.

How to skin a mountain lion

Fresh tracks of a large lion made in the snow.

First, you must catch your lion! I've been on four lion hunts all up and while we'd treed cats, never once did I have the inclination to actually shoot one with anything other than a camera. That all changed when I hunted in British Columbia with my good friend Cam Lancaster. On the tenth and final day of our hunt we treed Mr Pumpkinhead himself.

Lion hunters are a special breed. I love them. Love their smelly hounds, early starts (up and out by 3.30 am most mornings to cut tracks) and camaraderie. Cat hunters hunt; there is absolutely nothing else in life of any consequence. To them, the sound of hounds on the chase, echoing around some huge snow-clad basin, is pure magic. Like most hunters, they have an extremely close affinity to the game they pursue. It

OPPOSITE Face off. LEFT Stopping for a well-earned brew of tea. Travelling cross country on my snow machine was jarring with three broken ribs. My Canuck buddies just told me to toughen up!

Above us we could hear the hounds giving voice. Getting to them was going to be hard work.

He was dead, he just hadn't realised it.

is no disrespect to call a cat pumpkin-headed, especially if his head really is that big.

On this particular hunt I was using one of my all-time favourite calibres, the venerable .38-55 in a lever action: big heavy slug, 250gr (grain) travelling at a slow 1800fps (feet per second). A real old dunga! Firing one is like throwing a brick, however; big and slow does the damage. I centred on the cat's chest and squeezed off from about 15 metres. Down he came. Wow. So that's what the term 'like a cut cat' means. I turned him at the base of a tree with a Hail Mary shot and he spun, heading off down the mountain in huge bounds, that long tail giving him balance as he quickly put distance between us.

Cam turned. 'Did you even hit him *once*, Kiwi?'

For a split second I ran some doubt software through my central processor. Did I? Didn't I? Like hell I didn't. I smacked him fair and clear in the chest. 'He's dead, Cam. He just don't know it.'

And he was. Two hundred metres down the mountain we found him, not moving. I wept. A tear for the cat, a tear for my soul and a tear for the bond between Cam and myself.

Skinning a cat is not all that hard, nor different from, say, skinning a bear. Here's a quick one-two on skinning your cat after you've weighed him. Put all your lines in first. Down the inside of the hind legs, across the front legs and then all the way down the belly. Now draw your knife line all the way down the tail. By putting in all your cut lines first they'll be nice and straight, good and accurate. Your taxidermist will appreciate this, trust me! Now you can begin taking the skin off the legs, leaving the paws and claws intact at the last knuckle. Take the head off at about the second vertebra; you can cape it out later.

I tend to do most of the fine work where I can relax on a seat and get as good a job done as possible. Sip a brew, tell a yarn. You want to be able to look at those paws and claws in 15 years' time and not squirm at the rush job you did on the hill. Down to the tail, take your time here, you're nearly finished.

Now, don't throw away the back steaks. Mountain lion is pretty darn good eating. If, like me, you believe you take on some of the spirit and characteristics of the animal when you eat it, then you will enjoy this meal even more. If you don't, well hell, it does taste bloody good all the same!

Russ Bouver, a Canadian hunter with a big heart and a great sense of humour.

Working for a laird in the Scottish Highlands and learning about manhood from a bunch of hard-out guys.

3

HIGHLAND HI-JINKS

I arrived in London in February 1978, having left behind a beautiful Kiwi summer. In some ways it was love that carried me across the world, in the form of Teresa, a Pommie girl I'd met back home. I had 145 quid in my back pocket and a place to crash at Elephant and Castle with Teresa, her sister and brother. Before long I scored a job at Tavistock International Advertising, which had juicy accounts with clients such as Benson & Hedges and a few large Scottish distilleries. I joined a rugby team, too, playing fullback with the London Wasps club.

But London was suffocating me. I needed wide open spaces and the outdoors. Then one day at New Zealand House in Haymarket I saw an advertisement in the *New Zealand News UK* for an experienced fencer, who could also do some tree planting, based in the Highlands. I rang the number. What experience did I have, they asked.

'Heaps!' I replied. 'It's exactly what I used to do back home!'

'Well, jump on a train, laddie,' they replied.

So Teresa and I went our separate ways, having decided we were far too young to get involved in anything serious. I packed my boots and bags, and looked forward to discovering the country of my birth.

Everything about being in Scotland was wonderful. As soon as I crossed the border from England into the Scottish Lowlands, the soil was different, the people were different. When I arrived I felt like kissing the ground. I was home. To this day Scotland feels like home and I always stop north of Carlisle to kiss the ground, as I do in Auckland when I return from a trip abroad.

The town of Aviemore, where I was headed, lies around 145km north of Edinburgh, and around 60km south of Inverness, within the Cairngorms National Park. It's popular for skiing and other winter sports, and for hill-walking in the Cairngorm Mountains. When I jumped off the train there was snow everywhere. But I wasn't here to ski; I was here to begin a job that I had no idea how to do. Badenoch Land Management was run by a bloke called Jamie Williamson, who was married to a Kiwi, and, luckily for me, only ever employed Kiwis.

London, with its large population and crowded streets, was beginning to suffocate me and I knew I'd have to move on for my own sanity.

I met the foreman, a man mountain named Neil Rasmussen, who in turn introduced me to the rest of the crew. These guys were tough bastards and lived in an American-type trailer home outside the town. The day I arrived they had just got back from a two-month stint up north in the Highlands. They had been fencing in the middle of nowhere, and were back in town to collect their pay, eat and drink. And drink. And drink. I was looking at a bunch of hung-over good keen men lying about in a caravan.

Neil introduced me as the new guy: 'Boys, this here is the new bastard. He looks young and he is. I dunno how long he'll last, probably not too long.'

A pretty fine introduction, one which I heard Neil deliver a few more times over the ensuing year.

'Do you want a beer, mate?' someone asked.

'No, thanks,' I replied. 'I don't drink beer.' (I still don't to this day.)

'Have a whisky then,' he persisted.

'No, I'm fine thanks,' I replied.

Neil looked up at the boss. 'Why the fucking hell did you bring a young prick here who doesn't even fucking drink? God, he's already proving he's as useless as tits on a fucking bull. Now you'll expect me to teach him everything!'

Jamie's answer made me even more apprehensive: 'You don't need to teach him a thing — he's an experienced fencer.'

That night a huge snowstorm hit, and by morning a drift had blocked the caravan door. We couldn't open it. Neil reached for his chainsaw. I offered to climb through the caravan window. I squeezed through, dug the snow away, and opened the door. Neil had found a use for me.

As a result of the extreme weather, not a lot of fencing could be done. But once we cracked into it, Neil picked up pretty damn quick that I didn't know what I was doing and warned me I'd better learn quickly. Actually, that's putting it mildly; his actual words were: 'If you don't listen to what I tell you, I'm going to kick your arse so hard.'

I learnt quickly.

Kiwis give it a crack. We always have. We're brought up that way. We give it our best. Even though, as they say, common sense is not very common, Kiwis possess a fair bit of it. Years later, it's heartening to see many young New Zealanders still working on farms around the UK, fencing, shearing and dairying.

I soon clicked that when you're away in some obscenely isolated Highland location, working solid for months at a time, the only thing to do upon return to base is spend your pay cheque and live it up for a couple of days. We were always hanging out to be paid. Sure, we averaged £45 a week, but typically there was always some article of clothing to buy — boots, new socks, a warmer jacket — and the rest of our pay we blew on single malt whisky. Well, malt whisky for the first day, cheap booze thereafter!

With Christmas looming, and broker than broke, Neil and I told Jamie we'd like to borrow the 8-ton truck and a few chainsaws. Jamie asked what we needed them for. We replied it was best he didn't know. We went down to the Forestry Commission nursery, where trees — three to four years old — now stood around 2 metres tall. Once there, the race was on to cut them down. We threw them on the back of the truck,

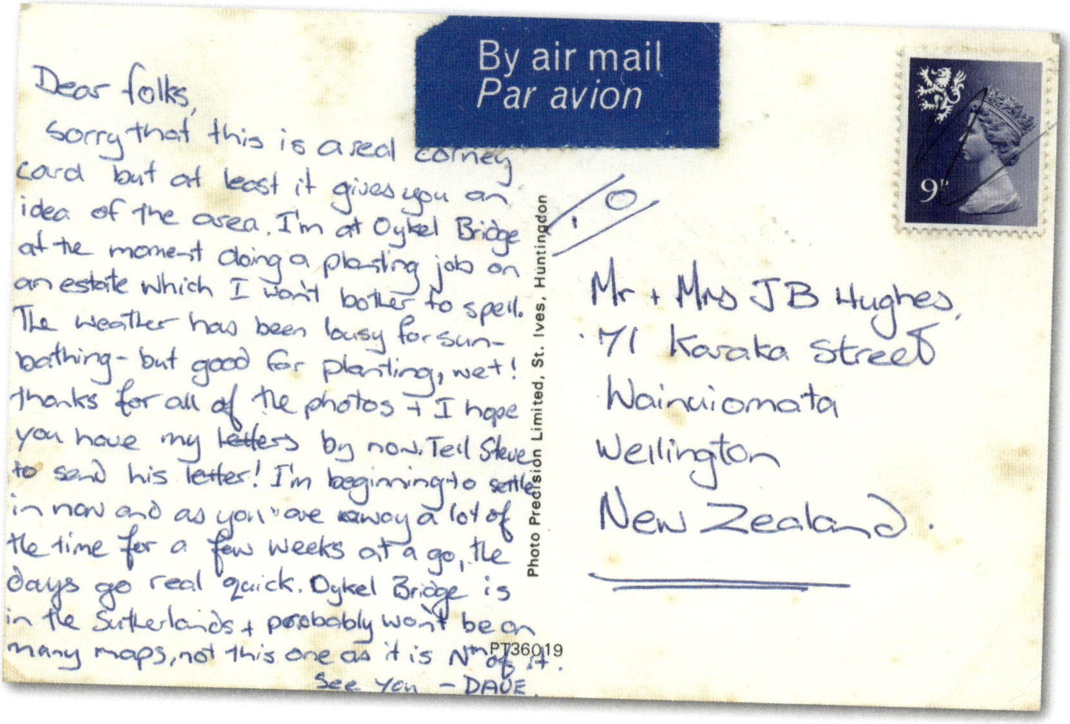

By air mail
Par avion

Dear folks,

Sorry that this is a real corney card but at least it gives you an idea of the area. I'm at Oykel Bridge at the moment doing a planting job on an estate which I won't bother to spell. The weather has been lousy for sun-bathing - but good for planting, wet! thanks for all of the photos + I hope you have my letters by now. Tell Steve to send his letter! I'm beginning to settle in now and as you're away a lot of the time for a few weeks at a go, the days go real quick. Oykel Bridge is in the Sutherlands + probably won't be on many maps, not this one as it is Nth of it.

See you - DAVE

Mr + Mrs JB Hughes,
71 Karaka Street
Wainuiomata
Wellington
New Zealand.

Photo Precision Limited, St. Ives, Huntingdon

PT36019

ABOVE Postcards became a quick way to get a message home to say I was still alive and doing okay.

drove to Inverness and sold them as Christmas trees for five quid each. Good coin, considering we had a few hundred of these things! With a £1000 worth of notes stuffed in our pockets, we filled the truck with diesel and dropped it back, with Jamie none the wiser. Back in town, we went straight to the pub, where, propped against the bar, was a team of Forestry Commission lads. They were not small guys. They were each six-foot-six Highlanders, and they looked utterly miserable.

We rocked up and asked, 'Why so glum?'

'Some bastard's been doon to the nursery, chopped doon all the fucking trees!' they lamented.

'Bastards! Och well,' we replied. 'You'd better have a drink on us.'

Another time, out the back of a place called Aberlour, we were once again skint and hungry. When I was a kid, one of my heroes was John Wayne. I love the movie *Hatari!*, in which Wayne is in Africa capturing live animals from his jeep. I described to Neil how Wayne bolted his seat onto the front of the truck and drove around lassoing lunch. A hungry Neil was keen to try yet another one of my hair-brained schemes. We stripped the Land Rover, got an old tractor seat and

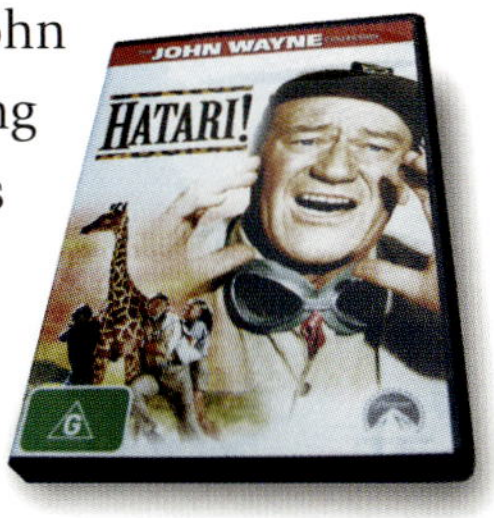

bolted it to the front above the bumper. Then we got a decent long stick, put a noose on it, and drove up and down paddocks trying to capture a sheep. These were not flat paddocks. These were stuck-on-the-side-of-a-mountain type paddocks. It took a few hours but we finally caught a sheep and butchered it up. We were pretty damned proud of ourselves. It was all gone in two days.

At the time, we were building a deer fence, so I suggested we chase down a few roe deer who'd wandered into the now-finished enclosure. We were young, fit and dumb, and we chased two deer for a few hours until finally they were running along the edge of the fenceline. As I crouched by a log with a pair of deadly accurate fencing pliers, Neil, panting as he ran, drove them towards me. I jumped up and smacked them in the head with the pliers — whack, whack, quick as you like — killing them both stone dead. Tarzan of the Highlands. We cooked the venison up in the caravan.

On another day we were repairing stock fences in picturesque Pitlochry, which was rather dangerously about half a kilometre from the local pub. On the other side of the road was a bloke doing a similar job. Wearing nothing but a kilt and a tam-o'-shanter, this rogue of the Highlands sported long red hair, bulging chest, bicep and thigh muscles, and must have been about six foot six. I couldn't resist.

Part of the deer fence we built outside Aberlour.

'Hey, sparrow! Race you to the pub, mate. Last one there buys the rounds!' I called out.

He beat us. As we entered this tiny drinking hole, Braveheart eyed the top shelf and pointed to a mind-numbingly long line of whiskys, 20 or 30 bottles in all. *Uisge beatha*. Water of life.

He grabbed the bottle at the start of the row and said, 'We'll start . . . here.'

Before long we were as pissed as chooks but nevertheless Neil insisted on getting to the end of the row of Scotland's finest. Then, of course, he insisted on driving back to camp.

Our old Land Rover. I'm sorry, Betsy, for all the hard times we gave you.

To get to our caravan, we had to negotiate our way through nine sets of gates, an occupational hazard when you are living near a castle on an illustrious estate run by a laird — a suspicious laird, who'd been watching our every move over the past month. Upon reaching the first gate, I jumped out, dutifully opened it, waited for the Land Rover (which we named Betsy) to drive through, shut it and then jumped back in the cab. As you do. But Neil was losing patience. I hopped out at the next gate and just as I was about to open it he said, 'Davey, I've got a better idea. We've got to rebuild these gates next week. Sit on the front and hang on whatever you do!'

He smashed the next eight gates to smithereens, leaving them little more than matchsticks. I had wood splinters all through my face. Neil thought it was a great joke. I was in a hell of a lot of pain. Minutes later, a tractor appeared over the hill, driven by a dude dressed in a satin dressing gown and slippers, and wielding a shotgun. It was the laird himself.

'You fucking Kiwi heathens! You bastards! You fucking nomads!' The shotgun was pointed directly at us. 'Get off my land before I give you a taste of what I'm viewing!'

I extracted myself from the bonnet of the jeep and Neil drove all the way back to Aviemore, abandoning the caravan.

To his credit, Jamie, himself a son of a laird and once classmates with Prince Charles, was very tolerant of our escapade. When we warned him trouble was imminent, he calmly suggested we go back and pick up the caravan.

'We're not going back! The crazy bastard has got a shotgun and it's loaded!' we replied.

'Come on,' Jamie said. 'Bloody stand up for yourselves. Give me a hand to pick up this caravan.'

In trepidation we drove all the way back to the castle. Inside, wolfhounds lay in front of a roaring fire and the laird sat like a king, dressed in all his finery. I couldn't help but look at the guns surrounding him. Nice guns, matey, er, your lordship. With heads down and tails between our legs, Jamie dragged us to the fireplace. The laird glared at us.

He's going to shoot us now.

'About last night . . .'

Oh God, don't drag us through all that again.

'I'm sorry for running you off. What you guys did was the sort of thing I would have done when I was a young fellow. Will you have a whisky with me?'

So there we were, four grown men, pissed as newts, hooning through this guy's estate smashing his gates.

So we got pissed again! As if this wasn't bizarre enough, he added, 'You missed a couple of gates last night. Let's go get them.'

Woo hoo!

So there we were, four grown men, pissed as newts, hooning through this guy's estate smashing his gates. And the next day we rebuilt them.

Though Neil may have enjoyed some of what the Highlands had to offer, one thing he couldn't stand were snakes, which were not an entirely uncommon sight, particularly adders. One night we returned to the caravan, jumped into our beds and then I saw a snake. Thinking about it later, it was probably just a sock, but after a few of the Highlands' best it wasn't easy to tell the difference. Neil sprang onto the tabletop, demanding to know the snake's whereabouts. I ripped the caravan apart but couldn't find it.

'It must have gone in one of the holes in the wall,' I said.

Well, Neil sprinted off that table like you wouldn't believe; he didn't even touch the ground. Then he was straight out to the Land Rover and back with a chainsaw. He cut every cupboard and door out of the caravan.

'I'm going to find that snake and you're going to kill it!' he yelled.

We carved the caravan to pieces. The oven, the fridge . . . everything was now outside. A thin aluminium shell was all that remained.

'Where's the snake?' Neil asked, out of breath.

'Must have got away,' I replied.

We rebuilt the caravan with fencing staples.

As you can probably tell, this life was way more fun than my life in London. And there were no fewer Kiwis. Another was Mike, a chemistry teacher from Wellington whom we dubbed 'Chemical'. A reluctance to join in our hi-jinks wasn't an endearing quality but Chemical possessed it. And he was so damned pedantic to go with it. Typically, when we'd been away on a job for months, stony broke till payday, we'd come to an agreement to raid the nearby chicken houses. Grab some eggs, maybe bop a chicken off. We'd always feel like bad bastards afterwards, having done the dirty on our neighbours, but at least we could eat. On less favourable days (read, days when it was too risky to steal chickens due to the increased security on the coops), we'd empty our pockets and see how much we had between us. Eighty pence could buy eight Mars bars, divided by three . . . that's two and a bit Mars bars per day, per starving forestry worker.

We'd eaten Mars bars for two days when Chemical could have shouted us a hamburger.

Payday, as always, seemed to loom a long way off in the future. Not a minute too soon Jamie would turn up with our bulging envelopes. After one particularly bad bout of starvation we discovered Chemical had a stash of over 500 quid squirrelled away.

'Well, boys,' he glowed as he walked into the kitchen one day. 'My stash is pretty damn full. Got enough in my booty now to head for Mexico.'

Five hundred quid he'd had stashed away and he couldn't bring himself to front the boys a tenner until payday. Some blokes I'll never understand. We'd eaten Mars bars for two days when Chemical could have shouted us a hamburger. I fumed. Then I got him back the next day.

A great part-time job on our days off was felling dangerous trees, trees that were overhanging houses or roads. Such trees needed to be felled by expert lumberjacks, or Kiwis who'd told the local council they were expert lumberjacks. For 50 quid we'd drop the tree. We'd shimmy up, cutting branches off as we went, get to within 6 metres of the top, hook a cable on the main spar, undercut a notch below, clamber back down and then wind in the cable on the tractor logging winch. Perfect. The top 6 metres would just fall straight down in a beautiful perpendicular, then we'd repeat the process, segment by segment, accurately dropping the entire tree to the ground. We're lumberjacks and we're okay. Bear in mind, some of these trees were huge, many between 45–60 metres tall.

'Chemical' on the job.

It was a beautiful spot, with a pub on the other side of the loch approachable by dinghy, a good thing given Neil's propensity for drunk driving.

So there was Chemical, 50 metres up, cable on, undercut made. I was just waiting for him to climb down. My hand hovered over the winch control. Mexico. Five hundred quid. Hamburgers. Couldn't help it. Put pressure on the winch. Bit more. Tension on.

'Hey, Chemical! She's going!'

He hung on to the trunk for dear life as the top peeled past him. I knew what was coming next. The rock. The whole top of the tree began to rock from side to side like a gigantic pendulum doing some wild primitive dance. Hang on to that, you miserable bastard. After four to five minutes of his passionate embrace, Chemical slid down the tree.

'What the *fuck!*' sputtered the white-faced figure trembling before me.

'Your undercut was too deep, Chemical. I've told you that before. Better watch it next time.'

Then there was the time when 'Dutchie' tried his darndest to kill me. We had moved from the caravan near Aviemore into a small manse on a wee loch named Loch Alvie. It was a beautiful spot, with a pub on the other side of the loch approachable by dinghy, a good thing given Neil's propensity for drunk driving. We'd row to the pub, have a session and row home in complete darkness. Typically, we'd get halfway across the lake before one of us would ask, 'Did you leave a light on?'

'No.'

'I didn't either.'

Cue rowing in circles before heading to the only place nearby with a light on: the pub.

We named our new abode 'Oor Manse', and Neil and I scrounged around for furniture while Jamie invited Dutchie, a forestry student and family friend from Amsterdam, to stay and work with us. He was friggin' useless, the sort of bloke who'd accidentally cut your boots with his chainsaw while working on a tree. One time Neil and I returned from a month's work to find he had commandeered my bedroom. I cornered him.

'Mate, that's my bedroom. My gear's here. There's another room in the house, you need to go and find it.'

Dutchie at first refused to budge from my room. When he finally did move he flogged my mattress and bed, something Neil and I discovered upon returning from the pub. Totally annoyed, I reclaimed my sleeping gear and staggered back to my room. As I stumbled along with my mattress, past the toilet, a hand holding a knife came out at me. It was bearing down with murderous intent. My hands were full. I couldn't protect myself. Then *smash!* That was Neil, knocking Dutchie out by smacking him in the head with a half-empty whisky bottle. Dutchie would have killed me, I am sure of it. The next day Jamie gave us shit for knocking the poor bastard out.

Dutchie's incompetence wasn't restricted to flawed execution plans. Along with trying to kill others, he often tried to kill himself. When work got scarce we'd labour on Jamie's family estate, building forestry roads. The chosen mode of transport for hauling the metal from the quarry was big old tractors with hydraulic trailers. One such road-building job was miles out the back of Jamie's manor, where a narrow bridge straddling a huge gorge proved a daily hazard. The approach was tight. When it was Dutchie's turn to cross, we urged him to do so in first gear.

'Dutchie. Listen here, you tulip-eating, dyke-building, clog-wearing git. It will take you forever, it's a long, long hill,' we said. 'But just let the tractor gears take you down the hill. First gear, *low* ratio. Got that? *Low*.'

Dutchie's response was resolute: 'Con boys, you don't tell me nutting, I'fe been droiving dese tractors for years back in Hollant.'

'Righto, mate,' we nodded.

Neil and I sat back, rolled a durrie and waited. Before long, Dutchie came down the slope. Have I told you it was a long slope? Have I explained it was narrow and terribly dangerous? Halfway down he decided he was travelling too slowly and attempted to change into second gear. Instead he found neutral and couldn't find first again. Couldn't find second either, for that matter.

The tractor just took off. Neil and I continued to puff away, taking bets on where he would eventually snuff it. I had a fiver on him not making the bridge. The only thing ahead of him was a sheer bluff. We thought, Dutchie's as dead as a dodo. He's going to kill himself. Good-oh. Then it dawned on us that we'd have to tell Jamie that we'd killed him. Reluctantly we stubbed out our cigarettes and tried to work out if there was any way to help. It was clear that the bridge was too narrow for Dutchie to make it across safely. He had far too much speed on. The trailer, filled with crushed rock, was now drifting sideways, with at least

Have I told you it was a long slope? Have I explained it was narrow and terribly dangerous?

O flower of Scotland
When will we see your like again
That fought and died for
Your wee bit hill and glen
And stood against him
Proud Edward's army
And sent him homeward
Tae think again.

The first verse of Scotland's unofficial national anthem.

half of it hanging over the side of the ravine. Somehow he'd managed to just about reach the bridge, so I'd lost five quid, but the 150-metre drop to the burn below still beckoned. Dutchie manoeuvred the tractor across the road and up the sheer bank, but as he did so his arms slipped through the steering wheel, and as he hit the bank he broke both of them.

And that was the end of Dutchie as part of our crew.

Two or three days later he headed home with both arms in a sling. The boss made us take him to the railway station, where Neil and I gave him absolute shit as we hung about on the platform making sure he got on the train. At least with two broken arms he couldn't come at us with a knife.

After he'd left, Jamie insisted we repair all the damaged fences Dutchie had managed to drive through — and there were plenty of them. Straight piece of road, ton of room either side . . . Dutchie would drive a tractor or Land Rover through the fence. We didn't mind fixing them, rolling about in hilarious fits as we recalled Dutchie's last ride.

The romance of spending another winter in the Highlands was beginning to wear thin, particularly when Jimmy the 'Dinnae tell me hoo ta drive a tractooor' Scot frae Aberdeen repeatedly took to sinking our half-track tractor in freezing bogs of peat. Not once. Not twice. But three times that idiot sank the bloody thing until only the exhaust was sticking out of the goo. This meant two to three days digging the tractor out, wearing nothing but your undies, smelling of bog peat and frozen stiff. After the third sinking I'd had enough.

'Jamie,' I said. 'You know how you owe me a week's holiday? I think I'm taking it from today.'

I wasted no time in catching a train to Stranraer, jumped on a ferry and took off to the Isle of Man. A week there among family and a change of scenery fostered in me an unsettling dissatisfaction with my current life, and I thought, *Bugger it*. I returned to the Highlands only to pick up my gear and say goodbye. Chapter closed.

Turning 19 in Scotland had taught me the value of men friends and the role they play in your becoming a man. It's a big thing, manhood, and each boy has to take his rite of passage. Without this rite, without this acceptance of your place among men, the transition to manhood can never be made. Tribes throughout the world have understood this for millennia, through initiation, through physical trials and tests. The rite of passage is not a right of passage. It is ceremonial and it is earned.

Bullshitting my way into another job, falling in love and hanging out on a Greek island.

4

ISLAND LIFE

The Vagabonds, my Isle of Man rugby team. I'm second from left, front row.

When I arrived on the Isle of Man I felt confident, even a little bolshie. I missed Neil and Jamie but this was the start of a new adventure. You should never look back or dwell on the past. It's great to know where you've come from, but don't look back. Take those experiences with you on the next part of your journey.

I moved to a wee place called Onchan, just outside the main town of Douglas on the Isle of Man. I soon learnt that foreigners were tagged 'Come-overs' and a work permit was required should you want to work

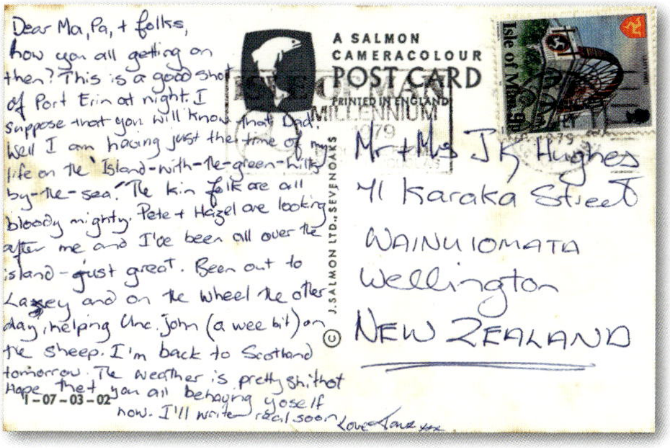

there. I went into the local government job bureau and was rejected for a permit by the man behind the desk because of my 'Come-over' status.

Port Erin, Isle of Man.

'We don't like Come-overs,' he said.

I looked at his name badge: Smith.

'Where does a name like that come from? You're from England. *You've* Come-over here yourself!'

'My parents were English,' he spat. 'But that has nothing to do with it. I was born here!'

By this stage I'd had enough. 'Listen, mate, my father is Manx. Our family trace ourselves back to the court of King Orry, we're not fucking Come-overs. You're a Come-over, now give me that permit or I swear on the sacred Braaid stones of Ellan Vannin, my family will be down here with their swords and bloody axes. This is a Viking stronghold!'

And that was that. I got the permit.

I scored a job on a construction site at a place called Port Erin. This time I bluffed my way into driving big old JCB diggers. As I sat on one for the first time my new boss told me to pull a trench and put some drainage down.

'Righto, mate, consider it done,' I said, wondering how it could ever be done. However, instead of walking off, as I thought he would, the foreman stood there! I looked at the multitude of buttons and thought, *This thing's got more switches, keys and knobs than my old FJ Holden*. The boss began to view me with ever-increasing scepticism.

'You've never driven one of these things, have you?'

I stammered a reply. 'Um . . . our diggers back home are quite a bit different, mate.'

He wasn't buying any of that. 'You don't know how to drive it, do you?'

I said, 'Give me a few minutes and I'll learn.'

He ordered me to step aside. 'I'll show you how to start it, show you what knob does what, but for Christ's sake by the time the boss comes back this afternoon, you'd better be digging that trench!'

Once again, I picked it up and learnt on the go.

Not unlike the Wellington advertising agency job, the reason I scored work was because the guy I'd replaced had broken his leg. Two months later he came back to work, and for the second time on my OE someone tried to kill me!

When the regular bloke returned, the guys on site were upset as — despite a slow start, I'd actually become quite a good digger driver. I'd also do odd jobs to help them out, a big plus on a construction site. If someone had to move a pallet, I'd lend them a hand with the digger. But this guy wouldn't help anyone. When he returned after sick leave, I was relegated to labourer. In the trench one day he wasted no time in trying to take my head off with the digger. I was wearing a Swanndri, ducking down doing a bit of digging, when the swinging bucket from a nearby digger did everything but knock my head off. I saw this shadow coming and wondered what it was, then bang! The teeth of the front bucket gripped the hood of my Swanndri and ripped it clean off. Let me tell you, they stuck those hoods on pretty damn good. If I'd lifted my head two seconds earlier, I would have lost it — as it was, he'd damn near strangled me.

He just looked at me and said, 'Ist thee a-right, son?'

He was the most useless digger driver, continually smashing walls, digging up gas and telephone lines. I'm convinced he did it on purpose.

The Eagle Tavern on City Road, London. Made famous by the nursery-rhyme lyric, 'Up and down the City Road, in and out the Eagle, that's the way the money goes, pop goes the weasel', a weasel being a tailor's iron which they would pawn over the bar for a drink when low on cash.

Apart from spending time with my relatives, and playing some rugby with the Vagabonds, I pretty much lived the life of a loner on the Isle of Man, more often than not doing my own thing, though I did meet a London girl called Jo who was on holiday with a friend. She visited me at Christmas, too. After 10 months on the Isle of Man, for the second time it was love that took me to London, where being a Kiwi was what landed me a job managing the Eagle Tavern in Islington while Jo continued her work as a nurse at the Great Ormond Street Hospital for Children.

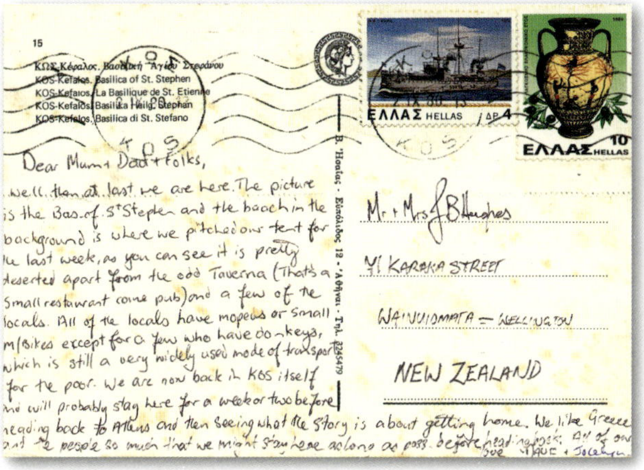
15

ΚΩΣ-Κέφαλος. Βασιλική Άγίου Στεφάνου
KOS-Kefalos. Basilica of St. Stephen
KOS-Kefalos. La Basilique de St. Etienne
KOS-Kefalos. Basilika Heilg. Stephan
KOS-Kefalos. Basilica di St. Stefano

Dear Mum + Dad + Folks,

well then at last we are here. The picture is the Bas. of St Stephen and the beach in the background is where we pitched our tent for the last week, as you can see it is pretty deserted apart from the odd Taverna (That's a small restaurant come pub) and a few of the locals. All of the locals have mopeds or small m/bikes except for a few who have donkeys, which is still a very widely used mode of transport for the poor. We are now back in Kos itself and will probably stay here for a week or two before heading back to Athens and then seeing what the story is about getting home. We like Greece and the people so much that we might stay here as long as poss. before heading back. All of our love Dave + Jocelyn.

NEW ZEALAND

ΕΛΛΑΣ HELLAS

St Stephen's Church ruins on the island of Kos.

Five months later we had enough money to travel around Europe. There wasn't a plan. We just zigzagged our way through Belgium, France and Holland, then down through Switzerland, Italy, Yugoslavia and across to Greece. After Scotland, it felt like a five-month holiday. It was summer so we lived in shorts, and on the Greek island of Kos our accommodation was a tent on the beach.

Every morning I'd head into the tiny village of Kefalos and go out with the local fishermen before light. The payment for doing so? An octopus. I'd take the octopus to the taverna to cook it, we'd drink some despicable cheap retsina and a few ouzos, go swimming and maybe look at a couple of ruins. And that was our life.

I'm a terrible tourist. I hate big buildings. If I went to Rome I wouldn't go near the Vatican or St Peter's (all that extreme show of wealth at the centre of a religion just gives me the absolute shits). I can't do museums. I do people. Luckily, the sorts of folk I want to meet live in small towns and the countryside.

Our bus crashed in Yugoslavia, pinning the driver's legs. We got him out, but he vehemently refused to stay in the country. So we took turns driving the bus clear through to Greece.

Europe is no different to the rest of the world, in that thieves and pickpockets are everywhere. Generally, Jo and I didn't have a problem, despite having no vehicle and having to rely on trains, buses or hitching. One night, however, a bunch of like-minded travellers opted to sleep on a railway platform in Athens. It seemed safe and warm, and much cheaper than the typical *pension*. Alas, a few hours later, Jo and I woke to find a couple of Greeks rummaging through some nearby rucksacks. I figured they belonged to the Pommie girls beside us. The Greeks had a knife, but I had a bigger one. I jumped up, growling like a lion and acting like a crazy man. I guess it worked; they scarpered. The girls had woken up during the fracas, and they thought I was a bit of a hero. They were producers for the BBC, and were doing a bit of a tramp around Europe.

Upon returning to the UK, Jo's intention was to move to Carlisle to study midwifery. But first we had severe food poisoning to deal with. Couple zero money with terrible diarrhoea and spewing, and you have a recipe for disaster. (Interestingly, in all my travels this is the only time such a bug has struck me down. And I got it in Calais, France — bloody typical!) We were so crook. Then I remembered the two girls we had helped in the train station, and that I still had their London details. They told us to come and stay, so we did until we came right. Then we hitchhiked north, Jo stopping off in Wigan to spend a couple of months with her parents, and me heading to Carlisle, on my 21st birthday, with the grand total of 27p in my back pocket.

Seared kingfish with horseradish sauce and cucumber garnish

INGREDIENTS

1 kingfish, filleted, skin on
1 250ml bottle horseradish pour-on sauce
1/2 stick celery
1 red capsicum
1 cucumber
2 tablespoons basil pesto
2–3 tablespoons olive oil
salt and pepper
wasabi (optional)

For this recipe I use kingfish with the skin on. I prefer the cut from down close to the tail end of the fish. Personally I find the tail, as with fish belly meat, suits my tastebuds. Maybe it's also because I love eating the crisp skin you get from cooking it this way — and the scales are a bit smaller at the tail end! If you've caught the fish yourself — well, it's going to taste even more delicious.

I love horseradish sauce. Mmm mmm! Rather than muck around making my own I use Cotterill & Rouse's pour-on sauce. Yeah, traditionally, it's supposed to go with red meat, but hey, trust me, it's equally good with fish!

Slice half a celery stick across into wafer-thin slices. Add to the horseradish sauce and stir in well. Slice some red capsicum quite thinly, then dice into small pieces no more than a couple of millimetres wide. Add to the sauce.

With a sharp knife (there is no other kind) slice a cucumber lengthwise into strips about 6cm long and, say, 3–4mm thick. Now carefully slice these thin strips into 3mm julienne strips (Yes, julienne is a fancy name, so imagine 6cm long cucumber matchsticks about 3mm square).

Now, I don't marinate fish with anything other than salt and a little crushed pepper. The only place I like to see a lemon is on the side of the plate for garnishing, or, of course, floating in a tall glass of Bombay Sapphire while I'm cooking. What I do use, however, is a little pesto on the skin side. Only use a top brand, such as Genoese, who use fresh basil and pure olive oil in their pesto.

Heat a pan with 2–3 tablespoons of olive oil. I use Swazi Oil. It's totally organic, high in antioxidants, as well as having a high proportion of monounsaturated fats — so it's very healthy for your heart while also being great for your soul. That, and the fact I've usually just spent 12 months tending the trees, talking them up (you really do need to talk to trees on a regular basis, if for nothing more than your own well-being), selectively picking the fruit . . . and creating the best oil possible, does make me a tad biased.

Cook the fish for a few minutes each side, turning just the once. Try to cook just the first 5–7mm of the outside flesh, leaving the inner fish beautifully raw. Don't have the heat too high as you want the skin to be crisp but not burnt. Remember, it will still continue to cook after you take it off the heat.

Once cooked, slice the fish into steaks about 10mm thick. Place two per plate, pour on the horseradish and celery sauce, and garnish with the sliced cucumber. For a taste explosion, add a wee squirt of wasabi on the side of the plate to provide an alternative flavour for the adventurous palate.

Simple sophistication. Quick and oh so easy! You are going to love this . . . and so will your guests.

LEFT The boys at Three Kings. CENTRE Three Kings, great in good weather but nowhere to hide when she blows! RIGHT Alan Jamieson: 'I'd have liked to have at least seen the shark that did this!'

Early mornings in Scotland, gorgeous as anything, but so damn cold you'd have to break the smoke off the top of the chimney.

Bullshitting my way into another job, and having an interesting experience with strawberry yoghurt.

5

TRUCKING GOOD TIME

The good news was my aunty gave me 20 quid for my birthday. The bad news was a bed and breakfast in Carlisle cost 25 quid a week. The owner, sensing I was short, offered five quid off for just the bed. When no response came, he asked how much I had in my pocket.

'Twenty pounds and twenty-seven pence,' I replied.

He said, 'Make it fifteen and that'll give you five quid for food.'

I needed work in a big fat hurry, so wasted no time in heading down to the job centre. A negative response awaited me, despite my owning a UK passport. It's worth remembering that during this period the UK unemployment rate was 12 per cent. Jobs were hard to come by. But there was a job going for a truck driver.

I said, 'That's me.'

The woman at the job centre asked to see my licence.

I replied that I could have it sent up from London, before pleading,

On the road in Cumbria.

'You've got to interview me for the job.'

A call was made to the employer, Farm Frost, a company that delivered frozen foods all over the UK. The woman in front of me nonchalantly hung up the phone, adding, 'I've spoken to the boss, the position's been filled.'

'You tell him the best guy for the job is standing right beside you,' I replied. 'In fact, he's on his way! Tell him that!'

She replied, 'I'm not telling him that.'

I insisted. 'Tell him that.'

I asked her to hand me the phone and dial his number. The gruff voice on the end of the line confirmed what I had already been told: an applicant for the job had been chosen.

'Okay, listen,' I said. 'The best guy for the job is standing right here and he's on his way to see you right now. Stay there!'

Peter Stevens was the guy's name and he told me I was the cheekiest bastard he'd ever met.

'Look, mate,' I replied, feeling as though I was making some headway. 'I'm the guy for the job. Unlike those others you've probably seen today I *need* this job. I'll be the best worker you've ever had. If not, you can kick my arse.'

The honest approach must have worked.

Next thing Peter said, 'I like you. What do I call you?'

I said, 'You can call me what you like if you give me the job.'

'Good.' He laughed. 'Welcome to the job, Kiwi Bastard. Turn up tomorrow morning at seven o'clock — you've got a road test with my supervisor.'

Fuck.

Here we go again.

I'd better learn how to drive a truck.

The vehicles were only eight-tonners, but I failed miserably. Carlisle is a tiny town with narrow, winding cobbled streets, and by the end of the lesson I felt I had let Peter Stevens down. Thankfully my ally came in the form of the supervisor, a Scottish lass called Maxine.

He told me I was the cheekiest bastard he'd ever met.

She said, 'You haven't driven many trucks before, have you?'

I had to admit I hadn't.

She said, 'I don't know if I can give you this job.'

'Max!' I said. 'I need this job. Ever since coming down from the Highlands I've wanted to work in trucking and this is my one opportunity.'

'You were in the Highlands! Where were you in the Highlands?'

'Aviemore — do you know the place?'

Maxine's eyes lit up. 'My family are from Perth.'

I'd never been to Perth.

'Yeah, know it well.'

She said, 'Okay, you've got the job but you'd better learn quickly.'

Farm Frost was responsible for transporting frozen chips and sausages to fast-food outlets such as Wimpy and McDonald's as far south as Doncaster, and as far north as Stranraer. The day after my driving test I hopped aboard to make my first delivery. Unfortunately, I didn't realise how high these trucks were. Weaving through the streets of Carlisle I approached an underpass beneath a railway line. As I navigated through the gap, I knew there was room for only one vehicle. The next thing a woman was coming straight at me.

Oh my God — she's not even looking.

When I flashed my lights, she continued driving straight towards me. To avoid an accident, I veered into a nearby median barrier and in doing so managed to write off the entire frickin' truck.

I veered into a nearby median barrier and in doing so managed to write off the entire frickin' truck.

Let me tell you, I was almost weeping. When the cops arrived, I couldn't even open the door because her car was in the way. And she was freaking out. Behind the cops, Peter Stevens suddenly materialised.

Here we go, I'm going to lose my job, right here, right now.

To my surprise — and elation — the cop went on to completely defend my position.

'Here's what happened, mate,' the cop said to Peter. 'Your driver had right of way and this woman didn't even bloody look. Your driver saved her life by swerving into the side of the tunnel. As a consequence, he's done a lot of damage to your truck, but he's a bloody good driver. He saved a life.'

So I kept my job that day — and became Peter's best driver.

I don't how many tons of frozen chips I physically carried each day from truck to restaurant, but I got super-fit and strong in no time. Each morning we'd leave the depot between 4 and 5 am. Many Wimpy restaurants didn't have big freezer rooms in those days, so a trip to the same establishment twice a week wasn't unheard of. Farm Frost also supplied dairy foods, yoghurts and cheesecakes to a range of UK supermarkets. Much like in the Highlands, I often had no money, especially since you didn't see your first payday until you had been working for a few weeks. When dairy trucks arrived back at the depot — with pallets of out-of-date cheesecakes and yoghurts — they would normally be thrown in the rubbish. But not if this Kiwi had his way. Every night I'd go to the bins and steal what had been chucked out.

One day another driver named Dave Smith said, 'Hey, Kiwi Bastard, what you doing?'

'Oh, you know,' I replied. 'Just taking a few desserts home, mate.'

'You did last night, too. You must eat well.'

I came clean, admitting that's all I ever ate, the yoghurt serving as

breakfast and the cheesecake dinner. Dave spotted me doing the same the next four or five nights and could handle it no more.

'Do you think your teeth could handle a steak?' he asked. 'I've told my wife about you and she said, "Bring that boy home for a steak."'

Those days were about survival. Sometimes you've got to live on your wits and think on your feet. Despite the tough times, we had a shitload of fun at Farm Frost. Pranks were a major source of entertainment, one involving the very man who provided me with a life-saving meal.

One morning I planted a fresh pig's ear underneath the passenger visor of Dave's truck. It sat there for several days, and being midsummer, it festered and got a bit maggoty and gooey. Each afternoon, Dave returned to the depot complaining about a wretched smell in his cab; he'd turned his cab upside down, but he still couldn't find the source of the stench. Then, about a week later, on his way back to Carlisle, he picked up two beautiful Norwegian hitchhikers in the Lake District. Sunglasses on, Dave felt pretty cool and suave. The gorgeous girls, however, had no way in which to block the blinding sun so one reached up and pulled the visor down. Cue maggoty pig's ear falling into her lap! She screamed, then her friend threw up everywhere in the cab. Dave stopped the truck and they both jumped out, demanding their packs and storming off.

Two words rang over and over in Dave's head: Kiwi Bastard. Unbeknown to me, he was already planning revenge. My Friday ritual was to clean my beautiful Mercedes Benz truck. I'd scrub the entire thing, inside and out. This particular Friday I'd just done so when I went upstairs to the admin office to go through my weekly sheets. I looked out the window to see a truck that looked exactly like mine — only this one was pink. Initially I thought some clown had parked his pink truck in my park. On closer inspection, I discovered what had really taken place. Dave had pilfered a whole pallet of 2-litre yoghurt containers and covered my entire truck in strawberry yoghurt: the cab, the ute, everything.

ABOVE LEFT There are times when you probably wish you really were a numb nuts. Legend of the Valley, Colin Baynes, with sons Angus and Lachie, gather sweet stuff for their toast. Makapua Station.

CENTRE LEFT Jim Martell shot this bear which left him pondering . . . 'til he figured it was a grizzly/polar bear cross. I'd read in the *Dom Post* Green Pages these bears were scrawny and suffered terrible condition. Guess they'd never seen one. Fact is, polar bears evolved from grizzlies maybe less than 100,000 years ago! A grizzly bear I once shot in south-east Alaska was genetically more closely related to polar bears of the far north than other grizzly bears in Alaska.

RIGHT Think your job sucks? Snapped this guy giving away blowjobs outside a brothel in Seattle (I was just walking past, okay!).

BELOW Taygen Hughes awaits rescue in the middle of the Makarora River. The driver's identity has been obscured to save further embarrassment. Makarora, New Zealand.

LEFT The giraffe has always fascinated me. Each time I travel to Africa it is not until I have seen my first giraffe that I feel I am indeed back on the continent. Selous Game Reserve, Tanzania.
ABOVE RIGHT Hyrax are a cute small mammal with a likeable character. Though at first shy, they soon become inquisitive and often end up hanging around camp. According to some, they are the closest living animal to the elephant. Laikipia, Kenya.
CENTRE RIGHT The nosey young water buffalo approached in a show of youthful bravado and total ignorance of firearms. Conway Station, Northern Territory.
BELOW She had her cubs close by so we gave her both distance and respect. Laikipia, Kenya.

Setting out to travel through Africa in the footsteps of the great explorers, and ending up in Khartoum jail.

6

THE AFRICAN DREAM

Jo and I were engaged to be married, but it soon dawned on us that spending our lives together was not to be. I would eventually want to return home; Jo, an only child, finally admitted she never wanted to leave England. It is what it is. I'd also been stung by the travel bug and needed more adventure than the north of England could offer. The horn of Africa was calling.

As a kid, my heroes were Speke, Burton, Stanley and Livingstone, though to some extent the latter, in my opinion, was a bit of a religious nut. Bit of a missionary zealot — the kind of folk who, in my opinion, have over the past couple of centuries pretty well ruined Africa. Why would you ever want to convert someone else to your beliefs? Sure, introduce health improvements and education in the new world, but to attempt to change a person's whole spiritual core? Malevolent arrogance.

Africa — the very word conjures up visions of wild lands, wild animals and even more wild tribes. I craved to wander through the deepest darkest parts of the continent. Over the next 13 months I would jump on the backs of trucks, the odd train — camel and tracked — and do the remainder by foot, aiming for South Africa's busiest port, Durban.

In those days the *Lonely Planet* books had only just come out, and the African version became my Bible. I caught a bus to Athens, before jetting across to Cairo. There, I needed a visa and a letter from the British government if I wanted to enter Sudan. Instead of waiting four weeks for red tape, I headed south, though the tourist hordes of Luxor soon drove me away. I headed for the expanse of the Western Desert.

African ferries are not the most reliable mode of transport. Those that don't sink often arrive days or weeks late. When the one I boarded in Aswan arrived in Wadi Halfa, Northern Sudan, it was akin to a national holiday. (The ferry sank the following week, and 1000 people perished in the croc-infested waters.) Banks shut their doors and a party ensued on the banks of the Nile, which would have been great had I not needed to catch the one and only train the next day across the Nubian Desert. Surprisingly for Africa, I couldn't even find a black market to buy Sudanese currency. With only Egyptian pounds, would I risk getting on a train with no ticket? In the end I had no choice; I desperately wanted to see Wadi Halfa from a rear-vision mirror. It was a town to be remembered only for paperwork, hassle and dirt.

The train was bound for the city of Khartoum — and I was bound for jail. Despite every other *muzungu* (white man) having no ticket, I seemed to catch the eye of an officious bastard who put me behind bars. I shared a room with 20 others; the toilet was a bucket and dinner was *ugali* (a porridge made from maize). Sudanese are incredibly friendly people, even the crims in my cell, and I was soon surprised to discover I had nothing to fear in captivity, even though, let me tell you, I was locked up with some fairly ornery-looking characters.

The ferry at Aswan, well, three barges roped together actually. It sank the following week.

After two days, I convinced a guard to let me go downtown to buy some local currency. I actually had a fair bit of dough in the form of US traveller's cheques, but wanted to keep such news quiet. The bank required my passport. My side of the conversation went something

like this: 'Sorry, that's in jail where I'm supposed to be — so I can't change traveller's cheques here? Where's the black market? Oh, you can go to jail for that? I am in jail, turkey!'

I spent the remainder of the days wandering around Sudan's capital, playing dominoes, drinking chai with the friendly locals and smoking hubbly bubbly pipes full of sheep shit and tobacco. Hey, it's not too bad. And I'm sure every now and then they dropped a little hash in the mix. I soon, however, saw sense and paid my jailer using traveller's cheques, retrieved my passport, and got out of there.

There's nothing like a few days behind bars to appreciate the luxury of a hotel. I hung out in Khartoum reading about my heroes, British army officer Charles George Gordon, and British explorer and big-game hunter Samuel Baker. The latter, in particular, has an incredible story, so let me bore you with just a little background to the man. Baker was a pretty resourceful sort of a bloke. Like many of his peers he was a man of many talents, but he's mostly remembered for discovering Lake Albert and for his adventures as a big-game hunter in Asia, Africa, Europe and North America. When his wife, Henrietta, died of typhoid fever in 1855, Baker was just 34. On a visit to a shooting estate in Scotland, Baker struck up a mateship with the Maharaja Duleep Singh. They travelled

The Nile, one of the most magical waterways in the whole world.

all over central Europe together and on the last part of their journey, to Bulgaria, Baker took the Maharaja on a jaunt to the local harem.

Baker immediately fell in love with one of the slaves up for auction, a white woman destined for the Ottoman Pasha of Vidin. He lost out in the auction to the Pasha but paid off the girl's keepers, grabbed the dame and fled. Ha! A man with fortitude, smarts and most importantly, some sizeable balls. A romantic. The man we all wish we were. Baker eventually married Florence in 1865. But his new bride wasn't about to become a housewife.

Her family was Hungarian landed gentry who had fallen on hard times, and Florence was fluent in five languages. She joined her husband wherever he went, and was known to carry a pistol. Ahh. Wild women, you've got to love them. If you don't, well hell, they'll more than likely shoot you!

The hubbly bubby brothers. Sheepshit and tobacco with a dash of hash.

A train journey to the outskirts of Khartoum set me back on track to discover more of Africa by foot. On a roofless railway platform in the middle of nowhere, with no trees for shade or privacy, I got desperate. I had to go to the toilet. But here's the conundrum: do you face the crowd, or vice versa? What made good form? It seemed as if the whole town was waiting with baited breath to see how the *muzungu* would handle it as I marched the obligatory 50 metres away from the platform. Then, with a certain colonial dignity coupled with fake aplomb, I turned to face them.

Ahh. Wild women, you've got to love them. If you don't, well hell, they'll more than likely shoot you!

Following the road down the Nile led me to places such as Malakal, a thriving little town on the banks of the Nile. By this stage I was tired of black bean stew so decided to shout myself some meat, the cheapest being goat's head stew. I was in heaven, picking out the eyes — two big, chewy, juicy, full and wonderful eyes, and what sweet cheek meat. Such luxuries were hard to find in Africa, as I would soon discover. I had a two-week stretch where I could find nothing to eat, nor drink for that matter, but mangoes. Nowadays every time I walk past the juice section in my local supermarket and spot the orange and mango flavour, I growl. Frickin' mangoes.

Staying in most places a week or two, I spent my days moving slowly, from village to village, oasis to oasis. Generally, the locals were friendly and hospitable, wanting to know about my world and country, and inviting me to stay with them. I struck up friendships, staying till the time was right to move on. I met people who had never met whites. They'd stroke my legs, because they'd never seen legs with hair on them before.

Having no plan, however, didn't mean I didn't have a purpose — which was to keep migrating south. I lived frugally. You didn't need a lot of money; dinner could cost as little as 10 cents. Bit of rice, a little flavouring, throw in some chickpeas . . . sorted! That would see you through to the next day. I carried a little bit of food and a huge knife. Apart from that, I had a tent, a lightweight sleeping bag, mosquito net and boots.

I'd always wanted to see Addis Ababa, but never did. An Englishman, American and I were denied entry at the Ethiopian border, the officials refusing to let us in without visas. Our American wasn't much use; he just yelled when things didn't go his way. I did sneak into other parts of Ethiopia, but not legally. At the time, the country was in the grip of a terrible famine. There were so many dead people. One day I helped pick up a very sick woman to put her on the back of a truck. She wore a loose cotton shawl and her stomach was showing. A scarf covered the rest of her almost lifeless body. As I lifted her high onto the vehicle it seemed as if the sun was shining right through her.

So there I was, skinny white dude, sitting in the back of a truck alongside vicious buggers carrying AK-47s and self-propelled guns.

As well as famine, Africa offered other occupational hazards. On the back roads near Nimule, on the Uganda/Sudan border, I ran into remnants of Idi Amin's guerrillas, mean sons of bitches, who, despite having everything, still demanded T-shirts, jeans and drink bottles. Basic stuff, yet basic stuff they would kill you for. One day I was hitching a ride on a truck on a bush track in the middle of nowhere, a no-man's-land between Sudan and Uganda, when we came upon a man lying in the middle of the road pointing a rocket launcher at us. The truck driver stopped, and between 30 and 40 guys filtered out of the bush and hitched a ride with us. So there I was, skinny white dude, long hair and a beard, sitting in the back of a truck alongside vicious buggers carrying AK-47s and self-propelled guns. Further along the road, one of the guys jumped up, banged on the roof of the truck and we stopped. I scanned the countryside around the truck. If we ran into government troops I knew I'd have to figure out a plan real quick. No worries though:120 metres off the side of the track, standing broadside on, was an antelope. Food. Everyone rushed to the side of the truck, cocked their guns and let loose, firing hundreds of shots at the animal. The noise and spent cases flying around the truck were unbelievable.

When the boys had finally finished shooting, I peered over the side. The antelope, still there, looked up, not at all concerned. He knew something I did not. Meanwhile my fellow travellers feverishly shoved new mags in, again took aim and again shot like hell . . . and missed. This animal had now had something like 1200 rounds fired at it. These guys were so angry. Finally the antelope clicked into survival mode, running into the bush before the boys got lucky, or a stray ricochet somehow found its mark. They turned to the white guy in the corner.

All I could offer was: 'It was a long way off. Easy to miss. Too far, hell boys, I would never have been able to hit it.'

They agreed, muttering, 'Yes, yes. Too far, too far.'

Fifteen kilometres down the road they were gone. Five kilometres further, and a makeshift stick barrier across the road meant another halt in our journey. Another border patrol — well, another group of stoned soldiers actually, though this time they were government troops looking to tax people coming through. As expected, they went through my backpack, fleeced my knife and a few other bits and pieces. Then the man in charge, clearly in the last stages of syphilis — big sores all over his face and what looked like half his nose and an ear falling off — pulled me to the side and pleaded for drugs. I said I didn't do drugs, before realising he meant medication. He was going to die, of that I was sure. I ended up giving him two packs of Dispirin, for which he was so grateful he demanded that the guys who'd nicked my stuff return it straight away. I always carry Dispirin or Nurofen now. Never know when you'll bump into someone with the clap.

Though it wasn't a race, my target of Durban in South Africa was still a long way off, and finding good food continued to be a challenge: more mangoes, bean stew, mealie and goat if I was lucky. Every now and then a falafel. When I reached Kampala, Uganda, civil war continued to rage. One night, five other white travellers and I peacefully smoked a bit of dak on our bungalow veranda, watching rockets fly and grenades explode on the edge of the CBD. Submachine gunfire rattled away, more than once a little too close for comfort.

We woke to the horror of dead bodies in the streets next to overturned cars. It's hard to believe how many people had been killed in Uganda, between 100,000 and 500,000 people under Idi Amin's regime alone. The new guy was no better. In fact, most locals I spoke to wanted Amin back. 'At least with Idi we had a reasonable idea of who was going to get shot; with this guy nobody knows who is next,' they explained.

I had no idea what I was getting myself into. *You're a long way from Wainuiomata now, Davey*, I thought. A young Kiwi guy blundering through a mad continent.

The only way to stay in touch was by mail, having given my parents and mates a list of the places I planned to go. Once I reached main cities I'd head for the nearest post office and their *poste restante* department. Receiving mail was just like finding a hidden treasure. I'd take those envelopes to a quiet place, open them and read all the news from home, devouring the words as if they were a special meal, knowing it could be another month before I would be able to connect with loved ones.

I next fetched up in exotic-sounding places like Jinja, Soroti and Tororo, on the Kenyan border. Originally I was going to hang out in

Burundi and Rwanda, but they were having similar problems to Uganda and I was tiring of gunfire — and of holding my hands up in the air. I realised it was just a matter of time before I became the object of some child soldier's wrath. When I crossed the Kenyan border I finally felt safe.

I craved to reach Nairobi, where professional hunters used to hang at the Thorn Tree Café and the old Norfolk Hotel. I stopped in Nairobi for three months and played rugby for Ngong Hills, alongside other expat Kiwis. I lived on the infamous River Road, the main drag through the poorest part of town, which is convenient if you happen to be looking for the seediest, darkest hovel or a location where murders and burglaries are commonplace. I chose it because it was cheap. River Road would hardly see a day where someone didn't pull a *panga* (machete or a knife) on you in return for your wallet. It just meant carrying a bigger knife than the next guy.

Watching your back is important everywhere, but looking after your health is always top of mind in Africa. I remember meeting a Kiwi dude in a boarding house who'd contracted the trifecta: malaria, amoebic dysentery and bilharzia. His teeth were falling out and he couldn't stop shitting green shit. An Aussie bloke staying in the same hostel helped me get George up to the hospital, but he was in such a state no one would see him. The poor bugger was at death's door. All the staff did was delay the inevitable, prod him and clean him.

Thankfully the Aussie was also a tenacious sort of bloke. He managed to get George back to London to the Tropical Diseases Hospital, though even that came with its challenges. British Airways wanted nothing to do with him. The Russian airline Aeroflot were the only people who would fly him.

Around 12 years ago I was at the factory in Levin when in walked this guy who said, 'You don't remember me, but my name is George Blair. I met you in Nairobi.'

He still needed work done on his teeth, but I gather his shits were cured.

In 1982 I reached Johannesburg, 13 months and 10,000km from where I had started. Despite continued war troubles, I had returned to Kampala, before heading east to Dar es Salaam, Tanzania. The Tanzam Railway took me to Mbeya, Tanzania, before I wove my way to Lusaka, Zambia, and finally Livingstone, near Victoria Falls. Hunger and low funds dictated that I had to continually trick my way into five-star hotel buffets to stuff buckets of bread rolls and jam into my backpack.

My plan to hitch from Johannesburg to Durban took a series of small trips, but I eventually scored a ride with a grandmotherly woman who needed a rest from driving. When we reached our destination, she gave me a phone number, adding that if I ever needed help to give her a call. 'My husband, er, fixes things,' she rather hurriedly finished.

After such a hard slog, reaching Durban was an anticlimax. It just wasn't Africa. The third largest city in South Africa was really just a sunny Wellington. With apartheid. It staggered me that I'd just travelled right through Africa and hadn't bumped into all those horrible black people (okay, apart from the odd mass-murderer); I'd just encountered *people*. Suddenly, white and black people weren't allowed on the same bus or to use the same toilets. It was a different world and I was about to find out the hard way.

Before long, I scored a job working in a restaurant in a black area of Durban. The restaurant was the first takeaway for black people, four of whom I worked with. We sold things that blacks would eat, not whites,

Entering Zimbabwe on foot. Down to under 70kg and beginning to look forward to the end of the journey — and hotdogs, doughnuts and chips.

He called me every name under the sun, took my passport and put me under house arrest.

including *vetkoek* — dough deep-fried in cooking oil. Part of my uniform was a .38 pistol in an ankle holster. Very Logan Brown . . . Not!

To keep fit, I joined the local rugby club, as had Murray Mexted at the same time, though clearly for a different grade. (By no means do I want anyone to think I ever excelled at the game. I've only played two internationals: once for the Isle of Man and once for Swaziland. The Isle of Man had three teams; Swaziland had two.)

It took time to acclimatise to Durban. For a bush baby, cities are frightening places, but at 69kg I needed to recharge my batteries and eat ice cream and fatty foods. At the end of three months I went to the immigration department to renew my visa and spoke to an Afrikaans guy, who in turn proceeded to rip the shit out of me. He called me every name under the sun, took my passport and put me under house arrest. Unbeknown to me, I'd committed a multitude of horrendous crimes and was in deep trouble. Additionally, I was working in South Africa illegally and had been associating with blacks. But how could I not? I worked with them; we played rugby together; I went to their *braaie* (barbecues) and weddings. They were just people. According to immigration, however, I was assisting ANC activists who were bringing weapons into the country.

It was heavy shit being under house arrest. I lived in backpacker's-type accommodation. I couldn't work, and resigned myself to waiting for my trial. Perhaps worst of all, I couldn't talk to anyone. I had no one to turn to. There was no such thing as a New Zealand Embassy, and with so many Poms in South Africa the British High Commission couldn't give a toss, despite the fact that I was travelling on a British passport. 'South African law,' is all they'd say.

I wasn't allowed to see my rugby mates or socialise with anyone I knew. I was scared about going to court. There was no evidence for the 'offences' I'd been charged with and all I could do was sit and wait — and accept my fate.

After several weeks the detectives and I were getting on well. Sometimes, despite risking their jobs, they invited me into their homes for barbecues where we'd talk about Colin Meads and the All Blacks.

'Davey,' they'd say. 'Man, you're such a good *oke*, and we hate this job sometimes, but you're going to jail! Not for long, six or 12 months, then we're going to deport you.'

Far out, I thought, *you really don't want to go to jail in South Africa.* A day before the trial I didn't even have a lawyer. But then I discovered a crumbled piece of paper in my pocket from the old woman who had picked me up outside Johannesburg.

Her husband fixed things.

She remembered me, and asked if I could join her and her husband for lunch. But first I had to convince my new best mates — the detectives — to let me borrow their car. They informed me they'd stay at my place while I could take their VW Golf.

'Be back within two hours,' they demanded, 'otherwise we lose our jobs.'

I drove to this woman's place, met her husband and over lunch told him everything: where I'd been, what I hoped for the future, and how much I liked South Africa. Most importantly, I told him I hadn't done any of the things I'd been accused of. My only crime — if it was one — was meeting black people. By the end of the lunch, he repeated what the detectives had said: 'I like you, man, you're a good *oke*. I'll make a call.'

And he did, to the Minister of Immigration in Pretoria. Despite speaking in Afrikaans, I could make out that he was saving the bacon of a very worried Kiwi.

'It's all sorted,' said the Fixer.

I was told to return to Durban, pick up the detectives and go to the immigration department.

I dragged myself yet one more time up the stairs to the big bastard's office, something which, in the past, had made me damn near puke. The only reason I did so at all was because he still had my passport. The office door opened, and this brute of a man smiled possibly for the first time in his life.

'Ahh! Mr Hughes! Come in, please! Sit down, cup of tea? Scones, perhaps? Please, make yourself comfortable!'

What the hell has happened here?

Brutus continued: 'There appears to have been a terrible misunderstanding. We have mixed you up with someone else. I'm so, so sorry but we can fix all this right now! I have your papers and your passport. You now have permanent residence in South Africa. Welcome

Note the Zim *trillion* dollar note! Now that's inflation buddy.

to our country! Feel free to come and go as you please!'

This was far out, though I wasn't out of the woods just yet. One final piece of red tape required me to have a piece of paper stamped outside of South Africa.

Before I knew it I was being chauffeur-driven in a Mercedes to Swaziland.

'It's a bureaucratic thing,' Brutus informed me. 'My driver Jannie will drive you out of the country. You will stay in a nice hotel — at my expense of course — get the paper stamped at the border, then come back.'

Before I knew it I was being chauffeur-driven in a Mercedes to Swaziland.

'So, Jannie,' I asked, breathing a sigh of relief once we were out of Durban. 'What's all this about?'

He said, 'Don't you know, man? It's the *broederbond*; the band of brothers. The brotherhood is a secret society in South Africa. They run everything, the government, the military — the guy you had lunch with is one of their head pooh-bahs. We're going to get drunk tonight mah friend, maybe find some whores, it will be terrific. I'll get to sleep with a black woman.'

So we did. Get drunk. We partied in Swaziland at a place called Big Bend, and in the morning I was to return to South Africa. Jannie, meanwhile, was covered in love bites and as happy as an Afrikaner hound dog.

'Come on, Davey, we're going!'

I replied, 'Do you know what, Jannie? I kind of like this little country. It's not part of South Africa, is it?'

Jannie replied, 'No man, it's a kingdom.'

I said, 'And you guys have no jurisdiction here, do you?'

'Not at all,' Jannie responded, clearly wondering what I was getting at.

'Thanks for the ride,' I said. 'But I don't want to go back to South Africa. I'm staying put.'

Little did I know my newly adopted country would shape my business 12,000km away and years later in peaceful Horowhenua.

ABOVE LEFT A group of very impressive impala bucks! Mount Kenya.

ABOVE RIGHT This young bull faces a huge challenge to reach old age. The constant threat of poachers, along with habitat encroachment and drought, means he'll have to learn quickly from the older bulls in the herd. He'll also need a bucket of luck — hell, he may be dead already. Selous Game Reserve, Tanzania.

CENTRE LEFT The Kori Bustard is one hell of a big bird. The males can get up to 20kg, which, as you'll agree, would take a fair bit of stuffing. Selous Game Reserve, Tanzania.

CENTRE RIGHT Shortly after finding fresh stag prints in a streambed I watched this 10-point stag come along. Like me, he was following the stag ahead of him. Did he ever catch up with the stag? I'm not sure, all I know is I never did! Piripiri Stream, Ruahines.

BELOW An eagle attacks a full-grown mule deer doe. Dale Wood and I watched several eagles harass, then attack, the doe, who did not appear weak or injured. Crazy Mountains, Montana.

LOU MCNUTT

Moving into a bordello in Swaziland and learning all about cannibalism.

7

HOPE IN A STRANGE LAND

Swaziland is a small landlocked kingdom, with South Africa as its largest neighbour on three sides and Mozambique to the east. Throughout recent history it has changed hands often. South Africa ran the joint from 1894–99, but at the conclusion of the Boer War in 1902 the Brits took over. It finally became the independent nation of Swaziland in 1963. Not long after I had arrived the sovereign, King Sobhuza, died. The warriors of the nation shaved their heads in respect at the passing of the Great Elephant. And so did I. *Hau*! *Hau*!

Since 1986, King Mswati III has ruled as sub-Saharan Africa's last absolute monarch. Political parties are banned, and the leader — who has been known to buy expensive jets while his own country suffers famine —

MIGUEL TORRES

The late King Sobhuza.

can overrule any law. Today, Swaziland has an unemployment rate of 40 per cent and a quarter of its adult population has been infected by HIV/AIDS. Where are you now, Great Elephant? *Hau, hau!*

These figures may make for bleak reading, but back in 1982 any place but South Africa seemed like heaven to me. Things looked up as soon as I left Durban; I was now officially off the hook, the charges had been dropped and I had my passport back. I could zip in and out of South Africa at will. Swaziland may have been my saviour, but I quickly needed a job and somewhere to live. In South Africa I had been more than happy to work in a labouring position, but in Swaziland such jobs were saved for the locals. I needed work that used my mind, not my hands. So I went to the offices of the *Times of Swaziland* and told them I was a reporter and journalist from London's *Daily Mirror*. Yeah, I know. I just needed a job! Based in the capital Mbabane, the *Times* was the *New Zealand Herald* on valium. Unlike its opposition, the *Swazi Observer*, the *Times* didn't take bribes from politicians or local chiefs to write whatever they dictated. I lost count of the number of times my co-workers were arrested or locked up.

TESSA JOUGHIN

The Reed Dance or *Umhlanga*, which takes place in Swaziland in the spring every year. Young childless unmarried maidens from all over the kingdom cut reeds with long knives and then gather to present them to the Queen Mother and dance.

The editor of the *Swazi Times* gave me a job as a journalist in the morning, and by the afternoon, Doug Loffler, the newspaper's owner, told the editor he needed an advertising manager. Doug was starting a new paper and two business magazines, and required an advertising manager for both publications. 'Obviously with your background, you're the man for the job,' he told me. Despite the fib to get the journo gig, the bit about advertising was actually true!

For the next eight months I lived at Ma Smith's Boarding House in Manzini, a small town south of Mbabane. It was the craziest place I have ever stayed in. Ma Smith was a huge coloured woman, weighing probably 155kg, who ran her guesthouse with an iron fist. Her boyfriend was a tiny Italian with a bald head who ran the local Italian restaurant. Whenever he slept over, and they argued — which was often — Ma Smith chased him around the house with a heavy cast-iron frying pan. If I shut my eyes, even today I can clearly recall the sound, resonating through the house, of that pan making contact with a human head. We weren't allowed women in the house after 11 pm and dinner was stew with rice; one night beef, the next chicken. At Ma Smith's, you knew what day it was by what was on your plate.

When his girlfriend caught wind of his antics she bit the poor bastard's nose off.

I shared a room with Dave from Liverpool, who worked in South Africa for the oil company, Sasol; John the meat inspector from Birmingham, and Hannibal the Portuguese panelbeater. To top it off, we had a wee Scots guy who became known as Hard Luck Hughie, a man with the hardest luck of anyone I ever met. When Hughie was flying into Swaziland to start his job, he stopped over in Nairobi. As he walked down the gangway, he tapped the air hostess on the arse, who then gave him a push, and he went arse over kite and ended up breaking both of his arms. The first day at work saw Hughie in plaster — and I'll tell you later how he almost lost his nose.

So what drove these expats to Swaziland from Portugal and England? Huge sugar plantations, pine forests and pulp mills, where a handful of Kiwis worked, too. Then there were transients like me, who turned up and thought, *This is as good a place to stop as any.* It was an easy country to live in; the rules weren't hard and fast like South Africa, and I could mix and mingle with whoever I liked. I got on so well with the Swazis, and I felt as if they were my people and that I belonged to their tribe. It was like the movie *Avatar*! Well, not quite.

The only downside was the 40km distance between my new job and Manzini. I could have moved closer, but enjoyed Ma Smith's bordello too much. I hitchhiked via bus or truck to and from the *Swazi Times* each day. Meanwhile, Ma Smith's continued to live up to its reputation, and much of the shenanigans revolved around Hard Luck Hughie. He had a black girlfriend and would spend half his time at Ma's and the remainder in a mud hut with his girlfriend. One night, however, Hughie got tanked and slept with someone else. When his girlfriend caught wind of his antics she half bit the poor bastard's nose off. Then she burnt every single piece of clothing he owned.

Dave was no better. He'd been sleeping with quite a few of the locals and continually suffered from crabs. The first thing he'd do when returning from a night out was spray his balls with a can of Black Flag.

Every night you'd hear him saying, 'Oo, oo, it hurts, but it works, it hurts, but it works!' Nothing was more certain than that it never worked; you'd hear him scratching through the night. I remember thinking, *God, stay there, crabs, don't jump into my bed.*

Dave had a tendency to come home drunk and take a leak in my cowboy boots. He just used to get on my tits. One night he'd had a skinful, and on coming home sat at the end of my bed. Minutes later, I woke to find a stranger in my room and freaked. I grabbed his body, smashed it into the wall and proceeded to beat the snot out of it. The body slumped to the ground. I turned the light on. Oh God, I thought, it's Dave. Blood was pouring down his face. At breakfast, Dave joined Birmingham John and me, broken nose, swollen lips, puffy eyes.

I said, 'Dave . . . about last night.'

Before I could construct the right things to say, he said, 'Yeah, some bastard rolled me on the way home from the pub!'

Clearly, there was no point putting him right. 'You want to be a bit more bloody careful, boy,' I finished.

According to the Daves, he was dead meat. I had to find Hughie first.

Another Dave — we'll call him Evil Dave — who was also a Liverpudlian, hooked up with Crabs Dave. When both the Daves and Hughie all got sacked on the same day from Sasol, they fled back to Swaziland in a stolen company van. They parked it up at Ma Smith's and the two Daves headed into town to figure out how to fence the van. Hard Luck Hughie, however, had other ideas. He took the van up to his new girlfriend's (one who didn't mind a noseless short Scotsman), got blind rotten on local poison and on the way home crashed the van, writing it off. Dave and Dave were livid.

Hannibal then offered to buy the motor for 500 *emalangeni* (the local currency) from the Daves, which they agreed to. Hannibal's mistake was giving Hughie the cash. The guy just couldn't help himself. With fresh notes in his hand, Hughie visited what seemed like every whorehouse and casino in Swaziland. What he didn't gamble or spend on women, he was wasting on booze. Meanwhile, the two Scouser Daves were looking to kill him. Hughie was in big trouble and I worried for him; his easy-going nature would not save him from these guys. First, he'd written off the van, then he'd spent the profits. According to the Daves, he was dead meat. I had to find Hughie first.

We searched high and low. Rumours circulated: I heard he was up in Nhlangano, so off I went. Crabs Dave reckoned he'd been seen at the casino and off they went, looking with a vengeance. We would each search the smallest tip-off, but no one could track down Hughie. One night, as we sat down to dinner, came the news I had been dreading: Evil Dave announced he'd found Hughie. Crabs Dave chimed in.

'Right, let's go and sort him out!'

I knew straight away they were going to kill him. 'Hang on, where's he at?'

'Manzini Hospital,' they answered.

I explained that he must be a bad way and said I'd join them.

Evil Dave said, 'Do what you fucking like, just stay out of my way!'

Off we marched to the hospital, where a German doctor said, 'So. You are the friends of Hughie? I'm so sorry — it's just one of those things. There's nothing we can do.'

'What do you mean?' we asked.

'Your friend — he is dying.'

To which Evil Dave replied, 'He's going to fucking die alright!'

I summed it up for him. 'Mate, if Hughie is going to croak it, then maybe that's for the best. You and Dave don't need to hang around. I know you want to deal to him, but he's a goner any way you look at it.'

Evil Dave scowled a Scouser scowl. 'You're a soft prick, Kiwi.' With that, they turned and walked out of the hospital.

More probing revealed that Hard Luck Hughie was suffering from an incurable, inoperable disease, no doubt picked up from his endless extramural activities. Or because he had screwed a monkey, as Crabs Dave put it. Hospital staff expected Hughie to last no longer than a few days. We busied ourselves making burial plans, undecided on whether to send his body home.

But where *was* home for Hard Luck Hughie? No one knew. A trip to the British Embassy was in order. Two more days went by and Hughie was still at death's door. I snuck up to see him, though he didn't recognise me or say anything. Another two days went by, and, if I wasn't mistaken, Hard Luck looked just a touch better than the day before. You know, he bloody well survived this incurable disease, possibly the only person to do so in living history. And with that, somewhat ironically, Hard Luck Hughie became one of the luckiest bastards I ever met.

And with that, somewhat ironically, Hard Luck Hughie became one of the luckiest bastards I ever met.

I worked at the *Times* for nearly two years, before employing a Swiss guy, Danny Schneider, to do graphic work on the magazines. I taught him English and he taught me German. We got on like a house on fire, soon realising how much we both deplored the way the *Times* was run. And that was it. We set up our own ad agency, catering to the banks and insurance companies that were currently being represented by the newspaper. In those days no one was doing advertising, everything was pretty ad hoc. Okay, no more puns. Our company was called Graphic Art and Design — or GAD for short. We became the GADsby twins, and you know what, it worked! Despite our financial situation being tenuous at times, we had a great time and it was a new adventure.

By this stage I had moved to a small cottage in Malkerns — a similar distance from Mbabane — and having long since tired of the bus or using my thumb, I invested in a motorbike, a Yamaha XT500. When business was quiet I'd take it for a blat and have an adventure.

One day while riding to work in Mbabane, I came across a roadblock at a place called Malagwane, on a steep hill just outside of town. A big fella, about six foot eight, with a machine gun stood on the road with his arm out.

'Halt!' he said.

I stopped in front of him, and he signalled me to turn the engine off. Typically, to do this on the old XT I'd have to pump the gas a couple times, then push the kill button. But on this occasion as I pumped the gas my thumb slipped off the kill button, my fingers slipped off the clutch and the bike did a handstand, then just took off! Ahhh, XT, I loved you so dearly when you talked that torque! The front wheel slammed right into this guy's knackers! Then the bike knocked him over and I rode right over the top of this policeman holding a machine gun. I fully expected bullets to start flying from his mates, who were standing nearby, but instead turned to find them laughing and mouthing, 'Go, get out of here! When he gets up he's going to shoot you!'

Now, I'd never seen this particular cop before, but invariably, as always happens, I saw him every goddamned day thereafter. Whichever town in Swaziland I happened to be riding in, there he was, this great big dude shaking his fist at me. At least he had a sense of humour.

He could have shot me and gotten away with it.

Along with fun times in Swaziland came events of a freakier nature. *Muti*, or traditional medicine, may be commonplace in southern Africa, but to a Westerner it's hard to fathom. The word *muti* comes from the Zulu word for tree because that's the source of many of these medicines. *Muti* ingredients, however, aren't always gathered from plants and trees. *Muti* murders refer to a ritual practice in which organs or other body parts are harvested for the production of traditional medicine. The medicine supposedly strengthens the 'personality' or personal force of the person who commissions the medicine. Politicians use *muti* to gain votes. Police might use it to gain a promotion.

One of Swaziland's prime ministers was once caught with *muti* while in power. Another time he was caught with human body parts beneath his seat in the parliamentary chamber. *Muti* murder victims vary widely in age and social standing. They are often young children or elderly people, both male and female. Some believe really powerful *muti* can be made from the flesh of albinos. Each of the body parts has its own significance; the most potent magic comes from parts that are cut off a living being.

Mutilation does not take place in order to kill the victim, but generally the victim will die of the wounds. Body parts most often removed include soft tissue such as eyelids, lips and labia — although entire limbs can also be severed. The body parts are then mixed with medicinal plants and cooked to create a medicine.

When I lived in Swaziland (and even today) *muti* murders were not uncommon. Close to Malkerns there was a cannibal camp, where human body parts were eaten by believers in *muti*. Sometimes, when the bike was stuffed, I was forced to walk through a nearby forest to get to work. I nearly shat myself every time. This will sound crazy, but I genuinely believe the reason I was able travel in and out of the cannibals' area was because of my blue eyes. If I ever got into a dodgy situation where these dudes watched me, or started to gather, I'd stare at them and they'd freak. Blue eyes seemed to scare the crap out of them. Eventually the cops caught the people involved.

Crazy shit happened every day in Swaziland; even so, I was constantly amazed at the number of *muti* killings. I doubt a day went by when someone didn't get bopped off for magic. A guy I knew from the University of Swaziland was kidnapped and taken into the woods because his captors

Close to Malkerns there was a cannibal camp. Sometimes, when the bike was stuffed, I was forced to walk through a nearby forest to get to work.

required some 'white man *muti*'. As they walked him down to their sacred tree, my mate resigned himself to the fact he was going to die. But his captors noticed he repeatedly stumbled and couldn't keep up.

When asked why, he replied, 'It's my ailment. I have multiple sclerosis.'

His captors swore, cursed and fell about the place. 'Oh, motherfucker, oh shit, you should have fucking told us that when we kidnapped you!'

My mate's fear turned to confusion.

'We need a perfect human being,' they explained. 'You can't have any illnesses or sickness. Now we're just going to beat you up.'

So they beat him up and stole his car. For the first time in his life he was happy he had MS.

I used to eat lunch every day at a place called the Swazi Chicken. The five owners included a woman who lit up the room every time she smiled. She was forever singing and often gave me extra pieces of chicken. Later I discovered all five restaurateurs had been arrested for keeping human body parts in the freezer. They said they needed magic in order to be the most popular restaurant in town. As a result, they went to court, were found guilty and sentenced to death. I found this out via a professional hangman I met in a bar in Mbabane. The man with the unenviable job was from South Africa. I commented that I had no idea such jobs still existed.

'I'm the only professional hangman in southern Africa nowadays,' he replied. 'It used to be quite an industry. These days I only do a dozen or so a year, though there will be five tomorrow; that's a new record for me.'

'It's got to be a tough job,' I said. 'Ever any light relief?'

He answered, 'No. Not in this job. Oh hang on a minute, actually last month I hung this guy in Botswana and, just as I was putting the hood over his head, he asked,

"Is this thing safe?"' The hangman laughed into his beer, thinking it was a cool joke.

I never saw my friend from the Swazi Chicken again. She was hung the next day. Ahhh, my sweet thing, I still miss seeing your smile when you sang that song you knew I so loved.

Come Saturday morning there was never a lot to do in Malkerns. So from time to time I'd get up while it was still dark and ride 30km into the bush, down various tracks to a mud hut run by a witch doctor. Seeing a witch doctor in Swaziland was not uncommon; seeing a white one was. Her story was a fascinating one: she was a nurse and her husband an undertaker. Working in Swaziland's rural areas demanded she work alongside witch doctors. A sound knowledge of white man's medicine meant she was highly respected and over the years she became the witch doctor's confidante, and was shown the tricks of the trade.

Her hut couldn't have been any more different to that of a white doctor: it was full of bones, snake and leopard skins, pieces of lion's and elephant's tails, roots, shrubs, rhino horns, pots of frogs and crocodile heads. It looked like a movie set. My own doctor back home in Levin, Andy van de Vyver, is African, but he tends to keep his snake bones well hidden in his surgery.

She would sit me in the darkest corner, where I would covertly watch her clinic. Through the doors walked throngs of people, including princes, doctors, policemen and politicians, everyone coming for the *muti* and magic.

I sometimes found a *muti* parcel around my house. They never contained body parts but rather things like a tied-up clump of hair, an old toothbrush I'd thrown away, or little roots from trees. Sometimes there'd be a dead frog in a bag underneath my goddamned welcome mat. I took what I found to my white witch doctor friend, who thankfully reported none were 'bad parcels'. Instead she informed me that a young woman in the district fancied me, hence the frog! Later I used *muti* to my advantage. I'd long fancied a young American university lecturer. I'd tried flowers, gifts, sweet-talking, yet whatever I did proved fruitless. She was completely uninterested — and that just didn't *happen* to me! (Okay, it happens all the time.) I needed help, so I confided in the witch doctor, who told me she'd make some fresh *muti* (without human body parts I hasten to add).

'But you'll need something from her,' the doctor advised.

I managed to get some of her hair and the *muti* was brewed. I then invited the lecturer to dinner, bought a leg of lamb (which was probably goat) and cooked a beautiful meal. I was surprised she had agreed to come, but not that she still showed little interest in yours truly on arrival. Then I put some *muti* in the gravy! We ate, had one glass of wine, and the brand-new pair of Levi jeans I'd bought that week were ripped off me in minutes. She just tore the dome off and destroyed the zip.

Does *muti* work? *Yarrra*, yes indeed! I've seen it work so often. Watched people get sick just because the moment they've found some *muti* it began working, bang.

Do I believe in it? Absolutely, 100 per cent.

Swaziland made me. Unlike South Africa, Swaziland gave me a sense of freedom and independence. People weren't scared of the police. There was a sense of justice. It was a kingdom with very little oppression. Living there amplified and heightened my senses. For the two and a half years I was there, every day was an adventure. I wasn't crowding into a train full of accountants and lawyers, going up to the seventh floor and skim-reading the newspaper. Every day, when I walked to work, the cobras and mambas wanted a piece of me. Returning home at night through the forest with cannibals nearby made me feel alive. You had to live on your sixth sense, be aware of the dangers and steer yourself away from them.

We all possess a sixth sense, but many drown or suppress it. We write it off as just a gut feeling. Well, *listen* to those guts, they're so right. That's all a gut feeling is — your sixth sense coming back. You can train it. Give me the skin tingling, the neck-hair hackling, the eye-widening, nostril-flaring awareness. Move closer to the edge. Get off the ledge. Pump that adrenaline.

San (Bushman) rock engraving at Twyfelfontein, Namibia.

When I first saw the gemsbok it was from the side — I believed I had found the fabled unicorn! When it turned and I noticed the malformed horn I felt fame slip through my fingers yet again.

Zebra liver with onions

INGREDIENTS

1 zebra liver
1 cup milk
1 tablespoon whisky or rum
4–5 large rashers bacon
2 onions
1 cup flour
1/2 cup red wine

Thinly slice 1 fresh zebra liver. (I prefer slices no thicker than one finger deep and a couple of fingers wide.) Soak your zebra liver in milk — this helps take away some of the sourness or metallic flavour. You can now also add a small bottle-cap of whisky or rum to the mix, should you wish. For a far more intense whisky or rum flavour, swig back a cap or two of the booze and just soak the liver in straight milk. Place the liver in the fridge for around two hours.

Cook 4–5 large rashers of bacon in a heavy cast-iron pan. When the bacon is cooked, remove it from the pan. Thinly slice 2 onions and cook the onion in the remaining bacon grease until just translucent, then remove. Roll the liver slices lightly in flour. Lower the heat of the pan and place in the liver. Do not add salt while cooking. Keeping the lid on the pan will help keep the liver tender. Turn the liver slices once, then add the onion. You can also chop up some of the bacon and add that.

Serve and eat as is, or make a light gravy just before the livers are fully cooked by adding a half glass of cheap red Australian wine to the pan and stirring it up for a grand finish (there's no point in wasting good Kiwi wine on this recipe).

Finally, keep an eye out for the inevitable lions and hyenas who will come to your camp once they smell this fabulous meal!

Zebra livers are an absolute favourite dish of my daughter Taygen. Mine too, for that matter. They are so exquisite.

Heading for the hills and a possum hunter's life.

8

HEADING FOR THE HILLS

In 1985, I arrived back in New Zealand, and the only thing I was sure of was that I didn't want to get married. I was 25 and I had been away for seven years. Something I'd always wanted to be was an advertising copywriter, but I had no experience. Mind you, that had never held me back in the past. I went to Ogilvy & Mather and J. Walter Thompson in Wellington and told them I was a copywriter fresh from the UK. When I was asked for my portfolio I said it was on a tea chest aboard a boat. J. Walter Thompson took me on, and waited anxiously for the boat. It was a sizeable jump going from production to copy, something which frustrated me. I'm a reasonably creative guy — and write pretty well — but I had never really had the opportunity to unleash myself. The company had some big clients, including Lever Brothers, and their brands Persil and Surf. I guess there was just too much learning on the job and I didn't excel. I worked at it for about three months until one day they asked after the whereabouts of that boat. Ironically, I thought I was doing okay.

But no experience is wasted, and writing soap-powder ads taught me I didn't want a bar of it. So I took things into my own hands and headed for the hills. Inspired by the old American trapping books I've always loved reading, I went possum trapping. Over the next while I moved around, setting up camp on the West Coast, the Ruahines, and out the back of Wanganui country.

Possum trapping is all about planning. If you're going into the scrub for three or four months you'd better damn well figure out how much food, fuel and bait you'll need. I'd fly in with two sacks of spuds, two sacks of onions, heaps and heaps of pasta and rice, and carbo up. The size of my meals was incredible. You need to eat plenty of carbos, as well as deep-fried possum, possum casserole, or possum pie. Breakfast was a huge bowl of porridge. If I was on my own, I'd bake a loaf of bread every two days, but after a few months I'd kind of get sick of it so I'd conjure up crazy bread recipes, like coffee bread or onion bread. The biggest luxury was a can of peaches.

Wintering over at Kinvig Hut in the Ruahines.

The number of traps I ran depended on the terrain. I could run 70 without a problem. I used a little Victor No. 1, a North American jump trap. Every trapper has a secret lure. I used flour with icing sugar, before adding cinnamon oil, rose oil and aniseed oil. Those three oils would work at different latent temperatures. On a hot night (anywhere above five or six degrees) your aniseed oil would really move. When things were chillier, your rose oil became dominant.

So many days were cold, wet and miserable. I spent endless hours fleshing and tacking out skins, checking those which were drying, double-checking

Hernes head rests in the misty morning of our camp. Hunting the roar of 2008 with Belgian Bob and Taygen.

they were drying under the tail properly. Day and night were spent ensuring the skins looked their absolute best. I was proud of mine. I wasn't happy with good — they had to be great. Once dry, I'd take them off the boards, split the tails, brush them, and prepare them for auction. Back in those days there were two auction houses which bought skins, Dalgetys and New Zealand Fur Auctions, run by Don Campbell in Seaview. If you bothered to turn up at Don's on auction day, lunch and booze would be provided. If your skins fetched a good price you drank their free liquor; if the skins fetched a bad price you drank their free liquor. Buyers glared at the smelly guys who'd just come out of the bush.

It was a great life.

Trapping demanded you lived off your wits. You were totally responsible for your actions. If not, it could be your demise. You felt invincible, not part of everyday society. Many days I was out on a limb, crossing swollen rivers and climbing through snow. I found amazing things: mistletoe, even a whole flock of blue ducks, some of which became tame and cleaned my porridge billy each morning. At least I had someone to talk to. As well as talking to animals, I also talked to the rocks, trees and rivers. Oh the rivers! Spend time on your own and a river actually starts talking to you. Sit down for a spell by a river long enough and it will tell you a story. On quiet days you will hear it playing, making noises like children. Rivers are alive; it's just that we have spent thousands of years not listening. Sometimes I'd swim out to a rock in the middle of a pool and stand there naked, in the middle of winter, and pretend I was some bloody symphony orchestra conductor. Thank God no one ever saw me doing it. Thank goodness the river didn't mind.

At times it rained and rained. I learnt to watch the moon and predict when a storm was coming. People seem to have lost that art. These observations are grounded in science. The moisture in the air creates a ring around the moon. Most people look at it and think, *Wow, what a pretty ring around the moon*. For a trapper — or anyone whose livelihood depends on the weather — that ring means you've got three days max before the shit hits.

Aside from chatty animals, the only entertainment I had was a transistor radio. Generally, at night I got a better reception. That was the only time I really had any down time before I hit the sack. There were no

Walkmans or digital downloads. Nowadays you can plug whatever you like into some speakers run on a little solar-powered generator pack.

Most people in this country hate possums with a vengeance, many going out of their way to run them over. I stop my truck and let them cross. Dairy farmers would hate to hear that, but it comes down to the fact we're talking about an animal — with a spirit and a life. I won't run it over just for the sake of killing it. I'm not a fan of anyone who kills something just to kill it. If there are 68 million possums in New Zealand — as many experts predict — why do we never see them dead on the side of the road in the numbers that we did when we were kids? Bah humbug! There are not 68 million possums. Going out on a limb, I'd say possum numbers are in the area of 30 per cent of what they were 20 years ago.

There are still a few guys out there trapping, but I don't think they stay out long. Most are either plucking or working for contractors. Most of the money is in plucking because of the huge market for possum merino. It's crazy: at the moment you'll get paid $110 a kilo for possum fur, while sheep's wool is about $2.50 a kilo. If that's the case, why aren't we farming possums? I'm still waiting for skins to shine again, and when they do, mark my words, I'm going to go back trapping. I've been waiting 20-odd years. Back in the '80s, however, when trapping was my life, it was just as well I finally came out of the bush.

Because I married the first woman I saw.

ABOVE Home away from home at Kinvig.
BELOW Sunrise at Longview Hut, and the boys are still in the sack.
NEXT PAGE On top of the saddle sat a decent wallow. Martins Bay, Fiordland.
FOLLOWING PAGES
LEFT Two crisp early morning bush shots. Robbie Suisted photographed the rifles and told me no rifles were hurt in the making of this shot.
RIGHT Mountain daisies near Howletts.

ROB SUISTED

ROB COATS

Possum stew

INGREDIENTS

1 possum, skinned and butchered
1 cup flour
handful horopito, chopped
handful kawakawa leaves, chopped
salt and pepper
1 teaspoon curry powder
lots of vegetables
1 onion
3 tablespoons oil
3–4 rashers bacon

Deep fried possum. Crumbed possum. Possum pie . . . and my all-time favourite, possum stew. While trapping I'd eat a lot of possum; it was handy, easy to bring back to camp and didn't necessitate taking a rifle around my trapline.

I once made the mistake of candidly answering a journalist's question about what possum was like to eat. 'Why, it makes your hair shiny and your shit slick,' I said.

Hell, I thought it was a pretty good throwaway line until Maggie rang me a few days later to say I'd been quoted verbatim in the newspaper. What made it worse, the article was syndicated nationwide and I received a fair bit of ridicule over the matter. It is, however, quite true. Eat enough possum and while it may not happen overnight, it will happen.

When I was trapping I'd only eat possums I'd shot or poisoned with cyanide. Would I still eat a cyanided possum? Not on your life! And you shouldn't try it either, not unless you're experienced with handling deadly poison — better still, stick to shooting them.

Hang the possum. Like all game, hung is best. Three to four days is ample. Use the hind legs whole (I don't bother too much about front legs on a jacko) and strips from the back. Place the meat in a plastic bag with flour, chopped horopito (pepperwood) and kawakawa (bush basil) leaves, and a little salt and pepper. Add 1 teaspoon of curry powder to the mix, and give it all a good shake. Quickly brown the meat on a fairly high heat. Add to a casserole pot with any vegetable you can lay your hands on, especially onions, and while at it, add 3 tablespoons of oil. If you have any bacon, 3–4 rashers cut into strips will really give it a boost. Pour in some water to a level just above the ingredients. Cook it nice and slow over the coals for about an hour and a half. If you're at home cook it at 150°C for the same time. Check the water level and add a bit more if it's looking dry, then let it simmer on low coals for another hour or so. All done. Eat with rice or mashed spuds.

Now get yourself ready for more bouncy, lustrous, shiny hair. Oh, and the other.

Telling Belgian Bob I will die if I dont have a whisky and find a woman.

9

WHISKY AND WOMEN

When I'd come down to the flatlands (anywhere with a town or a farm), I'd always feel 10 feet tall and totally independent. *By God! I'm a mountainy man, do ya hear! I can out-run, out-ride, out-drink and out-fight any man alive! Wah!*

So you're a little feral for a day or two . . . give the boy some space, oh, and maybe some soap while you're at it. It takes time getting reacquainted with the big smoke. First, you must retrain yourself. Hover on the footpath's edge, look left, look right, look left again, and then right again. Do that for a couple of minutes until you feel you have safely figured out which way the cars are coming from. In the bush you're not used to watching for cars. Once safely across, find some fish and chips and hot dogs, anything with fat. Your body is craving it!

This particular day I bumped into an old mate, Belgian Bob, and told him I needed whisky and a woman, though in no particular order. If I

Belgian Bob in one of our favourite spots under Mt Ruapehu. I'm sure the deer here are a sub-species, spindly wee stags. But boy! Talk about fun in the roar with everything up close and personal.

didn't get one or the other, I would die. *Die*!!! My eyes lit up when he mentioned a party. Even better, he hooked me up on a blind date with a girl called Maggie. My date had been informed that the bloke they'd been talking about was finally out of the bush after five months, to which Maggie replied, 'What does anyone *do* in the bush for so long?'

I turned up late, wearing a poncho, cowdy boots and a cowdy hat. I also had my sister Diana on my arm, which surprised Maggie, who thought the date was over before it began. She later told me I was the loudest person she'd ever met. I thought I was just a quiet bloke who talked to animals and conducted rivers naked. Maggie remembers me as the guy who boomed when he laughed, the whole room wondering what was shaking.

No one at the party knew what a trapper was. Meanwhile, I was enjoying music, whisky and the company of this young chick from Nelson, now teaching at Parkway College in Wainui. I was also trying to be smooth: 'Hey snake, do you wanna wriggle?'

Judging by Maggie's reaction, it wasn't my best line.

It took a while to adjust to civilian life after so long in the bush, but finally I adapted and began to dress appropriately.

'Er. Would you like to go dancing?'

This time the response was affirmative, though it hadn't crossed Maggie's mind that we would be going alone. Once in her car, she asked, 'Where's everyone else?'

I replied, 'We're it, baby, let's go!' Rock and roll.

Every nightclub in those days was called Whispers or Rumours, and we found one in Lower Hutt. I threw my arms and legs around like a hillbilly. Apparently I don't have a lot of rhythm. I must have really fallen for this girl because I even took my hat off. Normally I have an issue with such a rule in New Zealand bars. I just don't get it. I wear hats, always have.

As soon as you go into a bar, the barman says, 'Take the hat off, son.'

And I say, 'Here's the deal. I will take my hat off if you can give me one good reason why I should that doesn't include the words "Because those are the rules".'

What is it about hats that pisses these guys off? Actually, I know where this archaic rules stems from. It has to do with old gentlemen's clubs and the fact that they all had a picture of the ruling monarch hanging on the wall. In deference to royalty, one always took one's hat off.

When we left the bar at 2.30 am I asked my blind date if she liked crabs. I took her and her puzzled look to Days Bay. It was high tide and I knew there'd be people catching crabs. I told her we could buy some and cook them up. Sure enough, there were about 50 Indians and Samoans on the wharf, all with crab cages. We walked along the beach in the wee small hours and I told Maggie all sorts of bullshit: how I used to be a bodyguard for Stevie Wonder, and how it was fun until we went window-shopping and he'd smash everything with his cane. I told her I couldn't read or write. I quoted her a few poems by Keats. I think Maggie found all this pretty romantic.

We moved in together almost immediately. Then shortly thereafter I was offered a logging job in Karioi, near Mount Ruapehu. Despite falling for Maggie, I had been getting itchy feet and needed to get out in the bush again. I was bush sick.

The day before I left, I was looking around the flat for my trusty old boots and was having no luck finding them. To my astonishment, Maggie informed me she'd thrown them out. I'd lost toenails in those boots! Well, that was it, a woman deciding I wasn't going bush again? I was definitely leaving! Next thing I knew, Maggie was standing in front of me with a box in her hands.

'Your old boots were so smelly,' she said, 'I took them to the shop and said to the guy, "you'd better give me a pair exactly the same size and make as these"'. My anger subsided.

I never did take on the logging job. The moment Maggie bought out those boots I decided to stick around. This woman was something special. I rang my mate at Karioi.

'Mate, I'm going to hang around and see how this one pans out,' I said. 'Reckon I'm going to ride this bronco.'

After a week I said to myself, *I'm going to marry this girl.*

I got a job as a labourer for a construction company called Wilcox & Hughes, conducting similar stunts to those I learnt in the UK. I'm glad OSH wasn't around in those days. God knows how we were never killed.

Maggie and I had been going out for a month or so when we had our first trip away. The New Zealand possum-skinning champs were being held at Lake Brunner on the West Coast, and I'd managed to find a spot on the North Island team. I just knew Maggie had to see this event. I told her it'd be fun and she'd meet a bunch of possum trappers and crazy dudes; salty dogs like Barry Mercer, Charlie Emmerson, Frank Wolf and the irrepressible Mike Bygate, all legends in the possum world and deer-culling days. Four North Island representatives were to skin against those South Island bastards. Typically, those southern boys always did something to upset their opponents. This particular time they made us skin *frozen* possums, while they had the luxury of the thawed variety. These things were frozen solid! Jesus, did we have bloody sore fingers by the end of it.

Skinning frozen possums was a challenge.

Maggie sat in the front row as we skinned, a choice she would soon regret. Sometimes when skinning, the actual skin doesn't come off as cleanly as you'd like, and the only thing to do is grab the possum tight and whack it into the bench. Especially frozen ones, you bloody southern bastards! But because you're speed skinning, you'd better be quick. The next thing you know — if you're lucky enough to be sitting in the front row, as my new girlfriend happened to be — you're wearing a lapful of possum guts, balls, head, brains and eyes. I noticed a few specks sitting on Maggie's shoulder, so went over and informed her that perhaps it wasn't the best place to sit.

'Sit a bit further back, honey,' I said, removing a possum's eyeball from her shoulder when she wasn't looking.

Despite not taking the logging job, I was adamant I was going to further my education. School C just wasn't going to cut it. I'd read in a *Time* magazine I'd found under the bunk in Kinvig Hut in the Ruahines that the highest paid consultants in America were of the corporate-image variety, so I decided to become one — despite not knowing what one was. First I'd have to become a marketing guru, so I enrolled at Massey University and moved to Palmerston North. After a few months, Maggie said that our set-up was crazy and told me she was following me. She scored a job teaching at Waiopehu College in Levin. I moved out of my flat and we rented an old farmhouse in Taikorea, me riding my motorbike each day to Palmy, while Maggie drove to Levin.

It took a few years to pop the question. Most people have wonderful stories about how they got engaged. When Maggie and I are asked how it happened here's what we say: 'Well, we got a whole lot of Chinese for dinner, came home, drank three bottles of wine, got rip-roaring drunk, and Maggie started sobbing that all her friends were married and she wasn't. I said, "I'll marry you, you bitch!"'

At least that's the story I tell everyone. In actual fact, I got down on one knee and asked her properly. But first I needed to ask her old man for permission. Her father Les, a London Cockney, answered the phone just as he does to this day.

'Les, it's Davey here,' I started.

'Davey who?'

'You know, I go out with your daughter.'

I told him I was ringing to ask for his permission for his daughter's hand in marriage. 'But I don't give a shit if you say no because I'm doing it anyway. What have you got to say about that?'

It was Maggie's strong will that attracted me. She'd been married once already and had been through hell, so was strongly aware she wasn't going to make the same mistake twice. I guess I had to prove myself. In the past she'd gone out with town guys. I was different to most of the people she'd met. Truth be told, we just had a passion for life — and we still do. Together we looked for challenges, crazy things. She often tells me she doesn't want to lose the 'wild man'.

Damn, she looked beautiful!

Whenever I say I want to go to Siberia or Alaska, she says, 'That's what a wild man would do. What are you waiting for?' She's smart, realising that adventure helps me grow. 'Get out there,' she'll say.

Our wedding was held at my brother John's place in Wainuiomata. I flew in by helicopter — 20 minutes late. My soon-to-be father-in-law, a stickler for time, lamented after 10 minutes that the groom should always be on time. He pulled Maggie aside: 'I don't think this turkey is coming, let's get out of here.'

Maggie replied, 'He's coming, but he's got a plan.' Which was probably giving me a little too much credit.

In reality, I'd told my pilot I wasn't getting married until we could find ourselves some deer. 'Head for the hills, buddy!'

If we were successful I'd take it to be a great sign, an omen. It took a bit longer than I thought, but as soon as we spotted three hinds on a slip I yelled, 'That's it, brother! Let's head home, we've got a wedding to be at!'

Two of my best mates were groomsmen. I wore a suit and carried a Bowie knife because you've got to cut the cake with something. After the ceremony, everyone went back to their utes, took their good shirts and suits off, and replaced them with black singlets, shorts and gumboots. We lit the biggest fire and had the biggest party. Maggie and I cooked. We were broke and couldn't afford catering, so we provided all the fish, venison, wild pork, goat, eel, trout and pheasant. We ate like kings and partied all night long. It was a hell of a summer wedding.

And this is where Maggie and I continue to fall out — neither of us can recall the actual date. We've been married 24 years, yet have never celebrated our wedding anniversary because we can't agree what day it was! For us, it's not important to wake up and know it's our wedding anniversary. Every day we wake up and say it's a damn good feeling being married. Every day is our wedding anniversary.

ABOVE The rear end of a *bakkie* (ute or pickup) makes a great wagon for this family. For some reason though, the local elephant population simply can't stand these modes of transport and frequently chase the wagons. Should they catch up, they get all aggro and set about wrecking them. Such games elephants play . . . and no one knows why. Damaraland, Namibia.

LEFT Sven Engholm runs his dogsled school in a remote region of Finnmark. My cabin at the school looked like something out of a Hans Christian Andersen fairy tale. Handbuilt from logs he felled himself and with all the furnishings being designed and built by Sven as well, it is without doubt one of my favourite places on the planet. Karasjok, Norway.

An auspicious day, putting our sign above the shop on State Highway One.

Building Swazi with Maggie, and discovering it's so much more than a business.

10

SWAZI IS BORN

In 1992 I was doing some branding and corporate-image work from an office in Levin and Maggie, despite having three pre-schoolers at home, was looking for something to exercise her mind. One day it came to her we should start a company making T-shirts for hunters, as well as taking on other small printing jobs. Maggie came up with the name Swazi Print, telling me, 'You enjoyed your time so much in Swaziland, I think it would be a great name for a company.'

She was one step ahead, knowing the name was versatile. Swazi was a generic term, whether our target market was hunters, young kids or teenagers. Much like Coca-Cola, Swazi could mean anything and would go wherever the company went. Within no time our lounge was packed to the gunwhales with fabric, so we opted to move to the old Levin railway station which we took on a 10-year lease.

Around this time Warnocks, New Zealand's largest manufacturer

We set out to build garments that would last longer than anything on the market. It's all to do with our responsibility to our customer and our environment.

and retailer of school uniforms, had gone into receivership. All of a sudden schools from the East Coast to Wellington had no uniforms. Maggie got to work making freshly branded samples. We would throw the kids in the car and head off to Gisborne, visiting schools in the area with one set of samples. We made appointments with principals, and enquired where they were heading without Warnocks. In the past these schools had to take what Warnocks offered, but we were told, for example, that kids preferred longer, baggier shorts to Stubbies look-alikes. We wanted to make uniforms that looked smart and that kids would be happy to wear.

Bang! Our timing was perfect. Maggie employed me and paid me $50 a week, which is still my weekly wage, although I'm also allowed to go on a few adventures. I became chief patternmaker, something which still makes me laugh. Should I ever be feeling a bit down I head into the dungeons of Swazi and dig out some old patterns, before breaking into laughter. Here was an ex-possum trapper making A-line skirt patterns for a girls' school. It was all trial and error. I didn't know what I was doing, but I had the wonderful advantage of never having worked in the industry. There were no limitations or preconceived ideas of what a patternmaker or machinist did.

When new high-performance and technical fabrics found their way onto my desk, I began making my own hunting gear, amazed at how well it worked compared to my existing clothing. As any outdoors type will tell you, there's nothing worse than being trapped in a stream for days on end wearing sub-standard gear. Being an expert in getting wet and cold was finally about to pay off. We started making products, based on my experience, that were functional and comfortable.

Hunting and farming gear was closely linked in those days. If you wanted a raincoat, it had to be an oilskin or PVC parka. When new high-performance fabrics arrived they worked so well that I had a hunch there was a market for clothes for hunters. So we made up 60 sets of jackets and pants and took off to the Safari Club International Annual Hunting Show in Melbourne. When we turned up we were seen as hillbillies, especially in Australian eyes. A couple of hicks from Levin. Maybe ignorance is bliss. Maggie and I brimmed with confidence, perhaps stemming from the fact that I'd tested our gear and knew it bloody well worked. Other exhibitors had $20,000 booths. We had a trestle table with a makeshift sign that read 'Swazi New Zealand'. Every morning we'd jump out of our hotel bed, strip the sheet off, take it to our booth and drape it over the trestle table. Australian retailers looked at our gear, nodded their heads approvingly, but no one was buying. On Saturday, however, when the show was open to the public, we sold out within hours. The whole lot was gone. We then realised we had a product and needed to get home and build a brand.

When we returned from Melbourne we were fired up. At the time we only had one employee, who we happily told now had full-time work. Then came the serious stuff with the bank, which through it all was pretty bloody good to us. Starting with less than zero, they gave us a $4000 overdraft to buy machines and set up the outdoor equipment arm of the company.

Once the business was under way, pressure came in from every angle: financial, family, you name it. Three kids under four was enough work without adding a new business to the mix. Even with machines and cutting tables, we had to learn how to design garments. I visited every sports shop in New Zealand. I'd never done cold-selling before. Some shops paid attention; others were happy with existing stock, namely Macpac and Fairydown. I was either told that hunters didn't need this sort of gear or that 'We don't really like hunters anyway.' Some days I felt I was going nowhere, often sleeping in a truck in the pissing rain with a leaking canopy. But Maggie and I had a belief we were going to make this happen. Thinking about feeding and supporting three kids gave us no choice.

We'd throw the kids in the car and go on sales trips. We got to know every single playground in the country!

I got some great free advice right about then from an unlikely quarter. Steve Richards, owner of Huntech Clothing and at that stage our only competitor, had been pioneering high-tech gear for hunters for a couple of years. He told me to keep at it, to approach everything from a practical angle and, get this, that if ever I needed any help to give him a call. Our

LEFT Our first cattledog. From day one we've punched above our weight — you have to in New Zealand.
RIGHT We import all our garments from here.

companies have always remained competitive, with Steve in my opinion a very savvy businessman, brilliant designer and my most wily opponent. In latter years he just got so disheartened by what he saw as the lack of ethics in the hunting retail sector that he began to focus his energy in other directions. What a sad loss to the sport and industry.

Eventually we got enough stores ordering from us to get the thing going. And we didn't even have to tell fibs. Okay, maybe a few white lies, namely 'We have a full range' and a 'printed catalogue'. In reality, we only had one printer's proof and didn't want to print catalogues until we were sure we could sell the products. I think we just hit that sweet spot. It didn't take long to realise we'd have to punch well above our weight to make people believe we were an exciting, vibrant company with dozens of staff. Swazi was one machinist, Maggie and me based in a railway station we'd recently painted in the Bruce tartan. When you start a business you live on adrenaline, go to bed excited and wake up excited. Here we are, 16 years later and I still go to bed excited and wake up excited. Nothing has changed. The business is the same. There are different issues and challenges but it's still exciting. It's a chase, a hunt, seizing opportunities that perhaps other people don't see.

It's tough working with your wife and forming a partnership, especially when one of you (me) comes from a marketing angle and your partner comes from a production one. It's no secret these two facets of a business don't always get on. When you live in the same house (and sleep in the same bed) a disagreement over a garment can produce sparks. We're both fiery people and strong-willed. It took about two years to settle that down. I'll never forget those first few tough years when my mother sent weekly 'Red Cross' parcels. Paying the mortgage and food bill was a constant struggle.

Never one to pass up an opportunity, I'd drive to the Sander Tie Company in Paraparaumu each Friday to bag the leather offcuts they threw away. At this time leather ties were all the rage and I'd discovered the company just threw out their leftovers. Every Friday afternoon, Maggie and I would divide the takings into 1-kilo bags and run ads for them in the *Levin Chronicle*. There was a real fad at that time for sewing leather patches over jeans — kind of a cheap way to make leather pants I guess. Sometimes a knock on the door would turn out to be a huge dude with tattoos on his face, a Mongrel Mob or Nomad gang member, demanding a bag of leather, one of the 30 sitting on our lounge floor.

Fifteen bucks a bag, sell six and $90 could feed the family for a whole week. You do what you have to, to feed the vision.

Swazi grew quickly. Within two years we had 15 staff. We were outgrowing the railway station so we bought a larger factory. Initially we thought the building — at 400 square metres — was far too big. Within two years staff numbers had grown to 26, the maximum number of bodies we could fit in the plant. In the end we hired only skinny people. We finally moved into our current plant on State Highway 1, which measures 3000 square metres. We bought the building from Wisharts shirt manufacturers, as most of their business had moved to Auckland. Wisharts continued manufacturing upstairs (while we were down) but after 12 months they decided things were too tight financially. We were offered the entire plant, including every piece of machinery, huge steam-driven confangler machines (technical term meaning: I don't know what the hell they were) and pocketmakers. They had everything you needed

We painted the former Levin railway station in the Bruce tartan, and no one in town has ever forgiven us.

Our management team at Totara Street, Levin. From left, Maggie, Sharee Harper, Janine Wilsher, Lyndon Tamblyn and some unknown guy who just walked in off the street.

to make a shirt. Swazi was offered the whole lot for $20,000 (it was valued at around $2 million) as long as we took on their staff and business. This was a bargain, but in the end we decided we knew nothing about shirts — or the market. We declined the offer, but picked up some of their best machinists and we moved our entire operating plant upstairs, where we still are today.

In the 1960s and 1970s, Levin was the apparel centre of New Zealand. There were a heap of experienced people within the district. Huge plants with 300 to 400 staff were common, making everything from shirts to pyjamas. It was a booming town, but as the industry started to shrink those companies shut down or went overseas. One day I looked around and realised we were just about it. Wisharts, Lanes, Hagers, all great businesses, were gone. The industry was imploding. As the others shut down, I felt lonely. It's nothing you would wish for. To be honest I had hoped for a strong apparel trade in my town as it would bring key staff members in from other areas: great machinists and admin people, top marketing people and production planners.

Ironically, during Levin's tough years I never felt we were next. We've faced some huge challenges over the years, where the company has reached a point where everything was so finely balanced on a financial knife edge, and Maggie and I have had to make some tough decisions over staff reductions. And no doubt we will have more turbulence throughout the journey, that's the nature of being New Zealand-made. You don't climb mountains because they are flat and easy. You climb them for a better view of the world.

The apparel manufacturers I mentioned above all shut down for one reason: because they couldn't compete at the lower end of the market. Importers started bringing in clothing, not necessarily needed or wanted, but incredibly cheap. Many businesses that got into the import game have become dominant by opening in a town where local retailers simply can't compete. They and local manufacturers shut down, and all that's left are big ugly big-box stores everywhere. The people that used to have garment manufacturing-sector jobs and own their own retail businesses no longer do so. And the cycle continues; when you don't have a job the only place you can afford to shop is at a cheap import store, so these businesses keep growing — and growing. Vibrant provincial shopping communities have become homogeneous wastelands. Sorry, but I love this country and I cannot sit back and watch its very guts being ripped out without speaking my piece.

Levin, world headquarters of Swazi.

Grow a business in New Zealand and you'll need tons of capital, especially in the early years. We poured every cent into buying more machinery, employing more staff and expanding our range. After six or seven years, we needed to consolidate and we needed to start turning a profit — and using that profit not just to buy machinery but also to shore up the sides of the business. When a business grows at a fair clip, that growth can actually become a nightmare. You're just growing and growing and growing but the machine is eating up every cent that there is. You need to put the brakes on. You finally realise that, hey, this growth is getting us nowhere and how come I'm still earning $50 a week? So you put the brakes on, stop and have a good look at the business: rather than just growth as a strategy, let's look at where we want to be in one years', two years', or five years' time.

We had no idea at the time, but what Swazi was doing was innovative. For one thing, in this throwaway world, we had a reputation for manufacturing good, practical, durable gear that would last. And that's the key, because hunters, farmers and possum trappers don't typically have a lot of money. The best gear in those days was found in ski and outdoors shops. Macpac and Fairydown were pretty damn good brands, but their products lacked the durability for the rigours of hunting and were too costly for people in my sport.

The approximate cost of running Swazi from Levin is over a million dollars in wages. If we moved to China we could probably pocket that every year. But my interest in the business would wane pretty quickly.

It then becomes a numbers game, not a people game. *He tangata*. And I'm not interested in numbers. Our philosophy has never changed. Every now and then unions get involved, and although — like all good employers — we give our employees the absolute best deal that we possibly can, sometimes we have a union delegate breathing down our necks demanding more. Times like this make you rethink — is it really worth it going to mediation and bashing heads with these guys when the easiest thing would be to take the bloody factory overseas and never have to deal with these pricks again? At the end of the day it's worth it. After all, if I want to make a decision I don't need to talk to shareholders. If it feels right we do it — and staff have a big say in that.

Levin is our community. I feel a 100 per cent responsibility towards the people of this town. Levin is Swazi's heart, our world headquarters. This *town* makes the best raingear in the world. It is only a small matter, but we can shout it for all to hear. We lift our heads high and look out on the entire world. This town has craftspeople. Not only do we feel a responsibility to the people who service the day-to-day needs of Swazi, but also to the people who live here. I'm a great believer that money needs to go round in a circle; the moment you take a chunk out of that circle — and the connection is lost — the communities fall down. Government policies (I'm talking about *all* parties) seem to be based around gutting the provinces and shifting the masses to the major cities to where the jobs have been restructured. Gridlock time. Ever wonder why the poor buggers living in Auckland and Wellington require more and more of the country's resources to pour into infrastructure and roads? The economy takes precedence over people and the environment.

We had fun with our billboards outside the railway station, getting local artists to paint them.

I'm sure I can recall the economist Gareth Morgan once making a comment that any company that was not manufacturing offshore, or considering moving offshore . . . well, their owners were akin to village idiots. So be it, Gareth! But what a village I live in, my friend.

Every July at Swazi we have a mid-winter Christmas party. At one of them I was talking to a woman who has been with us for years. She's now a proud grandmother and she told me how pleased she was that her grandson was going to Te Aute College, the first to do so in her whanau. The only reason he could go was because she had a job and could pay for him to attend. Without that job, that wouldn't have happened. For her, the dream had come true. We could take our factory away and make things in China but if we do that we don't just take jobs, we take away dreams. Who am I to destroy a person's dreams? Who's to say the boy at Te Aute College is not a future prime minister, or a doctor, or the researcher who finds the cure for cancer?

I dream that people who work for me have the chance of a better life. Maggie and I have discovered Swazi is not a manufacturing company. It is a tool, an instrument, and we need to make that instrument as financially stable as possible so we can make a difference. We need to use it in the best way we can, whether through supporting conservation projects, or sponsoring a school or an athlete, or building a hut in the Tararuas (more of which later). We need to use this tool for more than our own purposes, for more than just personal wealth. We could be far wealthier if we said 'bugger it' and moved our manufacturing to China, but it's not about us, it's about this country. If you put people before profit, the profit will naturally follow.

Maggie and I have discovered Swazi is not a manu-facturing company. It is a tool, an instrument.

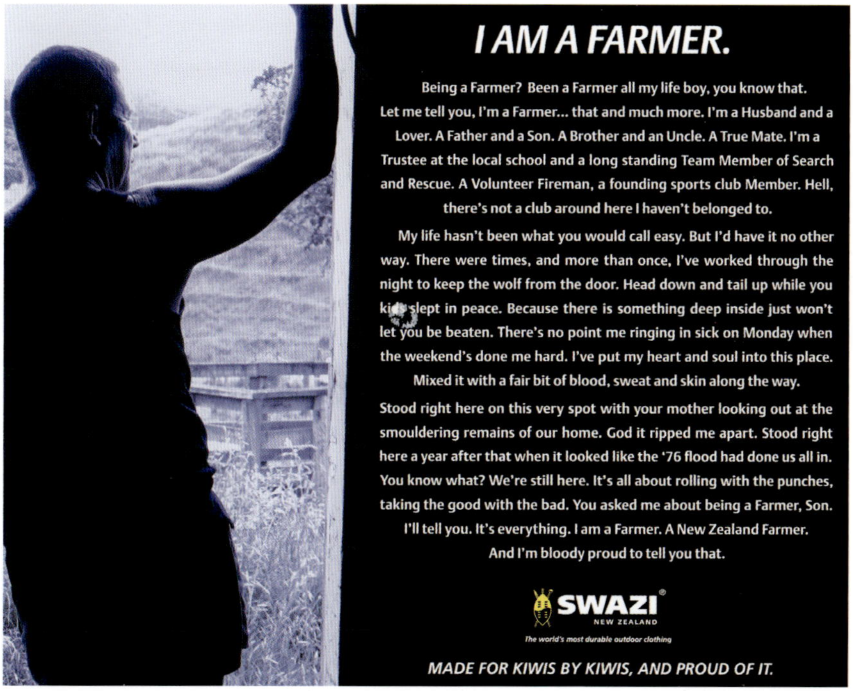

I AM A FARMER.
Being a Farmer? Been a Farmer all my life boy, you know that. Let me tell you, I'm a Farmer... that and much more. I'm a Husband and a Lover. A Father and a Son. A Brother and an Uncle. A True Mate. I'm a Trustee at the local school and a long standing Team Member of Search and Rescue. A Volunteer Fireman, a founding sports club Member. Hell, there's not a club around here I haven't belonged to.
My life hasn't been what you would call easy. But I'd have it no other way. There were times, and more than once, I've worked through the night to keep the wolf from the door. Head down and tail up while you kids slept in peace. Because there is something deep inside just won't let you be beaten. There's no point me ringing in sick on Monday when the weekend's done me hard. I've put my heart and soul into this place. Mixed it with a fair bit of blood, sweat and skin along the way.
Stood right here on this very spot with your mother looking out at the smouldering remains of our home. God it ripped me apart. Stood right here a year after that when it looked like the '76 flood had done us all in. You know what? We're still here. It's all about rolling with the punches, taking the good with the bad. You asked me about being a Farmer, Son. I'll tell you. It's everything. I am a Farmer. A New Zealand Farmer. And I'm bloody proud to tell you that.
SWAZI
NEW ZEALAND
The world's most durable outdoor clothing
MADE FOR KIWIS BY KIWIS, AND PROUD OF IT.

Developing the business, and combatting rivals who want to take us down a peg.

11

LOYAL

A little bit of national pride never hurt anyone.

We are determined to continue to manufacture in New Zealand. If we had to stop making Swazi here, I would shut the place down. But it gets harder. Staying New Zealand-made gets tougher. With more compliance forced upon us, staying competitive in a global market will never be easy. As each week passes, these matters seem to take up more of my time. Some of it is driven by the Employment Relations Act, which I think sucks beyond belief. It treats New Zealanders like idiots. Here is a scheme based on good faith instead of good relationships. But you can't put a finger on good faith. There needs to be a contractual balance between employer and employee, one built on common sense.

I think things have tipped too far in the employee's favour. All this does is create a rift between management and staff. Unfortunately things don't always work out. Hiring and firing are tough decisions. If we have to let someone go, I'm the one who needs to make those calls. It's the worst job in the world when it happens, yet these days the process is often devoid of reality. You can't sit down with someone and tell them how it is anymore. We're so wrapped up in cotton wool and process rather than reality that you just cannot possibly be open and truthful about someone's behaviour.

We once had a staff member who intimidated others, including her manager. It got to the point where one guy was exhibiting physical signs of stress and became very nervous around this woman. He brought it to my attention, and we tried for several months to change her attitude. But some people won't change. At that stage we let her go. Lawyers then got involved. Perhaps if I paid her $5000 it would all go away? Then I thought, *Do I really want to live in a country where the easiest way out is to pay someone off so they can go somewhere else and bother others?*

It went as far as the Employment Court, where we won. It had cost me in the region of $60,000 in legal fees and lost productivity. We won the case, yet we had not one cent of costs awarded to us. The final decision was that if this woman had to contribute anything in costs, in a case she herself had brought to the court, it would put her under undue financial stress. You don't win a prize for guessing what the outcome would have been had she won. Have I mentioned the Employment Relations Act sucks?

I'd like to think Swazi staff are proud of what we do. I look at our general manager Sharee Harper and still remember the day she walked in looking for a job as a machinist. Now she pretty well runs the company and I couldn't do it without her. Or Cathy Dunne our accountant, who should have been a marketer because she's far too bright to be an accountant . . . Being a machinist is a craft and something that is downplayed by many Swazi employees. Though I tell them we make the best gear in the world, some still say, 'I'm just a machinist.' They're not, and to prove it, I devised a label that reads 'Proudly crafted by . . .' followed by the name of the machinist. They take pride in, and ownership of, every garment they make. As for Maggie and me? I'd hate to see Swazi without us.

Business for me comes down to a measurement of success. When I walk through the factory door and hear people singing, I know Swazi is a successful business. Success can't be found on a balance sheet. Success

Loyal. The first time Mags and I met hunting guide Emma Morris was on a girls' hunt at Ngamatea Station. She couldn't wait to show us her Swazi tat. Blew me away.

is your people being so incredibly happy about coming to work that it's uplifting, uplifting to the soul. I'd choose hearing someone singing at the top of their voice over million-dollar profits any day.

Swazi started doing okay, but the real shock came on the day I decided I actually needed to measure business efficiency. I've always believed if you can't measure something, you can't improve it. We installed a bar-coded tracking system at Swazi, which meant that every piece of fabric that came in was coded and could be tracked. As it travelled through the production cycle, we could measure the efficiency of cutting, the amount of fabric we used, how much waste was involved, and then as it came through onto the production floor, we could measure every single machinist's contribution to manufacturing that product. The first measurement came out, giving our factory floor a 54 per cent efficiency rating. I thought we were doomed, yet when I spoke to other people in manufacturing I discovered 54 per cent was pretty damn good. I was horrified by that. We have a productivity problem in New Zealand; our numbers mirror those of Portugal, whose inhabitants stop for lunch, down a bottle of vino and have a three-hour siesta before doing a couple of hours work in the afternoon. How then to increase our productivity?

We needed to change the way Swazi staff worked. This was not something that happened overnight. Most people resist change, and it proved a struggle to convince the staff there was a better way, but four years down the track our efficiencies are always in the high nineties. Three or four years ago we had 80-odd staff; today it's around 70 with the same output. Measure it. Improve it.

When it comes to marketing your business, purists will give all sorts of definitions of what marketing is, but at the end of the day you have to move products and stay profitable. Marketing must be reflected in sales. I believe that marketing falls under branding. Those who believe marketing falls under a higher form of intelligence are sadly delusional! I don't care how good your marketing is. I don't care how slick your branding is. If sales don't result, then it's not working. Swazi's marketing team consists of the receptionist, the accountant, the person who makes the tea, the person who dispatches the garments, the person who checks the garments and the person who cuts them. Marketing is something we all do, and the essence behind branding is something we all understand as well.

Our branding strategy was that we wanted to be different. We used to have a couple of billboards outside the railway station. I was forever getting artists to draw murals. If New Zealand beat Australia at rugby league, the next day there'd be a huge Kiwi with a rugby league T-shirt on. Most people want to be different but being so requires you to change — and watch out, because people will start gawking at you, talking about you, and many people are not prepared for that. With change comes opportunity — you just have to look for it. Embrace change.

If you're starting out in business you must also ensure that the media becomes your friend. Don't take them for fools or suckers. Be truthful with them. Do not use them for your own gains, but if you've got something truly innovative, or something truly newsworthy, go to the highest mountain and yell it out. The media in this tiny country of ours do an outstanding job. Long live their independence!

Whatever it is you are marketing, remember: there's no such thing as a boring product, and no such thing as a boring service. Find a cool, fun way to market it and your customers will appreciate the fact by keeping on coming back. Even banks can have a human touch. They sell money. Imagine if they weren't so obsessed with making huge profits for their shareholders. Imagine if they didn't have to make $800 million profit this year, they only had to make $700 million and the other $100 million was going to make them the coolest bank in the whole frigging world. What's the difference between $700 million and $800 million? A small espresso machine in the corner?

Small things make a big difference. They give you a kick and a lift. We've developed a membership section on our website called Clan Swazi — it's the greatest thing because I get to touch my customers. If a Clan customer decides they really want to talk to me they smash a 'break-glass' fire-alarm icon on the Clan page, an email window comes up and they send me a direct message. Sometimes there are a few emails to answer, but I answer each and every one. I don't think many corporates in New

Whatever it is you are marketing, remember: there's no such thing as a boring product.

OVERLEAF Swazi Clansman.

IDITAROD
SWAZI

Zealand could say that. How would you get hold of the CEO at Telecom? There are barriers, try penetrating the fortress. If a business wishes to run itself based on what people want — and let's face it, most do — they need to allow customers to touch the owner of that business, to respond to customers' requests, questions and comments. I also send each Clan member a $20 voucher for their birthday. I want to make them happy. We get a huge response. Maybe it's a Buddhist thing; the true thanks for any gift or present actually lies with the giver.

Pretty early on in the piece I lost my ego. Perhaps I should say, my arrogant edge! I learnt to listen more and more to our customers, to their needs. Design and innovation is about providing solutions for the challenges outdoors people face. That makes most of our customers experts, so why the hell wouldn't you listen to them? The advice is free, for God's sake.

Swazi Clansmen can email me directly by smashing the glass on the Clan website. I promise to get right back to them — unless of course I am in some desert, up some mountain or at sea.

I try to come up with solutions that no one else has thought of. Looking back, we should have guarded our intellectual property (IP) so much better. I guess I was old-school, naively thinking no one would copy our products. After all, that would be theft. Theft of a design is theft. Oh, you sweet, innocent, dumb child! Other companies started copying our gear. I should have been more litigious, but more often than not I would just get emotionally hurt, but not legally defend my rights.

You often hear people say imitation is the sincerest form of flattery. To me, it's theft. Imitators have stolen something which is most dear to me. If you've ever had your place broken into you know the feeling you get when your secure, safe and sacred place has been violated. That feeling is the same when someone copies a product you have mothered, nurtured from the moment it was just a small idea you had on the side of a hill in the bush. You created the pattern, drew it up, made a prototype, tested it, tested it again, redesigned it, tested it again, before putting it out into the market knowing it is the best it can be. Then someone comes along and copies it.

The first time it happened was with a product called a Driback, a bush pant with a waterproof seat. We seal the seam so no water gets in, so when you're sitting on wet ground (or a bike or tractor with a wet seat) you don't get a wet arse. Within a year or two customers remarked on how well the trousers worked. The logical thing would have been to protect our IP. We didn't and next thing, all of our competitors were making their version of the Driback. You assume people have ethics and morals. You are trusting, but that can be a weakness in business.

Today I am still trusting. I don't want to change that, or be a pessimist or a cynic. Who wants to look for the bad in people? I search for the good. Most of my memories, be they life, family or business, are the good memories. The bad memories I block out and move on. Never regret the things you've done, only regret those not yet done. Whatever the calamity or issue, if you can't undo it or fix it, quickly forget it and move on. Quickly means instantly, by the way. Right now.

In October of 2004 I got a call from New Zealand Customs asking if I was now manufacturing in China. I was flummoxed. Why would they ask that? The chap replied that several boxes containing Swazi products had arrived in the country from China. The customs official wanted to know what I was up to, as the labels all said 'Made in New Zealand'. I asked him to track down exactly where those boxes were going, which turned out to be a company in Te Awamutu connected with Te Wananga o Aotearoa, the Maori university. How weird was that?

When we got in touch with a spokesperson for the company he abruptly replied we must be under the illusion that these particular garments were our ideas.

'Mate,' I said. 'They are — I designed them.'

I was shocked. The guy told me they had organised the manufacturing of the garments at the request of the Hunting & Fishing Group, who at that time were one of our biggest customers.

Alarm bells rang. The obvious question was: what the hell were they doing getting our gear sent to China and why were garments coming back into New Zealand with Swazi Made in New Zealand labels on them?

Within an hour I was sitting around our boardroom table with Hunting & Fishing CEO Andy Tannock and Janine Wilsher, our business manager. Tannock wriggled uncomfortably, telling me the products were sent to China so as not to be copied. Apparently, it was a mistake, they'd come back. I let him wriggle a wee bit more. Simply because, man, that was a pretty silly response from Andy.

Quickly means instantly, by the way. Right now.

'Why don't you just send them a picture of the garment instead of the real thing?'

An answer was not forthcoming. The only thing to do was come down hard.

'I'd hate to get litigious and involve lawyers as we've dealt with each other for quite some time, but here's the deal: you get onto those manufacturers in China and tell them to make significant changes to those garments otherwise the Hunting & Fishing Group and Swazi will end up in court.'

The result was a bunch of extremely ugly garments. I do believe they still make them that way!

It was so funny watching these guys dance a sidestep. They did, however, go back to the manufacturer and cut all sorts of things off, add an extra zip here, a slit there and some more pockets there . . . The result was a bunch of extremely ugly garments. I do believe they still make them that way! In that sense, I guess we won. We'd had a good relationship with Hunting & Fishing and it's gutting when a relationship falls over.

There's a difference between copying and getting suggestions from customers on how to improve products. We spend an unhealthy amount of time in the field ourselves, and take our customers' ideas seriously. It's a long process. Sometimes it takes two or three years to get a garment to a stage where we really think it works. Where it gets annoying is when copycats don't even bother changing the colours.

Swazi's decision in 2009 to allow customers to buy direct from us over the internet was difficult, but as one of the last apparel manufacturers in New Zealand, we had to look at a long-term strategy for survival. With some of our retailers and also our competitors making outdoor gear overseas, we could see our margins getting squeezed annually.

We knew we had a great product — and our customers felt the same way — so we opted to become both manufacturer *and* reseller, keeping a relationship with only one major New Zealand retailer, RD1, the trading arm of Fonterra. Writing 'divorce' letters to our retailers was tough. The company owed them a lot for helping build the brand, but for us it was the only way forward.

Our export business is internet-driven but it's critical to be visible in our overseas markets. That's why every year I continue to travel to overseas hunting trade shows.

I'm amazed how many people write to Swazi. We have a survey card that goes out with each garment, which we use for suggestions. Mid-season we'll get 200 cards a day. Every one is entered into our database, and when we come to the design stage for a new range the following year, we pull up that database and look for relevant suggestions. Often we'll send the new garment back to the person who made the suggestion and say, 'Hey, buddy, you suggested a deeper pocket. Well, here it is with a deeper pocket. We need you to test this for the next six months and see what you think, please get back in touch.'

Export plays a vital role for the future of New Zealand's economy. Villmarksmessen Outdoor Show in Oslo, Norway April 2011, with Are Venemyr and Kristina Kydland of Jakt & Friluft stores.

A great day in business is getting a letter from a customer like this:

> Dear Mr Hughes,
>
> I'm just writing to tell you about my son who had a terrible car crash last week and was pinned underneath his ute in a dark, damp gully in the Wairarapa in the middle of a swamp and spent the entire night there with horrific injuries, but when we found him in the morning and they flew him to hospital everyone said the only reason he was alive was because his gear kept him warm through the night, keeping his body at a temperature where he would survive — so I'm just writing to say thank you.

That's a great day. It's not about sales. Sure, you get a kick out of having a great sales day, but the best day is when we do something that has purpose and merit. Or how's this for a letter from a customer who over the ensuing years has become a very close and dear friend:

> Dear Swazi
>
> I just wanted to let you know that your products have performed splendidly for me in the most adverse conditions here in SE Alaska. Once, while sneaking up a salmon-choked stream in south-east Alaska the innovative hood design of my Swazi Tahr anorak saved me from being mauled — or, even worse,

killed by a very mad and very agitated brown bear.

I'd been moving fast, as we were short of daylight and wanted to get my hunter and assistant guide, Nick King (a Kiwi by the way!), to a point where we could gain a better view over the stream. I had just climbed the crest of a small hill when all of a sudden I caught just the slightest of movements out of the corner of my eye.

As I turned, I swung the .458 Magnum off my shoulder. Looking down the sight all I could see were four canines and two blazing eyes. I shot instinctively. The first shot went down the bear's throat, exiting through the neck. This slowed the enraged animal up just enough to enable me to chamber another round and put in a second followed by a third shot.

The attack happened so fast and was over so quickly. I think I had barely got in two rapid breaths before I noticed movement again in the scrub at about 25 yards. Two full-grown cubs came charging out of the brush, swinging their heads and woofing aggressively. I yelled loudly at them, waving my arms and gesticulating. After what seemed an eternity they slowly backed away before disappearing into the brush.

I now measured the distance from the claw marks in the mud, where my first shot had hit to where I was standing. Just over 2 meters. The charge had not been precipitated by any sound and I can tell you now, but for the well-designed hood on the Tahr anorak the bear would have hit me with all her force. Your well-thought-out hood design allows for just the right amount of rain protection as well as good visibility for the hunter.

Keep up the good work!

James Boyce

Alaska Master Guide

OPPOSITE Jim Boyce with the bear that almost got him. After the incident Jim wrote to me to say how he reckoned it was our coat design that had saved his life. Subsequently we became the best of friends and have shared many a hairy and scary time hunting in the primeval rain forests of south-east Alaska.

What a cool letter. Our gear works. The hood design Jim Boyce talks about has a number on the pattern piece that reads 'Mod#9'. Nine bloody revisions of a hood to get it perfectly right? That's why it's the best hood on any rain jacket in the world. That's why I get pissed off when lazy dickheads copy our gear.

LEFT If only Bobby Fithian's cache in the Middle Fork could talk. Damn, it would tell some amazing stories! Bobby has a good one about being chased up the cache ladder by three grizzlies who didn't even budge when he fired shots at their feet. In fact, they began climbing the ladder. It wasn't until he began wailing like a fire engine that they ran off! Alaska Range.

RIGHT I do believe it's not until you see some of the trees chiselled through to build their dams that you can even begin to comprehend how efficient the beaver is as a logger. Kuiu Island, Alaska.

BELOW Laurence Frank, my daughter Taygen and I were tracking hyenas in the Great Rift Valley, on the outskirts of Nanyuki, a town pretty much bang smack on the equator. I just loved the texture of this rock, so when I found a hyena skull . . . well, it's my tribute to Lucy. Nanyuki, Kenya.

Learning how amazing having kids can be, and figuring out how to make them independent.

12

FAMILY

In 1988 Ryan, our first child, was born. We were living across the road from the maternity hospital so when Maggie's waters broke I took her over in a wheelbarrow — no shit. There was a rugby test on that night and Maggie was adamant she was going to watch the game before giving birth. I took a notebook and counted and recorded the intervals between contractions. All her life Maggie has been incredibly fit and her labour was pretty much drug-free. When Ryan was born he shot down the table and I literally caught him. Maggie and I were in shock. We looked at this beautiful baby, then at each other. At the same time we said, 'It's a baby!'

Our doctor turned to us. 'What did you think it was going to be — a rugby ball?'

No one prepares you for the birth of your first child. You

Ryan at Lake Taupo. Was this where he first thought of becoming a marine biologist?

Show us your muscles!

can go to antenatal classes and learn about bathing and breathing, but parenting isn't a game of rugby where you can train and get ready physically. When it finally happens the feeling is one of warmth and utter amazement. Here is something real, something living. I'm sure it's the same for every parent, but the birth of your first child is incredibly special, as is every one thereafter. The first night the nurse gave Maggie the wrong baby — she could tell by the smell. At first the nurse didn't believe her, but Maggie was proved right.

'Reckon you may get a trick past them two old outlaws, but those youngen's, well, I'll be damned if they don't look like hellions!'

In those first few weeks Ryan and I had the best chats. I've always found baby talk condescending. Talk to children the way you want to be spoken to. From the beginning, Maggie and I had a dummy-free zone. I hate seeing babies suck them. This child is trying to communicate; how can it if you stick a dummy in its mouth? Take out that dummy! No. There are no excuses, take out the dummy.

That first night with Ryan, all I remember is lying awake listening to him breathe. If he didn't for a few seconds, we'd both jolt out of bed.

'The baby's stopped breathing!'

It's not until your second child comes along that you become an old hand; tip him upside down, give him a pat, make him burp. Then give him the other tit. The first is so fragile. Then number two comes along, by which time you've realised they bounce. They're not china dolls.

Ryan is his great-grandmother's maiden name. His middle name, Wilson, is my mother's maiden name. Then our little pixie Taygen was born. Her name in Celtic name means 'little princess'. I didn't like the original spelling (Tegan), thinking she may get called Tegal chicken, so I changed it. Third-born was Tavis, again a good old Celtic name meaning the son of Thomas or the son of David. My name is David Thomas, so I think it's a really cool name.

Like many families we struggled financially, but those years with three babies were the best. We spent a lot of time with them. Nowadays, whenever I meet new parents I tell them to blow farts on their kids' bellies, bite their bums, do as much as you can now because there comes a day, usually when they turn 17, when all of a sudden your daughter won't let you blow farts on her tummy.

It's quite something when they learn to walk. Taygen was just eight months. People would watch this small girl on the go and say, 'That's not right, how can someone that tiny be walking?'

On Ryan's first day at school, I sat in class next to his Australian teacher, Miss Davis. The topic was trees. Winter was just beginning and leaves had started falling.

'Some trees don't have leaves that fall off,' said Miss Davis. 'They're called evergreens. Some trees' leaves *do* fall off in the winter. Does anyone know their name?'

Ryan put his hand up and said, 'They're deciduous.'

Miss Davis asked, 'Can you spell that?'

This five-year-old kid on his first day at school walked to the blackboard and wrote 'deciduous'. I looked at the teacher and smiled: Lady, he's all yours now.

'This may end up being a problem.' She squirmed. 'A smart kid who can spell.'

It may sound hard to believe — a young kid spelling such a word — but I guess we always looked at learning as fun. We would forever be reading to the kids. I wouldn't even hesitate to give away half of all I own

I'm just so incredibly proud of these three. Sure, they all have a weird and wacky sense of humour, but that's their mother's fault.

Taygen has always loved hunting. She's a far better shot than me, dresses out the meat better than I can . . . hell, I don't know why she even bothers to take me along. Erua Forest, on a trip with Belgian Bob.

ROB PEETERS

SWAZI

to be able to get the kids to sit on my knee so I could read to them again.

Whenever I am asked which stage of my kids' lives has been my favourite, I reply, 'From the moment they were born . . . up until now.'

As everyone knows, there's a stage in a teenager's life where he or she reverts back to when the time when they couldn't talk. They grunt instead, but they soon get over it. We've never really told our kids off, believing it doesn't achieve much. We have brought them up with positive interaction. We never missed a sports day. We never missed the day they left kindy or the day they started school. We tried our best to be there as often as possible, but then, that was the beauty of being self-employed. But here's the deal: once a kid is three years old, that's pretty much it. If you've failed to instil respect, manners and the difference between right and wrong, you're going to struggle. I reckon parenting starts in the womb. If you decide to start teaching them a lesson at age 10, tough luck, you're too late.

Taygen pole-axed this kudu with one shot to the neck.

As with any family, it hasn't always been plain sailing. I remember when Taygen asked Maggie for a tattoo for her twelfth birthday. Her answer, one that would be heard in many a Kiwi household, was 'Go and ask your father.' Maggie knew full well I'd laugh and say no. Instead, I decided that if Maggie couldn't make a decision, then I would.

'Honey,' I told Taygen. 'You do understand you can't wash a tattoo off? It's there for life.'

'Yeah, I know that.'

'And . . . you're not allowed "Fuck You" on your forehead or "Get Stuffed" on your knuckles.'

'Dad,' she reasoned, 'I just want to get this nice little heart tattooed on my belly.'

'Okay, jump in the car.'

We drove to Palmerston North and visited a tattooist mate, Sid Holland. I'm sure you have to be 18 to undergo such a procedure, but I held Taygen's hand while she had it done. That's a lot of pain for a 12-year-old kid. When Sid finished up, Taygen and I drove home and she sprinted inside, lifted her T-shirt and proudly showed her tattoo to her mother. You can imagine Maggie's reaction, but I've always believed this 'Go and ask your father' philosophy is not the way to deal with things. Perhaps it should be, 'Come on, let's go and *talk* to your father.' Ultimately, Taygen was 12, it was something she wanted, it wasn't going to hurt anyone else, and she realised it was forever. To this day she doesn't regret it.

All three kids had shot their first deer by the time they were 12, but in no way were they forced to. Perhaps in their minds they thought I wanted them to. Afterwards, I explained that they now knew where meat came from, but to only join me in the bush if they wanted. Ryan never showed an interest and Tavis loves his fishing, so when Taygen took a shine to the sport it surprised the hell out of me.

My daughter loves hunting.

She's such a wee thing and to watch her dress a deer, get home and hang it is quite something. Several days later when she butchers it, separates the various cuts, vacuum seals and freezes it, I'm left thinking *This girl really knows what she's doing.*

To be honest, I'd like to think that whatever the sport, Taygen would just want to be with me. Or maybe she has the hunting gene. Her friends probably think she's a bit weird, especially when they see photos of her with blood up to her elbows, carrying a stag's head over her shoulders. Then again, the kids she grew up with expected her to do such things having come from a hunting family. At school, she and the boys were viewed as the Addams Family, often turning up to show and tell with crocodile heads, mammoth bones or a the skin of a zebra that Daddy had shot.

We used to have heaps of parties at home for the kids so they could invite their mates over. Living in the country means you can't drive home afterwards, so we'd often wake on a Saturday morning with 22 kids to feed scrambled eggs and baked beans to. Kids seem so much better behaved nowadays. They're smarter than we were, though I do laugh when my friends with sons say, 'The boy's got a few girlfriends on the go — I don't know what he's doing, but damn, I wish I was him!' It's always a different story when it comes to their daughters: 'She'd better be home by ten!'

She's such a wee thing and to watch her dress a deer, get home and hang it is quite something.

ABOVE When Tavis turned 15 he hunted his first bear with the master himself, Jimmy Boyce. Things got interesting in the dark forest. Very interesting! 'Tavis, don't you dare tell your mother about any of this . . .'

LEFT The Faz skinning a spiker he'd shot with Jason Smalley at Retaruke.

RIGHT Ryan shot his first deer when he was 12. It was a truly great hunt, and he amazed me with such sense of purpose, yet he hasn't shown a great interest in hunting since.

Why would you want to put a snare around your daughter's ankle?

Treat girls and boys equally. Sometimes they get up to things they shouldn't, but those are lessons they have to learn themselves. Taygen has had just as much freedom as the boys. If you treat your daughter differently to her brothers, she's going to rebel; she's not going to tell you the important things you need to hear. She's not going to confide in you or her mother, and that's a shame. But I do worry for them. It's a scary world and there are some evil goddamned people roaming our streets. I've got some pretty firm views on justice and rehabilitation. For some, it doesn't work. Why even bother? If someone has been anti-society for 20 years I don't need them to change; I need them to be somewhere where they will not harm other people.

God, I'm just so proud of each and every one of them.

My kids are spoilt, but we've made them work for what they've got and they've always held down jobs. They all got their own cars quite early on, but that's a necessity in the country, and they all paid for their cars by getting jobs. Three kids at university is quite a drain on parents, but we still like to spoil them and make them feel good as much we can. And the best way to do that is share time with them. I do hope they do something useful with their lives. Tavis (20) is doing a degree in broadcasting and film in Christchurch. Taygen (21) is doing commerce and marketing at Canterbury and Ryan (22) is doing a Masters degree in marine biology and marine ecology. Did I think they would do those things when they were younger? Absolutely not. Given Ryan has forever captivated people with stories, I thought he'd become a writer. Then again, maybe he'll end up telling stories about marine biology to inspire young kids. Taygen, in commerce and marketing, has done exactly the opposite to what I would have thought. Tavis is the dude, super-creative and fun, and will one day be as highly regarded as Peter Jackson. God, I'm just so proud of each and every one of them.

The kids all own a part of Swazi. But while it would be great to create some sort of dynasty, it's far more important for them to live a happy and full life doing what they want to do, not what Dad wants them to do. They don't have to run a clothing company because their mother and I run a clothing company, but they do owe it to us, for the investment we've made in them, to live a great life at a hundred miles an hour. I believe one of the most important things to realise about parenting, or life for that matter, is that you can't live your children's lives for them.

Live the life you want and you'll find you're able to give your family more than they could expect. Focus on your own life and goals. Decide where it is you want to go and you'll raise independent children, rather than someone looking to their parents for constant approval. I don't tone down my trips just because I have a family. When the kids were really young, I didn't head off on any great overseas adventures. It wasn't until they were two or three that I started going back to the wild places. The day I left for Outer Mongolia all three of them came down with chickenpox. For Maggie, the five-and-a-half weeks until my return couldn't come soon enough.

The most important thing should always be family. We're currently putting together our own TV show, *Adventures in Wild Places*. We're going it alone. An American producer noticed a teaser clip and phoned me to ask if I would front a hunting show on their outdoor channel. Apparently they liked my accent, humour and adventures. As tempting as the offer was, taking part in the American show would mean leaving Swazi. Filming 13 episodes a year would mean being away from home far too long. And what would the upside be? Fame, wealth and notoriety, I guess, but at the cost of dividing my family and taking me away from the people I work with. It was never even a contest; my family is always going to win. Fame and wealth are such small things in the big scheme of life. Family, friends and community will always be my measures of success, with business and financial gain coming fourth on the ladder.

RIGHT 'Texas Dan' Ellis gave me this ancient arrowhead from the Pedernales Valley. Carbon dating has shown it to be over 8000 years old. OPPOSITE Shooting my *Adventures in Wild Places* TV series. This opening scene is at the Otaki River with my favourite truck, Bodacious.

YOU'RE IN SWAZI COUNTRY
ISUZU
SWAZI
ARB
Bell

DAVE ABBOTT

Cam Lancaster was a man to ride the river with. A mountain of a man — hell, at times he was a volcano too!

I love the San Bushmen saying about how the stars are the campfires of those hunters who have gone before us. When I stargaze, I focus on the brightest star on Orion's Belt. It's Cam's fire.

I was honoured to be his friend.

Men of the Outback. Live-capturing buffalo on Conway Station, Northern Territory, Australia.

A Tundra Mile

In the North lies a land that beckons me deep
Dreams I've had often of a journey in sleep
Ah, to test your mettle, put spirit to trial
Take hold of your breath and walk a tundra mile

In a valley wider than a full day's tramp
At a halfway creek our caribou camp
Onward 'bou course by in relentless style
As south, ever south they tread their tundra mile

Across a wilderness reddened by leaf and berry
We stalk close to the herd not yet wary
Bulls at the rear they pass in orderly file
With consummate ease, purpose intent to end this tundra mile

Friend, should ever you bear north, a month out of Nome
To the land caribou, wolf and grizzly call home
Stride slow, peel your eyes every once in a while
Stay true, breathe it in, taste deep your tundra mile

Kiwi Jima. It's about time this young nation called Aotearoa began to care about its own people.

BRIAN HUGHES

Getting kicked in the guts over an army contract, and putting people before profit.

13

WIN SOME, LOSE SOME

The day when six Kiwi soldiers perished on Mount Ruapehu was a wake-up call for the New Zealand Army. On 13 August 1990, 13 soldiers and naval ratings became disoriented near the mountain's summit in gale-force winds, sub-zero temperatures and whiteout conditions. They dug snow caves for shelter and sang nursery rhymes for comfort while two men walked for 11 hours to get help. Three days later, rescuers found the group, including six who had died from exposure. Later a military court criticised the course instructors, saying they lacked the skills or experience to cope with extreme mountain conditions. It also condemned the army for not taking radio equipment.

The timing of the news was ironic, coming on the eve of the Government Job Summit. *Dominion Post.*

LIFE D1-D2
A3
Dom Post 26/2/09
ON THE EVE OF THE JOBS SUMMIT
Army shifts $2m contract to China
What do I tell my staff, asks clothing manufacturer
Tracy Watkins previews the jobs' summit B5
Don't expect miracles A2

The New Zealand Army soon realised if they were to run training camps on the highest part of the plateau at Waiouru they needed to clothe their soldiers properly. But once they started delving into clothing brands they discovered they didn't have a lot of expertise. A lot of the gear they used was cheap and nasty. It was made from a material called Milair, and came out of the UK; much of it literally delaminated in your hands when sewing it up. How the hell could you put a product like that on the back of a soldier? Some time later they decided they really needed to invest in a better fabric.

The supply of the army's clothing was through an Australian company called Yakka, which was based in Auckland. They'd set up a supply company called YASL to supply New Zealand Defence, and when YASL needed to develop better uniforms made from better fabrics, they approached Swazi. By this stage we had a lot of army guys running around wearing our gear, including the SAS, who loved it. Our garments worked better than any others in the field. Feedback got through to the army bosses that these guys at Swazi knew what they were doing. In 2003, we were given some pretty rough drawings and came up with some gear that, in my opinion, was going to be the best and most innovative wet-weather gear that any defence force in the world would have. The arduous process of testing and approving commenced, and we put a lot of our own hard-earned IP into the designs.

Our boys train and operate in conditions quite dissimilar to those found in the Wellington CBD.

And that's where the argument still lies today: was it really our IP or had we sold it to the army? No matter, at the time the gear worked incredibly well, fit the purpose, and kept soldiers in comfort in any terrain or conditions they faced. Then the bureaucrats decided to cut costs, opting

to make the jackets shorter and omit other special features. For me, this was an issue. I don't think the civilians down in the Wellington Defence ivory towers realise that rain doesn't always fall straight down from the sky; sometimes rain comes *up from the ground*. Wind works in crazy ways, too; heavy rain often bounces off brush and undergrowth. The bureaucrats decided to save money at the expense of the grunts who'd be wearing the gear at the coalface. I can visualise it now, a decision made around a cafeteria table while dunking their gingernut biscuits in their tea, after having finished the daily crossword no doubt. The result was still a very good product, but in my opinion it wasn't the best it could possibly be. *Es optimus, qui esse potes*! Be the best you can be!

In February of 2007 Yakka was purchased by another Australian company, Pacific Brands. Back home in Aussie, PB went on to lay off staff in their thousands. At one stage the company owed its bankers somewhere between $700 million and $900 million, though it's hard to get an exact figure. Things got pretty dire and for a time, on paper, the company was worth a mere $150 million, so they had big problems. To alleviate the pain, their bankers agreed to roll the loans over (two or three times) in the hope they'd pull themselves out of the hole. Meanwhile, 3000 to 4000 people were being made redundant.

The writing was on the wall: Swazi faced having to drop prices or YASL would take what we were manufacturing to China. I flew to Auckland and walked around the huge YASL warehouse with the YASL procurement manager, Trevor Steed. Trevor would stop in every aisle and comment that once this garment or that garment had been made in New Zealand, but now, why now, it was made in China! I felt sick inside as I knew which company had originally made that shirt, crafted that smock, sewn those pants. New Zealand workers who had performed well, yet demanded more than a few cents an hour. *He tangata*. My people.

I felt sick inside as I knew which company had made that shirt, crafted that smock, sewn those pants.

In the end, I don't think it mattered what we did with the army. We were making such small margins there was no way we could lower our prices and make a living. It was a $2-million contract, but there was very little profit to be had. How the hell could we further chop margins and stay New Zealand-made? YASL kept pushing until we said we couldn't make the product any cheaper. Generally these types of purchase contracts are run not so much by the army, but by the civilian bureaucrats sitting in

I TRUST THE PEOPLE WE HAVE ENTRUSTED TO LEAD US BECOME PEOPLE WHO ARE COMMITTED TO SERVE US.

Wellington. One has only to look at some of the force's ill-fated purchase contracts over the past few years for frigates, troop ships, LAVs . . . the list goes on. For me, these sorts of faceless and nameless people generally don't approach things either from a patriotic, strategic or commonsense point of view. In my view, they worry only about numbers and so had no issue with taking the manufacturing of New Zealand soldiers' gear offshore.

This was a real kick in the guts. We'd put so much of our own craft, our own innovation, our sweat, our care and our loyalty to New Zealand troops into making gear that would now be ripped away and taken offshore. As well as losing the contract, New Zealand was losing some of its own IP. If the contract stayed within New Zealand, the money it would generate would far outweigh the savings YASL could make offshore. Independent industry capability studies showed that short term you save immediately, but spending the money here in New Zealand meant long term you actually benefitted the country 1.4 times more than sending it out. That, however, never came into account.

Once it became common knowledge that we'd lost the contract, TV, radio and press were banging down my door. I was feeling let down, but the next day I received a phone call on my mobile, a rarity given that I never give the number out. The caller was a very senior officer in the New Zealand SAS.

'I'm just ringing up to say that me and the boys think it's a crock of shit what the government has done,' he said. 'You guys make the absolute best wet-weather gear in the world. We know that because we wear it everywhere. We want you to know we're behind you and there's an open invitation any time you're in Auckland to come to the mess and have dinner with us. We'd like to show you our trophy room.'

'Got any guns in that trophy room?' I asked.

'We've got some *big* guns.'

I haven't taken the opportunity to visit, but am pretty sure I will. They sound like an interesting bunch of turkeys.

Despite such support, losing the army deal really hurt. You like to think you love this country, but it takes me back to what happened in the First World War at Gallipoli. I carry with me a bullet from Anzac Cove, one which, by my own reckoning as a hunter, has passed through a body. In that war young men, some only 15 and 16 years of age, volunteered for what they thought would be a great adventure. As they lay in bunkers and trenches in Passchendaele, Flanders and on the beaches of Gallipoli, they cradled their young mates in their arms, watched blood drain from their bodies. These guys weren't thinking about value propositions, they were thinking they were dying for a reason. They were dying for future generations, for freedom, for something which cannot be measured. That something is the heart of this country.

A lot of those guys couldn't take it. They were shellshocked, cut down by machine guns and ripped apart by barbed wire. A number of them ran and were captured by the British, who asked the New Zealand generals whether they should be hung or shot for deserting their camp. The Kiwi generals didn't want the dishonour of it being known that some New Zealanders had deserted the cause. So they said, 'Shoot them.' And they did.

At exactly the same time, 129 Australian boys ran and were captured. When the Brits caught them they said to the Australian generals, 'Well, we've just whacked a whole lot of Kiwi boys for this very offence. Do you want your boys hung or shot?'

The response from the Aussie generals couldn't have been more different. 'These guys are sick,' they said. 'These guys are Australians. They're our brothers in arms and we're taking them home. Touch one hair on their heads and the entire Australian army comes home.'

Today it's the same old story — we don't know how to look after our own people. As New Zealanders we fight for one thing, and that's to be liked. We do it all round the world and we're doing it again now. I loved it when we stood up against nuclear warships. We don't believe in apartheid. We don't believe in suppressing homosexuality. We believe that the native people of this country were wronged and we need to right it. We fought each other during the Springbok tour but look back now, even the most ardent fan, and you have to admit that those were hard times but that the decisions we made were the right ones.

But we still want to be liked and we're going back down that track again. Our culture, along with the mana of leadership, has disappeared. We don't need people pretending to be Barack Obama. We need people

These guys weren't thinking about value propositions, they were thinking they were dying for a reason.

standing up and saying, 'I am here because the people believe I will make the right decisions.' Doing so is not easy but history proves that the right decisions benefit the nation forever, while wrong decisions will haunt us forever.

I bet Willie Apiata's mates were thankful it was him and not a politician on the battlefield while they were lying there, wounded, under enemy fire. The latter would still be there arguing about 'not getting involved' or 'this could affect our trade deals'. Doing the right thing is sometimes the hardest thing. A man does not shirk his responsibilities.

Losing the army contract was about more than just the fiscal loss. Business is a game. Let's get that straight. It's a vehicle we drive on a journey through life, but sometimes you've got to get out of the car to see what's worth living and dying for. The answer is our people. They count for so much more. That's why it saddens me when I see us putting our people after profit. The world has finite resources, yet we just throw things away if they don't work. Yes, the labour's cheap but we're running our resources into the ground.

We clothed the army for three or four years. We still do the odd job for them, but putting what happened into words here will probably put an end to any further work. To be honest, it was pretty much the end of it when I spoke on TV's *Close Up*, *Campbell Live*, and National Radio. I realised the consequences of doing so. In reality, a host of companies were getting squeezed by YASL, but none would talk. Most of them opted to keep whatever crumbs were left on their table. And how can you blame them? For some, their contract with YASL was all they had.

What do you reckon the chances are of us getting a crack at producing the gear for these boys? Forbidden City, Beijing.

I'd love to have a free hand and redesign the New Zealand Army's gear one day. I understand what you need from your clothing to lift a rifle, crawl

Crimpy was greased lightning with this quip on the eve of the Job Summit.

on your belly and run like fuck! At the end of the day, we knew our craft but when bureaucrats and private companies wedge themselves between you and the person wearing your gear you're never going to deliver what's needed.

We have been asked to help build some extreme cold-weather garments capable of keeping a soldier warm and comfortable in temperatures of up to –40°C. We're making the jackets straight off a supplied pattern and I know from my own experience of cold –45°C days in the Arctic and Montana that these garments won't work. My dilemma is, do I tell them? I feel honour-bound to do so.

Was there an upside to the whole messy saga? In some ways the situation was liberating. And at least I never had to stand in boardrooms, bend over and take it for my workers. From out of all this, we needed a new opportunity for the company. We had to change our business model. We asked the hard questions. Do we pull the pin now or are we going to dig in? Are we going to fight? Senior management weren't about to fight merely for themselves; they were fighting for the people on the factory floor, because at the end of the day that is the New Zealand we are fighting for. It's not just a group of machinists, it's New Zealand, and this is our small way of doing it. Our world is here in Levin. *Kia kaha. He tangata.*

Building Clan Swazi and having a good old cry in Southland.

14

NUTTERS THINK ALIKE

DAVID A TAYLOR

Clan Gunn, war or peace. You're either with us — or you're against us.

There are over 10,000 members in Clan Swazi. We set it up for people interested in stories — not just ours, but stories from all our customers. Anyone can join, and it often surprises me who does. As a company we need to make sure we don't come across as smug, or believe we're the only ones who feel passionate about the outdoors and hunting. There are a ton of people in New Zealand and all around this wonderful world who feel the same way — the clan merely provides a conduit.

I remember a clan member emailing me about his five-year-old daughter who wanted to go hunting with Dad, but could she please order a micro shirt in pink? Pink. She wanted a shirt just like Dad's with the thumb loops. Oh, and she also wanted a pink beanie. Clearly Dad was a little embarrassed to make such a request but even more so, it was obvious his love for his daughter ruled above all else. In the email, the father explained he'd told his daughter numerous times that Swazi's clothing was more often than not green or camouflage, not pink. But this girl was persistent — as are most five-year-olds — and she pleaded her father to at least 'ask the hairy man in your books; he's the boss, he'll do it'. Somewhat reluctantly, the father broke the glass on the Swazi website and sent me a message. He went on to say he'd been pushed to make the request, but in no way was he expecting me to fulfil it.

'But at least I can tell my daughter I asked,' he finished.

Well, I can't resist a challenge. You may have guessed Swazi doesn't stock a hunting range in pink, so I emailed our fabric suppliers in Thailand and asked for a couple of metres of micro fleece for a one-off. It would need to be dyed up, but so be it. We made the pink micro shirt and beanie, and sent it to young Maggie in Mosgiel, who is now over the moon to be the only person on the planet with a pink Swazi micro shirt. I don't know who was happier, her or me. The entire Swazi team shared in her happiness too. Unbeknown to me, Maggie's mother was a breakfast DJ on More FM in Dunedin, and the day after her daughter received our parcel she let half of Otago know about it. What goes around comes around, I guess. It was, and remains, a beautiful story, but you guessed it, it did not end there! We shared the story with the clan in our monthly newsletter and within the space of two days more than 100 dads had requested the same pink set for their daughters.

Clan Swazi's great advantage is being made up of like-minded people. I know, for example, I'm not the only bloke who has ever been stuck in the wet with a freezing arse. It is, after all, the biggest muscle on your body. If you happen to be crossing rivers day in and out, your arse stays cold *the entire day*. For this reason Swazi came up with Jewel Bags — underpants for men which dry quickly and keep the nether regions toasty. The female equivalent are called Bushies.

I do around 30 or 40 speeches a year, most of which are often a fair way from Levin. Nothing, however, could be further off the beaten track than the Hump Ridge Track on the edge of Fiordland National Park. I was asked to speak by the trust that runs the track and its huts, and ended up giving two talks, one at lunch and one in the evening.

People paid for tickets and were flown in by chopper. It was a bloody amazing event. Southlanders are well-organised, super people. Towards the end of the evening, an auction took place during which a bloke at the back of the room put his hand up and enquired about the jacket I had on. The garment in question was a one-off high-tech windproof jacket we'd made especially for our Southern Traverse team.

'Why don't you auction it off?' he asked.

'Well . . . because it's mine,' I said.

ABOVE Guest speaker at the National Bank series of business talks.
BELOW Maori Women's Development seminars. *He tangata*.

'Put it up for auction — you might find people bid for it.'

Oh, what the hell, I thought, it's for a good cause. I took the jacket off, and when the auction began I expected it to reach a couple of hundred bucks. Next thing, the bidding was up over $1000 and the dude who instigated the affair made the winning bid.

I cornered him later in the evening, curious as to why he wanted the jacket so badly. 'You could have just given me a couple of hundred bucks,' I said. 'I would have given it to you.'

He said, 'Listen, I paid more money getting here.'

The buyer explained he was from Auckland and had bought the tickets for the event on TradeMe. 'I bought the airline tickets and flew down myself just to be here,' he continued. 'A few years ago I returned to New Zealand with my wife and family. Having just finished writing a piece of software which took 18 months to build, I needed a bit of funding to finish it off. So I went to New Zealand Trade and Enterprise and a bunch of other people, showed them my software idea, but no one was prepared to offer any financial assistance. They all said the software was nothing new and a market didn't exist for such a product.'

The dude wearing my favourite jacket then spent the next eight weeks locked in his room with the curtains drawn, beating himself up. He'd spent a huge part of his life designing software which would never see the light of day. He was gutted. Then, one day, his wife walked in and demanded he get out of bed and watch something that was on TV.

'It's just started and it looks cool,' she told her husband.

The programme was a *60 Minutes* show about Swazi. He sat down and watched it. Months later, here he was telling me how the doco

Heading up the Tazlina Glacier, Chugach Mountains, Alaska. Some of the prettiest country on the planet.

had changed his thinking: 'I was inspired by your attitude — and your philosophy of never saying die. No matter what the challenge, you can overcome it. You just need to focus and pull on all your reserves.'

When *60 Minutes* finished he went back to his room, opened the curtains, sat down and finished writing the programme. No sooner had he completed it, than Fairfax in Australia and other major corporations were on the phone gobbling it up.

'I made millions of dollars,' he beamed at me through wet eyes. 'And I'm here because I wanted to say thank you.'

Arrrgh! Fuck, I'm a softy. I started to cry, then so did he. We were holding on to each other and howling like banshees. I was blown away that a few words from me, just being myself, on a TV programme could motivate

'Mum, I'd like you to meet my new girlfriend . . .' The guy on the right is a DBG. Yes, that's Deep Background Guy.

I find speaking at small rural schools a precious and uplifting experience. Aka Aka School.

someone to that level. Sometimes you don't think anyone is watching. Often I feel like an ostrich; my head is in the sand and I'm so busy doing things without noticing that people are actually sitting around talking about Swazi. Perhaps knowing that people are watching keeps you going. When a young cowboy falls off his horse, he gets up and keeps going. Sometimes when you've been thrown and winded, the bull will come back to have a go at you. Most of the time, though, if you get up, brush yourself off and keep a level head, plain old guts and belief will see you through.

A clan member once turned up to the Swazi tent at Mystery Creek and told us the story of how he nearly died on a day trip hunting in the Ureweras. When he started talking I remembered having read about him in the paper. He told me he'd been walking along, when he happened to look down at his gun and thought, *Gee, that doesn't look like a safe way to carry it*. The next thing you know he's blown half his arm off above the elbow. He began walking out of the bush, but kept falling over, at which stage the bones protruding out of his arm would stick in the ground and he'd have to wrench them free. At one point he even thought about cutting his arm off; at least then he'd live if he managed to escape. He pulled out his knife and contemplated cutting the last threads of his tendons. But he couldn't do it.

When he finally reached his car, he found his buddy, who'd got out of the bush ahead of him. They quickly drove to a house, where he called an ambulance, letting emergency staff know they were going to continue driving towards Rotorua and would meet the ambulance on the way. They hadn't gone that far when all of a sudden an ambulance came around the corner. (We're talking the back road to Ruatahuna here!) *That was quick*, they told the ambos. *Well, we've had no call from dispatch*, came the reply, *you guys are just lucky we bumped into you*. They later found out that dispatch had thought their call was a hoax. No ambulance had been sent. What was even more serendipitous was that the two ambos they had bumped into had only just returned from a tour in war-torn Bosnia. Their expertise? Dealing with gunshot wounds.

When he finally made it to hospital, his recuperation took months and he felt pretty damn low. Losing an arm was still a possibility, as was the realisation he would never hunt again. Then a parcel turned up. It was a Swazi jacket, and inside a card signed by every single staff member.

> *You need to get up on your horse if you've been knocked down. See this thing through. You need to go hunting again, because it's obviously what you enjoy. Everyone at Swazi cares about you and wants to see you out enjoying hunting again. Enclosed is the jacket we want you to wear when you get back in the saddle.*

As he relayed the story, customers in the tent — as well as my team — got very emotional and tears flowed. Damn. Ah, what the hell, bear hunters are allowed to cry, you know.

Ah, what the hell, bear hunters are allowed to cry, you know.

Two more Clan Swazi members, Donald Polson and Blair Gibson, sent me their incredible story after the devastating 2004 floods. Farmers from Whangaehu, they had been busy trying to move stock using their speedboat during the worst of conditions. When their boat overturned and sank (with Donald's Swazi jacket inside) both clung to a nearby broken tree for dear life. A dead sheep floated by, and the men grabbed it, skinning the animal for its pelt to keep them warm in the now-freezing conditions. Four years later a drought hit the area. They were walking down the river one day, when they discovered the tiniest section of the bow of a jet boat visible in the sand. It had been buried all that time. A digger was fetched to unearth the boat — and, to Donald's surprise, his Swazi Tahr anorak. Off home he went, gave it a quick wash and, what do you know, as good as new!

These stories make me realise how important shelter and warmth are in the bush. Which brings me to the subject of an old hut in the Tararuas by the North Ohau River. As a hunter's hut, it was great. Sure, the walls were falling down and you had to sleep on old ponga ferns each night, but it kept the rain and wind out. DOC, as part of their cleansing routine throughout the country, had decided to take such huts out as they were regarded as a danger. Whoo whoo whoo! A scary hut!

Horowhenua Hunting Club members work on the finishing touches and then, voila! The newly constructed North Ohau Hut — what a cool project!

I decided to pay a visit to DOC, pleading with them not to remove the hut, and saying that Swazi would pay for the maintenance each year. They thanked me very much, but said the hut was beyond repair and would be pulled down. So I suggested we build a new one. To my surprise — and full credit to Wayne Boness at the DOC office — they agreed. We decided we couldn't do it on our own, so we got the Horowhenua Hunting Club from Levin involved. The club and its members raised some coin through pub charities and Swazi kicked things off with a $5000 grant. Plans were drawn up and we burnt the old hut down. Club president Bruce Mitchell and I walked up and down the North Ohau River until we found a new site we were happy with. The rest of the club agreed it was a pretty damn good location, boasting something every hunter wants, a nice possie overlooking a nice river flat. Cup of black billy tea. Set of binos . . . life is good.

This project backed up my thinking that young trampers and hunters needed a hut fairly close to the road, otherwise, especially when inexperience is an issue, they wouldn't have the confidence to travel far into the bush, either on their own or in small groups. The new hut was within easy access of the road, but far enough away so most vandals would stay out. Once the hut was complete, Chris Carter (the then Minister of Conservation), Darren Hughes (local MP) and Brendon Duffy (local district mayor) officially opened the hut and we had a bloody great big party.

Since that day, hunters have shot deer right by the hut, down on the river flat. It's well patronised and has been a success story. I like to think the community owns their own recreation. Too many people sit around

The kids at Matatoki School, just outside of Thames, spectacularly dressed for their Possum Bustin' weekend.

waiting for the government or the council to do something about putting in facilities. Sometimes you have to get off your arse and do it yourself. In this case, the community showed what they could do, helped immensely by a proactive and enthusiastic hunting club.

Joining Clan Swazi is one thing, being crazy enough to want to work for us is something else. If you want the latter, you'd better have a fire in your belly and a flame in your eye! I'm looking for the devil. Anyone who works for us has to have a bit of the devil in them. They need a serious — *serious* — amount of humour, otherwise they just won't fit in. We have a lot of fun. When looking for staff, I'm on the search for someone better than me. Perhaps some people are frightened to employ someone more skilled and experienced than themselves. Maybe they figure the new guy will want to run the show; I'm looking for someone better than me to teach me. Above all else, I want a good listener.

Recently, when on the hunt for a new sales manager, we had 66 applicants from New Zealand, Canada, the UK, South Africa and Australia. It's incredibly hard to compile a shortlist. It requires knowing exactly what it is you're looking for. Three applicants were absolutely amazing; any one of them could have done the job and probably fitted in well. Typically, when we reach this point we ask, does this person

'You sippy sippy that red juice Davey, I'll stick with the beer.' Colin Meads — the man is a legend.

have the ability to be a Swazi person? Will they *get* us? Will they get our customers? Will they create a bond between themselves and our clients? If the answer to any of these questions is no, it doesn't matter how much experience a candidate has — we move on to the next person. And if we can't find the right person we wait. A hole, as they say, is better than an arsehole.

The first person to interview a prospective Swazi employee is our receptionist. Let's say the interview is booked for 2 pm. If the interviewee turns up at two, we won't actually meet and greet them until five past. They have to meet our receptionist, who will take them through to our photo hut to look at the photos our customers have sent in. Polite chit-chat will ensue, while the receptionist explains the team is running a few minutes late. What I'm looking for is how the applicant talks to my lady on the front desk. It's amazing how many people talk down to your receptionist, because she's *just* a receptionist. She's actually my litmus test. If they don't pass that test, I don't care how good they are in the interview — they've failed.

Personality, though, is not something you can crack in a couple of interviews. Generally we don't even begin to think who's getting the gig in that first interview. It's the second interview that is most telling, because by then we're relaxed. It doesn't take place in the boardroom. We favour an office or the cafeteria. And we just chat to people. We find out about them as a person; their family, social life and what does and doesn't turn them on. Ultimately it boils down to two questions: where are you going and could you go there with us? If the applicant can answer those two questions with conviction, the person will get the job.

What if someone bluffed their way into a Swazi job, as I did numerous times on my OE? Can a bluffer see a bluffer? I think they probably can. It's like being a card shark. Unless they're so much better at bluffing than you, spotting them is easy. I don't think anyone is capable of bluffing that well. Generally the jobs I picked up were of the manual type. One or two have been in journalism, where life is decided by living on your wits. When I scored those jobs I sold myself without references or background detail. Our interview and employment procedures are too unyielding for someone to sneak through.

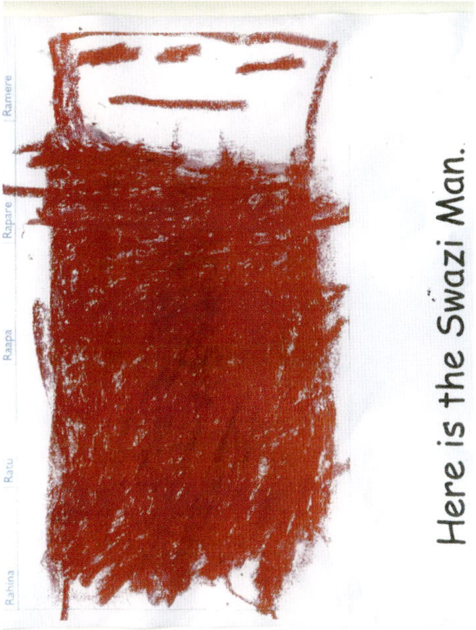

ABOVE LEFT Special rules for whom, me or the bears? Wyoming, USA.

ABOVE CENTRE It's just like looking into a mirror . . . Nathan from Hope-Kumeroa School with his awesome caricature — of me.

ABOVE RIGHT Rudnaya Pristan, one of the most polluted places in the world. This lead smelter has been the main industry — and, of course — cause of the pollution, since the 1930s. As we approached within several kilometres of town everything seemed touched with a deathly pall and we sped through the area, not wishing to linger. Russian Far East.

CENTRE After a week of Chital-hunting in the sweltering heat of Northern Queensland it was great to finally get to town and have a bath in a flash hotel. Apparently the water colour in said establishment was quite the norm for that part of Australia . . .

BELOW Steve Foster between a hard place and a hard place as he battles this bull tahr with his ice axe. Southern Alps, New Zealand.

DAVID HAMILTON

Handing out peter heaters and polar-fleece bras, and learning how to move an audience.

15

WHO THE HELL DO YOU THINK YOU ARE?

I dislike the term celebrity. Real celebrities are usually actors playing someone else. I feel for guys like Jonah Lomu who walk around airports wearing headphones, not because they want to listen to music, but more likely because they get tired of people coming up and asking questions or shaking their hand. I'm well known in the hunting and outdoor circles, but to the average punter I'm just that guy who features all too often on the TV show, *Border Patrol*. Although I don't see myself as famous, I did learn pretty early on not to be flippant with people who stop to chat. In New Zealand especially, when people come up and say, 'Hey, Mr Swaziman,' many have had to overcome incredible shyness to do so. I try to give them the respect they're giving me. To be flippant would be just downright distasteful. Do I always *want* to say gidday? Of course not, but it goes with the territory. Even if the most boring fart on earth approaches, I make an effort to at least listen, and

Already thinking about back steak on the BBQ and sliced salami with Monique the Pickles' wonderful chutney.

hopefully engage in some sort of conversation. Thankfully most people I meet are bloody interesting!

I don't, however, have much tolerance for talking to someone wearing the competitor's clothing. I know, I know, I should! Yet when I see what they're wearing — especially if it's what I suspect is a Swazi rip-off — I say hello and move on. It's a personal thing and one I continuously struggle to get around. Sometimes people wearing the opposition's brand put their hand over the label, apologising for wearing it while talking to me.

I normally reply, 'No, you shouldn't — have a great day.'

It's terrible, but it's just the way I am. Maybe it's the Scottish genes. You're either with us or against us. After all, the Gunn motto is *Aut pax aut bellum*. Either peace or war.

People call me the Swaziman an awful lot. Inside, Davey Hughes screams, 'He's not the Swaziman — he's Davey Hughes! For Christ's sake, call him Davey or Mr Hughes!'

ABOVE Waiting for the fog to lift.
BEIOW Dungeness crabs . . . Mmmm!

You soon get used to it. Sometimes, usually when I'm tired and feel I can't be bothered, I give myself a wee kick. You cannot let your brand down. I represent Swazi. Even while doing the Coast to Coast in 2010, I was still Mr Swazi. As each elite cyclist rode past me — and believe me hundreds did — every one of them said, 'Gidday, Mr Swazi, you're going well!' What I dislike most is when Maggie and I are out together and someone stands between us. With their back to Maggie, they continue talking as if she doesn't exist. In that situation I will typically say, 'Excuse me, allow me to introduce my wife, Maggie — who's standing *behind* you.'

That's just rudeness.

'Celebrity' does, however, have its perks. Getting into the Koru Club with one or two more people than you're allowed may sound incredibly snobbish, but when you travel as much as I do it's great to relax with a couple of buddies before your next flight. I'm a Leo, too, so being well known is almost like being stroked. Watch me purr! I love being in the limelight. Conversely, I like also hiding in the background, like when I was an extra in two *The Lord of the Rings* movies. I was what is known in the movie trade as a DBG — deep background guy!

In the beginning, though, there was no face of Swazi. We started with a logo, and that was it. It was Maggie who noticed that companies like Ridgeline and Stoney Creek didn't have a personality fronting them. From then on, my face was in the catalogue and we decided to really push that side of the brand.

It helps immensely being the spokesman for the company, not just because I'm outspoken, but because I hunt. That in itself says to hunters and farmers, 'he's one of us.' I'm part of their community. I don't live in an apartment. I don't work on the seventh floor of some building in Auckland importing a bunch of clothing at the click of a button. I hunt. I get cold, wet and miserable in some of the harshest environments in the world, and our customers know and respect that. I feed out to my deer and cattle in winter, and I run an olive grove. I'm constantly fixing a beat-up tractor and moaning about not enough grass, too much grass . . . When I say a particular jacket works well on the farm they all know, of course it's going to frigging well work.

The long arm of the law reached out to touch me as I pulled my crab pots along the Portland Canal, a remote part of the border between Canada and the US. A floatplane circled, then landed. Out jumped a state trooper, Sgt Dennis Rowe, who casually undid the holster on his pistol, stepped onto his pontoon, and announced he was going to check my fishing permits!

On an exciting hunt with Scotty Robinson, we got onto this boar with a bloody nice set of hooks.

There is still plenty of tall-poppy stuff out there, mostly within your own community. Then again, if you know it exists, you can handle it. Generally, it's with work. Before we started selling direct, I felt that a lot of the major corporate farm suppliers envied the fact that I ran Swazi and had a national profile. I was in the news. I wrote stories for magazines. *60 Minutes* did a doco on me. I was well known. In their minds, I believe, I was a tall poppy who needed to be taught a lesson. And it really came home to me. We had a great relationship with Farmlands, which was, and still is, a fantastic company. They have around 35 stores and turn over hundreds of millions of dollars per year. Swazi and Farmlands enjoyed a great relationship, especially with their former CEO John Newlands.

I felt privileged to attend his farewell dinner, even more so when I was asked to address multi-million dollar corporates in a farewell speech in John's honour. Afterwards, when I sat down to eat, a Farmlands manager sat next to me and made it quite clear, I felt, that I needed to be taken down a peg or two. The others at the table were amazed by his attitude. It seemed to me that he resented the fact that I had been asked to speak. He was a smooth dude, but I felt he struggled with the media attention I received. It rammed home to me there are people out there who don't like the fact that I lift my head above the parapet. Some want to chop it off.

Perhaps in a bizarre way being a 'celebrity' makes me a better citizen, because with it comes responsibility. People look up to you, especially youngsters. If I were to be caught poaching or with undersized crayfish or paua, I would destroy some people's faith in what they feel good about. Not just in regards to me, but in regards to themselves. Maybe they'd think, *I don't believe in taking undersized paua, yet the Swaziman did and he's famous, so it's okay*.

Do my kids see me as a celebrity? Of course not, although Taygen was a little surprised on our last trip to the United States when a school group ran up and asked me to autograph their T-shirts. The look on her face was obvious: Why is Dad *signing* these kids' shirts and hats? I guess my children have come to notice it more now they're out in the world. It gets interesting when Taygen's university lecture is about Swazi, her lecturers telling the room about a company destined to fail because it manufactures clothing in New Zealand and not China. Taygen, a little puzzled, is sitting in the lecture thinking, *That's my Dad you're talking about*. Tavis, too, has had Swazi come up in his lectures, but strangely enough in his school (the creative arts) his lecturers say, 'Isn't it cool these guys are standing out there and doing this?'

Mind you, they also teach Marxism at that school so maybe it's not such a great endorsement.

It rammed home to me there are people out there who don't like the fact that I lift my head above the parapet.

I do sometimes wonder what will happen to the Swazi brand when I'm no longer here. From a marketing perspective, it is something we're aware of. The separation between the brands will inevitably come about when Davey Hughes is weaned from the company. Somehow or another — and we talk about this at length — the best way to move forward would be to have me as the spokesperson, but not too involved in the day-to-day running of the brand. And that day will come. We're all ageing. But it has to be done right. Many companies have made a success of it. Dick Smith has done it, as has Michael Hill. Tony's Tyre Service (which was actually run by a bloke called Steve) sold four years ago, but Tony (Steve) still fronts the ads and is a spokesperson for the brand.

Public speaking was something I never anticipated would make me so nervous. Initially I found the pressure to entertain immense; the simple need to surprise a crowd or tell a bloody good joke was a huge weight on my shoulders. I guess being different — long hair, cowboy hat, weird props — makes me stand out, but in the end what you say has to come from the heart. When I stand on stage, I want to make people think.

At the first talk I gave, the main billing was a Well-known Sporting Guru (WKSG). I felt like his understudy. WKSG turned up as pissed as a chook. He stumbled about and struggled to get onstage. Eventually they managed to get him up there, though the first thing he did was fall down. When he stood up, 450 people were watching, many of whom had brought their children along. WKSG then launched into a joke so filthy that parents had to cover their children's ears. Then he slurred a

BELOW Dall Sheep-hunting camp in the Chugach Mountains, Alaska. Tad Gilbert and I landed in a Piper Cub at a strip named 'Half Chance'. I quizzed pilot Mike Meekins on the name and he replied, 'You get half a chance to land, if you stuff it up you've got no chance at all.' Thanks, Mike. BELOW RIGHT I'd always dreamed of hunting a buff with extra-wide sweeping horns. Sometimes dreams come true.

wee bit more, before saying something along the lines of he wasn't much of a hunter, but his grandfather had been a terrific shot. Grandad had hunted all over Africa and he still had the old man's gun complete with lion scratches all down the stock. He went on how it was a good thing his grandfather was a sound shot, because everyone knows those blacks and niggers can't shoot . . .

It should be said that well over three-quarters of the crowd was Maori. You could have heard a pin drop. Luckily the MC took WKSG off after four minutes. All I heard backstage was, 'Our next speaker is Dave Hughes from Swazi Apparel!' I was terrified, saturated in my own sweat. I looked as though I'd been in the shower, my fawn cotton shirt was stained with sweat. When I stepped on stage, 450 angry people glared at me. Oh, God. I started walking up and down the stage with my head in my hands. For the audience, it must have been like watching a yacht race. I continued to walk up and down, up and down, sometimes the entire length of the stage. Then I walked up to the mike, with no idea what my brain was planning on saying.

When I stepped on stage, 450 angry people glared at me. Oh, God.

'That's going to be an incredibly hard act to follow,' I began, and they all burst into laughter.

Thank God, they weren't going to kill me.

It was a great night — and I was hooked. I grew to love the buzz of entertaining people and making them laugh. It was a high, and has been the same ever since. People want to hear your stories and live vicariously through you. Nerves are always there, but when you stand up and start — bang! With experience comes the knowledge that having butterflies in the bottom of your stomach is actually a healthy thing. Cherish the feeling. It means you're alive, awake, and on your game.

Oddly enough, speaking is such a physical thing. How that can be so is difficult to explain to someone who doesn't do it on a regular basis, but afterwards I am totally whacked. All I want to do is sit down. When I speak, I give my all. Rural schools are the most challenging — and rewarding. The kids are so honest and don't miss a trick by asking sticky questions. Sometimes you try to skirt around them, hoping the kid won't keep up. Seconds later the same child puts up their hand and says, 'Mr Hughes, thank you, but that's not the answer to my question.'

And they ask everything!

The Tazlina Glacier, in the Chugach Mountains, Alaska, with its huge seracs and extra-wide girth. Makes an awesome backdrop. This is one of the reasons I hunt.

'Where do children come from?'

'How old are you?'

'Are you married?'

'Is your hair real?'

'How much money do you make?'

'What sort of car do you drive?'

Kids ask questions adults would never dream of asking.

Adults get a whole lot more serious. Many don't want to offend you, so their questions become more general. Not many queries from an adult stop you in your tracks. Most people are pretty scared to ask questions, so quite often I'll take spot prizes, like the Swazi G-string, peter heaters, bras made out of polar fleece, or funny things we have made at work. I tell the crowd, 'whoever asks a question gets a wee spot prize.' I keep them in a bag and the first one to be pulled out will get them all laughing — and then everyone wants to get a prize so they all start asking questions.

Kids, on the other hand, never stop. If I show them a skin they'll ask if the animal bit me. What was it like when you skinned it? Does it smell? Kids ask questions that involve the senses. Sometimes their questions are so honest I have to stop myself and go, *Wow, what an amazing thing to ask!* Things they ask make me think. Sometimes I take furs and bones, and hand them out. Kids like to see and touch. Guns and knives are not bad props either.

Making a Swazi commercial. Phil Wilson shot me with the net gun, hooked me on a strop under the chopper, then stole my Swazi coat! Times like this you need a really good pilot, and Toby Wallis fitted the bill.

I'm lucky in that I have a reasonably good memory and rarely need notes. I think on my feet, something I believe has helped me as a hunter. If you're stalking an animal and the wind changes, you've got to change real quick. It's no different when giving a talk. You feed off the audience's mood and energy. If they're not giving any, move on, you're lost. Once, having arrived home from overseas, Maggie drove me straight from Auckland airport to a talk in Turangi. I didn't think I was doing too badly, yet after 20 minutes, I looked at everyone's eyes and they were hollow.

Oh my God, no one's laughing at my jokes. No one is asking questions. Either I suck, or this is the wrong crowd. *I shouldn't be talking to these dudes.*

Despite desperately wanting to go home and hit the hay, I carried on. I thought the evening was a real fizzer. A year or two

later, a guy walked into the office at Swazi, and in a monotone voice mumbled, 'I was at your talk in Turangi and the boys are still talking about it. It was the most exciting evening we've ever had and you really rocked.'

God, you could have clapped, you could have laughed, you could have had a glint in your eye while you were listening!

'Texas Dan' Ellis and Whitney Sandulak, up the Ahuriri Valley. Danny trained hard for a year, came to New Zealand and climbed the mountain (four times actually!) to hunt his tahr.

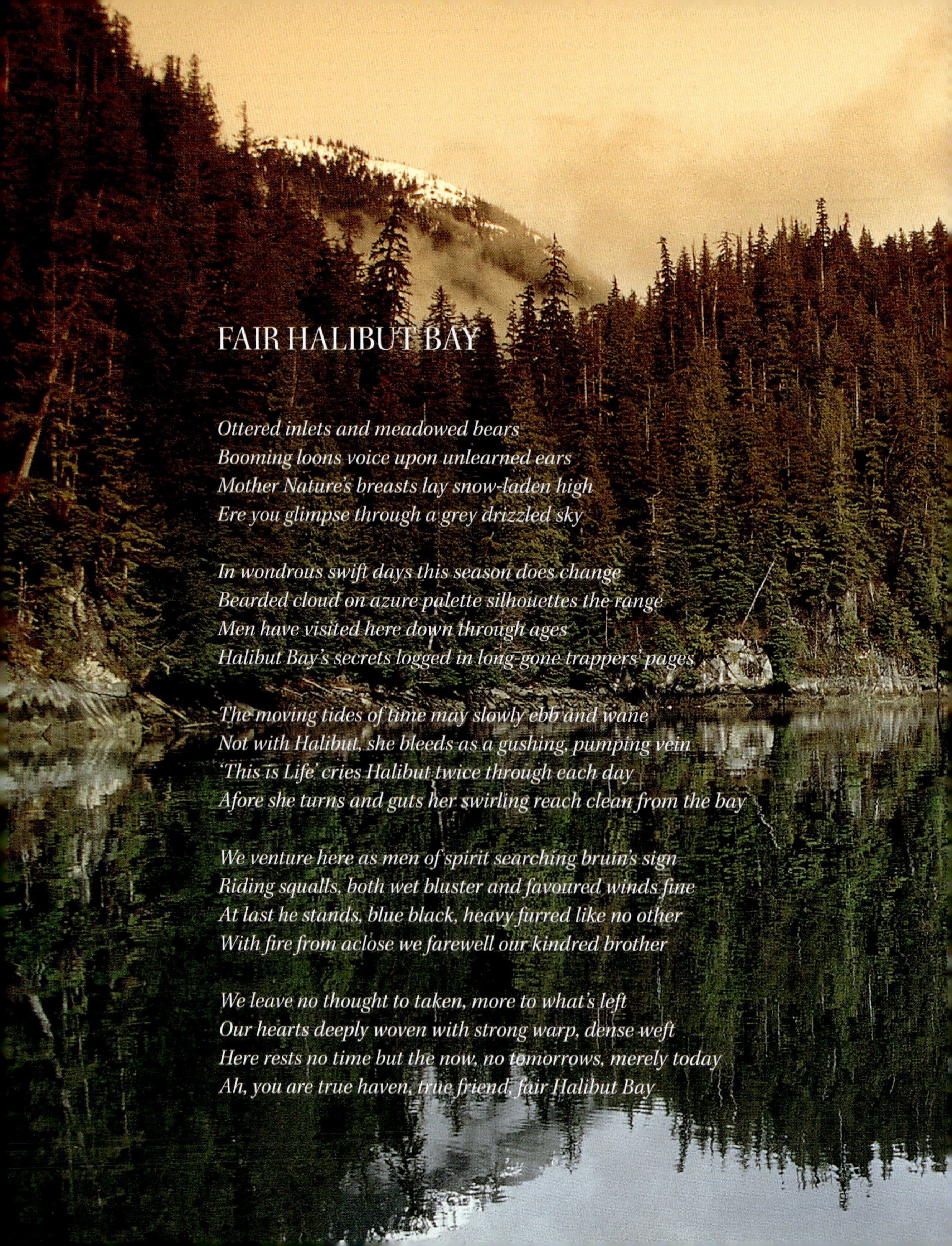

FAIR HALIBUT BAY

Ottered inlets and meadowed bears
Booming loons voice upon unlearned ears
Mother Nature's breasts lay snow-laden high
Ere you glimpse through a grey drizzled sky

In wondrous swift days this season does change
Bearded cloud on azure palette silhouettes the range
Men have visited here down through ages
Halibut Bay's secrets logged in long-gone trappers' pages

The moving tides of time may slowly ebb and wane
Not with Halibut, she bleeds as a gushing, pumping vein
'This is Life' cries Halibut twice through each day
Afore she turns and guts her swirling reach clean from the bay

We venture here as men of spirit searching bruin's sign
Riding squalls, both wet bluster and favoured winds fine
At last he stands, blue black, heavy furred like no other
With fire from aclose we farewell our kindred brother

We leave no thought to taken, more to what's left
Our hearts deeply woven with strong warp, dense weft
Here rests no time but the now, no tomorrows, merely today
Ah, you are true haven, true friend, fair Halibut Bay

Making an arrivals card declaration puts New Zealand Customs on red alert.

16

BORDER PATROL

BELOW Plains Indian Meet-Tenderiser. If you were to meet them on the plains, chances are they'd tenderise you . . .
OPPOSITE Wolverine skin. Pound for pound probably one of the toughest animals on the planet.

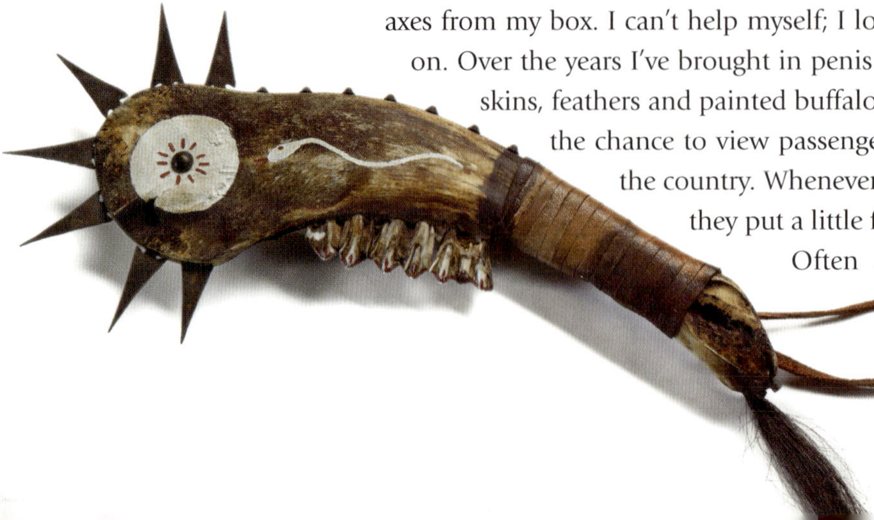

Coming home to New Zealand from an overseas hunting trip is always an adventure, especially when the TV show *Border Patrol* is involved. During the first series I was greeted by a cameraman who asked if I minded being filmed coming through Customs. No problem, I said. Then they watched as I unloaded skins, furs, buffalo heads, guns and axes from my box. I can't help myself; I love having the Customs dudes on. Over the years I've brought in penis bones, mammoth tusks, bear skins, feathers and painted buffalo skulls. MAF and Customs get the chance to view passenger lists before people arrive in the country. Whenever they see my name on a flight they put a little flag next to it.

Often an officer will greet me in the arrivals area and say, 'Mr

Hughes, the guys want to know if they'll be working overtime tonight.'

To which I normally reply, 'Yeah, it will probably take about an hour by the time you guys check all my bags and guns.'

In countries like Zaire and Uganda I sometimes shit my pants, but when I touch down in Auckland I get quite excited. For starters, there's the arrival card. Generally, when it comes to the MAF section, I tick 'Yes' for everything: skins, horns, guns, knives and every other category. I seem to spend my life in the red lane; it's been 25 years since they let me through green.

But one thing on that arrival form has always bugged me: occupation. I've always felt that it's nobody's business what I do for a job, so why fill it in? For many years I put 'pirate', and got a few hard stares and a few tellings-off by immigration, but I thought, *Oh bugger it, I* am *a pirate! That's what I do. I'm a private pirate, dammit!* After 9/11, though, I figured it wasn't fashionable to be a pirate anymore, so I changed my occupation to 'buccaneer'.

One time Swazi's GM Sharee Harper and our designer Jan Chammen and I were returning from a trip to Thailand, where we'd been looking through a fabric mill. When we landed, for the first time in my life I tried to go through the green lane. I'd put 'buccaneer' in the occupation box and as the immigration official looked at my arrival card he'd sneered, 'Hmm, buccaneer, eh, Mr Hughes?'

I jangled my wolf-tooth earring. 'Oh arrr,' I replied. 'Buccaneer!'

Out came the biggest red pen I've ever seen.

'Welcome home to Nu Zillund, Mr Hughes,' the official said as he proceeded to draw a large red circle on my card.

I knew what the red pen meant. Despite on this occasion having nothing to declare, I couldn't break my double-decade run of red-lane affairs. Putting 'buccaneer' hadn't exactly helped. Idiot.

When I reached the MAF desk a bloke pointed me in the direction of the red lane. Predicting how things were going to shape up, I offered: 'You don't understand. I don't have anything to declare. Please, I just want to *see* what the green lane looks like!'

It had always been a great mystery, like the ladies' toilet — what's behind the door? (That doesn't sound quite right, does it? Okay, like a ladies' toilet in France . . . hole's getting bigger here isn't it, but hopefully you'll be getting my drift. If not, I guess this is where you put the book down.)

'See that big red circle? Red lane please, sir,' was all he said.

Then he looked at the girls, Sharee and Jan. 'Are you with him?'

'Yes,' replied the girls.

'Red lane, too, please, ladies.'

Sharee and Jan exchanged worried glances. Travelling with the boss had its drawbacks, and they were about to see how things can quickly go from bad to worse.

At the next corner we were confronted by a Customs' blitz. Passengers queued and officious bureaucrats checked passports and cards. When an official reached me he spotted the big red circle and 'buccaneer' in bold letters. A grunt followed. Then he went to the centre of a room where the grand pooh-bah Customs guy stood. They scanned my passport and pointed at me.

Bugger. Think I have my boarding pass somewhere . . .

When he came back over he said, 'Mr Hughes, are you aware, sir, that falsely filling in an arrivals card can lead to a fine of up to $100,000, three years imprisonment, or both?'

I said, 'Yes I am.'

'Do you still wish to declare yourself as a buccaneer, sir?'

'Oh arrr,' I said in my best pirate voice. 'I do!'

Flummoxed, the officer saw no option but to go back to the grand pooh-bah. Both of them tapped things into their computers.

He returned once more, this time saying, 'Sir, do you still wish to go with your occupation as buccaneer?'

I confirmed his request. 'In actual fact,' I added, 'you need to talk to the person who designed these forms; you don't have enough boxes here for me to fill out my actual occupation. In the industry my *exact* title is *swashbuckling* buccaneer!'

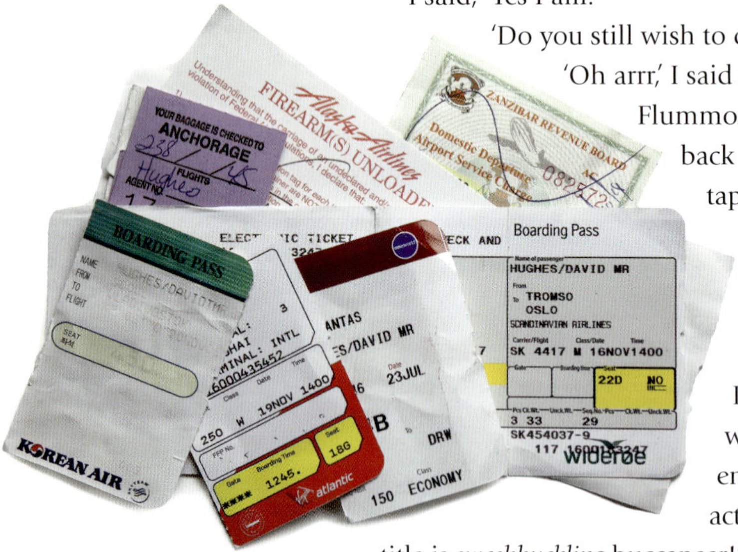

This upset Mr Customs. 'Can you tell us what it is that a buccaneer does?'

By now the passengers waiting to be checked out by Customs had begun to gather in a semi-circle around me. They glared, pointed and

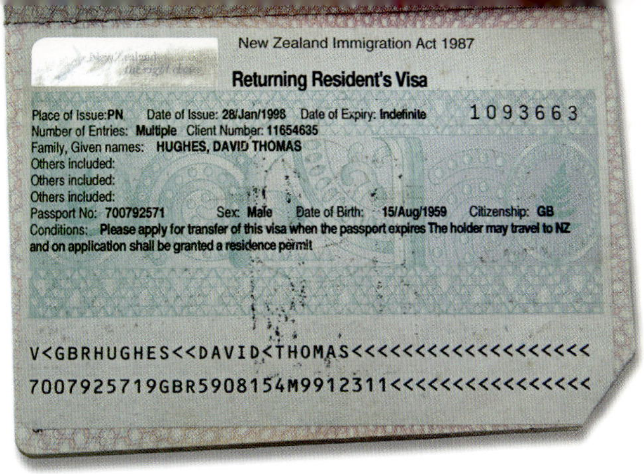

New Zealand Immigration Act 1987

Returning Resident's Visa

Place of Issue:PN Date of Issue: 28/Jan/1998 Date of Expiry: Indefinite 1093663
Number of Entries: Multiple Client Number: 11654635
Family, Given names: HUGHES, DAVID THOMAS
Others included:
Others included:
Others included:
Passport No: 700792571 Sex: Male Date of Birth: 15/Aug/1959 Citizenship: GB
Conditions: Please apply for transfer of this visa when the passport expires The holder may travel to NZ and on application shall be granted a residence permit

V<GBRHUGHES<<DAVID<THOMAS<<<<<<<<<<<<<<<<<<<
7007925719GBR5908154M9912311<<<<<<<<<<<<<<<<

My visa allowing me to return to New Zealand. I figured that after annoying one or two too many bureaucrats and politicians becoming a citizen might be prudent. That way they couldn't kick me out permanently!

whispered to their partners: *Yeah, they've got that big tall blond guy. You know, the druggie, he's just come off that Bangkok flight. He's probably got condoms full of heroin stuck up his arse.*

I continued standing in front of 60 or so people. They continued to stare, as if pleading to know what a buccaneer actually did. I'm not going to lie; I was captivated by the moment, so I jumped in head first. 'Imagine this,' I said to the crowd. 'You're six days off the coast of Cuba when suddenly you spy a sail ahead. "It's the Spanish galleon," the forward lookout cries! As our boat approaches, men come rushing up from her midships and the enemy pulls out their flintlocks. They're primed and they're after our blood! Smoke fills her decks as they fire. The lead flies and shrapnel tears at our rigging, smashes into our beam. You hear grappling hooks being thrown, pikes and cutlasses being drawn — and it's all on, me boys, it's all on! The ropes go overboard and we pull up next to the scurvy-riddled Spaniard dogs and there is one hell of a bloody fight. Blood washes the decks red. "Every man who is alive tonight will feast on peaches and peacock," yells the cap'n. That, my friends, is what it's like being a Buccaneer.'

The crowd was now either totally transfixed or utterly confused.

'Six weeks later,' I quietly drop my voice and continue, because what the hell, even I'm liking the sound of this story now! 'We're off the islands of Manila. It's so quiet. There's a fog, a deep fog, you can't see a bloody thing, not even the front of the boat. The only sound is the lapping of the waves as they hit the bow. But you sense deep in your bones something is afoot. Then, through the fog and mist, you see it, just a glimpse. Is it a raven? No! It's a flag! And it's black, dammit! It's the Jolly Roger! Pirates! Here they come! And the men are rushing up again, and the screams, oh the screams! Curses, cutlasses and flintlocks! And smoke! It's all on again! Fight, men, fight, this is it! Your lives depend on us fighting together. Here they come, but we defeat them once more! Thank God for buccaneers!'

The room was utterly silent. I turned to the Customs official, took a breath and finished.

'And that, mate, is what it's like being a buccaneer.'

The queue of passengers nodded and clapped ever so politely,

muttering to each other.

The official, meanwhile, still had work to do. 'Mmm,' he said. 'So where are they today, Mr Hughes?'

'I beg your pardon?' I asked, preparing my answer.

'Where are your buccaneers?'

I paused.

'My buccaneers,' I say, putting my finger on my ear, 'are on my bucking head, you silly bastard!'

Full credit to the guy. He lifted the barrier tape and asked us to bring our bags through. Sharee and Jan looked so dejected, knowing full well they could expect rubber gloves, strip searches and months in jail away from their loved ones. Guantanamo Bay had not yet been fully developed, but they would be shipped somewhere just as bad. *Why, oh why, did we travel with the boss; we all know he's a crazy sonnavabitch.*

ABOVE Rebbit. Rebbit.
BELOW A walrus penis bone, or *oosik*.

But instead the Customs officer took us to the X-ray machine, where he personally put all our bags through.

'Here you go, Mr Hughes,' he signed off. 'Here's your passport. Ladies, here are your passports. You guys have a really good day, and Mr Hughes, you carry on buccaneering, sir.'

I've since struck up a pretty good relationship with Customs and MAF — well, most of them. In fact, I've become an advocate for them, and given talks and radio interviews on what can and can't be brought into the country. The fact of the matter is these guys are experts: declare everything and let them do their job. I never try to sneak things through.

My ugly mug has been on *Border Patrol* four times, but my biggest concern is people watching the telly and thinking, *Why doesn't that guy get a real job? All he does is travel the bloody world and bring back interesting artefacts.*

Explaining how I am a whole person when I hunt.

17

WHY I HUNT

I am amazed my parents didn't have a problem with me hunting and trapping possums at the age of nine. We hunted with handmade bows and arrows, some of which were pretty mean-looking weapons. To construct them we'd get four-inch nails, smack them flat to make long blades, then split a piece of dowel, put the arrowhead from the nail into the dowel, shape it and bind them up with copper wire. We'd chase the possums up trees, stand at the bottom, and fire. How we never put anyone's eye out I have no idea. Death for the possum would be quick. You'd drive the arrow pretty well clean through it. We'd take the skins to a buyer. When the skin wasn't enough to pay for a new trap, we washed windows around the neighbourhood and cleaned cars just so we could keep hunting.

Back then society expected children to be independent, to be responsible for their own actions. Today, we tend to want society to take more responsibility for what other people do, and likewise, we take less responsibility for what we do ourselves. So we've created a whole lot of rules and we've put cotton wool around everyone just in case anyone has an accident. We've taken away some of that independence, freedom of thought, some of that 'You'll have to look after yourself because no one else will' attitude. I think it's sadly been eroded.

From an early age the longing to go bush just drew me in, and that passion for the wild places has never ebbed. With friends from the Wainui neighbourhood (I'm in the checked shirt).

Even this morning, when my son Ryan says he's off to the mountain to do the Tongariro Crossing, I ask, 'Have you got a PLB (personal locator beacon), a first-aid kit, a decent raincoat and thermals? What safety gear have you got?'

Ryan's reply is always the same. 'Dad, I'm 22 and for the past 22 years you've taught me what to take into the bush, so don't worry about it.'

It's good to see Kiwi kids still have that independence.

It may have been a different story though if Ryan asked to go possum shooting before reaching double digits. From those early days hunting possums in Wainui, I appreciated it wasn't necessary to shoot animals to prove to your dad you were a great hunter. When the men I idolised shot something, they ate it. My older brother was into pig hunting, though I preferred deer, perhaps because it was a more peaceful hunt and you could do it on your own. Generally, pig hunting dictates you being with someone else and a pack of dogs. I'm not a loner, but I do enjoy my own company.

I am often asked why I hunt, to which my reply is, *Why don't you?* I am a hunter. I am here to share, to make sure people can eat, and that the community, the clan, or the tribe keeps going. It's a primal thing. Giving meat away gives you a great sense of pride. After 40 years of hunting I still don't have the definitive answer. The best thing I can come up with is — I hunt because I can. I'm a whole person when I hunt. There's a moment when everything clicks, when you start to *see* things.

One thing I really enjoy is putting my rifle down and trying for a fish. Not always successful and definitely far from skilful, I relish the thought of catching a trout or salmon for dinner. Kodiak Island.

It's not only the animals you start to see, it's everything else. As corny as it sounds, you read the forest and become part of it. Occasions like this and my inner-greenie comes out. Deep down, I know I'm a tree hugger. I love taking my boots and socks off, and digging my toes into leaf mould on the bottom of any forest, especially beech forest. Get right under the top layer of leaves and smell life. You'll find bugs, worms and all sorts of things going on underneath. I don't know if it's primordial, or just me wanting to get back down into the earth. Every now and then I even eat a bit of dirt, just to see what it tastes like. Pretty weird, I know.

Hunting and being in the wild is not about being nature's guest in the forest. Hunting and being in the wild is part of me, the most natural part. Which is not to say I'm a good hunter; I'm actually pretty average, though when things get gnarly and every action must be right or you'll end up being either dinner or trampled into the dust, I tend to make the right decisions. I know some amazing hunters, people who can track

Not far from home in prime Sambar country.

animals for hours until they find them feeding, then shoot them. I can't do that. My strength is tracking animals that have been wounded or shot. And I do seem to have a hell of a lot of luck hunting, something which has stood me in good stead over the years. As a hunter you don't hanker for hunting, you hanker for the outdoors. I'm not focused on mountain goats, but on thinking about mountains and wilderness.

My navigation skills are based on gut rather than training. Kids today are far better equipped with the likes of GPS systems, but for me it's the knowledge I can handle whatever situation may arise. Besides, you're never in the middle of nowhere; you're always in the middle of somewhere. And how cool to be *somewhere*. When I used to go bush, I'd tell Maggie I would see her on Monday. To which she would reply, 'Any idea which Monday?' and I'd say, 'No, but it will be a Monday.'

Some people hunt so they can kill; others kill so they have hunted. Who is right? At the end of the day they've both done the same thing. It's very

DAVID HAMILTON

Taking the long ridge home in Retaruke, with Eugene Doyle and Jason Smalley.

personal. The last thing I'll do is judge anyone on why they hunt, whereas *how* they hunt is a different story. After all, here is a sport with no referee or crowd. In Alaska you are forbidden to hunt the day you fly. Doing so would give the hunter an unfair advantage having spied animals from the plane, unlike in New Zealand, where you can shoot from a helicopter.

I've hunted with guys who love long-range shooting and will shoot a goat from a kilometre away, across three gullies. Let me tell you — that is a long way to shoot and many factors come into play: wind, heat and humidity, just to name a few. Sometimes those guys don't get it right and gut-shoot the goat. The animal will wander into the bush wounded and bleating. And I say to them, 'Oh God, we've got to get over there and finish that thing off.' Then we peer at the gullies between us and the goat and your mates say, 'It'll be dead by the time we get there,' by which time I'm normally thinking, *How can you do that?* No, I'm not a fan of long-range shooting. I like to get as close as I can to an animal to shoot it, because I know I'll kill it — and that's a big thing. Get as close as you possibly can and then get 10 metres closer.

I suppose in a weird sort of way there is an 'animal-du-jour.' As a kid it was cool to go goat hunting. I've been invited, as I'm sure many Kiwi hunters have, to properties which were overrun with deer and goats to get rid of a few. You'd go somewhere for the weekend and shoot as many as 300 goats. But the fun quickly wore off. Shooting animals for the hell of it did nothing for me. I have mates I've hunted with since I was 15 who love nothing more than a good bomb-up, but I can't do it. If I happen to be there I'll shoot one or two goats, but that's it. I may look for a decent set of horns — or a nice skin — but I can't shoot hundreds of goats and feel good about it. Yeah, I know, but that's just me.

Hunting never becomes boring, but shooting an animal for the sake of it does. All animals have a spirit, and as a hunter you must respect that. I'm not religious, in fact, I'm a fervent atheist, which doesn't mean I'm not spiritual. There's the great spirit of the forest, the spirit of the sky, the river and finally the animal. Shooting an animal for the sake of it shows a lack of respect. The rule in our house has always been: you shoot it, you eat it — which made things difficult when the kids shot starlings and sparrows with slug guns. It doesn't matter whether you're shooting a possum or a bear. Which reminds me of a story . . .

A good mate of mine, Mike Bygate, one of New Zealand's funniest characters and all-round good bastard, was trapping on the West Coast just out of Reefton. Mike has muscular dystrophy and over the years the condition has really slowed him down, but he's still out there doing it. In fact, he's still contract-possuming at the age of 50. Mike went through a bad patch where he couldn't whack the possums on the head with a donger very well, so he made himself a pistol out of a .22. One day we were out the back of the Paparoas and he was checking one of his lines. A huge dark brown possum lay in the trap, so Mike — who has a pretty bad limp — pulled out his pistol and got ready to do the deed. Unfortunately, as Mike arrived at the trap the possum woke up, got a hell of a fright and ran straight up Mike's leg. So he shot the bloody thing. But he missed and shot himself in the foot! Sure enough, there was a hole in his boot. I told him to lie still.

Mike's screaming, 'Oh my God, I can feel it! I can feel the blood, it's filling up my boots! I can't look, you've got to strap it up, Dave, put a bandage on it!'

Again, I told him to hold still, before undoing his boot. I took his sock off and looked at his foot, and there, along the side of his foot, unbelievably, was a slight graze where the bullet had passed. Perhaps because of his muscular dystrophy, which caused him to often hold his feet at funny angles, the bullet had just creased him. He grimaced before asking how everything looked.

I said, 'Mate, don't look, you don't want to see this. I'm going to have to bandage it up.'

We got all the way to Reefton, but not without a struggle. Mike's limp was exacerbated by the supposed injury. As he held onto my shoulder I asked whether he wanted to go to hospital, or home. Helen, Mike's wife, was a nurse.

'Take me home first,' he replied. 'Let Helen look at it.'

So we rocked up to his house. Helen met us at the door and Mike's first words were, 'I've been shot, babe.' Before Helen got too carried away I made Mike lie down on the kitchen table, putting a towel under his head and generally making a real fuss of him. As Helen unwound the bandage slowly, Mike covered his eyes with his hands.

'Oh, Helen,' he said. 'What will happen? I won't be able to trap for

As Mike arrived at the trap the possum woke up, got a hell of a fright and ran straight up Mike's leg.

Nothing beats hunting a big bull tahr, his mane blowing in the wind, all the while being on top of New Zealand, gazing down on huge valleys and across glaciers.

months! I think it's smashed a few bones in as well. Ah, what a fuckin' mess, babe.'

When the final part of the bandage came free, Mike's bare foot was revealed, and a tiny white crease was visible where the bullet had slightly grazed him. Helen gave him endless shit and Mike has never forgiven me.

Hey, at least I never wrote about it in a book, Mike . . .

I have trapped tens of thousands of possums, but wouldn't know how many animals I have shot. I don't shoot birds. I'm not a great duck hunter, but don't have an issue with people who are. In areas like Southland, it keeps communities alive. It's the social event of the year. No one gets married on the opening weekend of duck season; if a bride turned up to the church she wouldn't be able to find the groom because he'd be shooting with his mates. I don't shoot giraffes or elephants, mostly because I have no reason to. Giraffes seem peaceful and cool, whereas elephants ruin crops and kill quite a few villagers as well as hunters — even when they aren't hunting them at the time. Elephants outside game parks are a totally different animal, very unpredictable, and I have no doubt hunting them would be one of the biggest adrenaline rushes around — yet I just don't have a hankering to go ellie hunting. Perhaps I've seen too many elephants killed by poachers.

I'm lucky enough to have hunted the world over and to have seen some of the most magnificent creatures to walk the face of the earth. But without a doubt, the greatest hunt, the best experience — and you don't necessarily have to shoot them — is hunting tahr, the Himalayan mountain goat, in the Southern Alps of New Zealand. It is the sport of kings; nothing, but nothing, comes close. I have often wondered why I enjoy it so much, settling on the fact that nothing beats hunting a big bull tahr, his mane blowing in the wind, all the while being on top of New Zealand, gazing down on huge valleys and across glaciers. We live in a stunning country and have the most amazing animals living among those lofty peaks. When you're up there, you're in tahr country, pitting your wits and experience against them. It's not that tahr are exceptionally difficult to hunt; it's the terrain. Learn your mountain skills well and respect the mountains at all times. Tahr country is tiger country.

I find it intriguing when people say they are anti-hunting, yet are engrossed by watching lions take down zebras on the Discovery Channel and Animal Planet. They sit glued to the screen, despite the fact that in most of those kills it's ages before the animal finally succumbs to the lion or the cheetah. Watchers of the show — I guess you'd call them animal enthusiasts — are so enthralled to be watching an actual hunt. Okay! That's exactly what it's like! You *are* that cheetah and it *is* incredibly exciting. It's not so much the kill, but everything leading up to it: the planning, the preparation, executing the ambush or the stalk. The difference is that, as humans, we believe the animal must be taken with a minimal amount of duress and pain.

Unlike many sports, you'll never find TV cameras focused on the hunter either — as they are in those reality shows. Most of those guys probably wouldn't survive without the support of a production crew, well, not longer than a few days. Half of them would hang themselves because they'd be scared shitless on their own. I guess it's best to remember they're TV hosts. I must admit though, I do enjoy some of them. Bear Grylls on *Man v Wild* makes me laugh. No disrespect, because he does do

Hunting with Ray Mears, with Mt Ruapehu in the background. Ray has got a great balance of adventure, love of the outdoors and hunting. His passion lies in sharing his experiences and vast knowledge with those who have not yet had the opportunity to visit the wild places for themselves.

some cool stuff, but hey, it's the best damn comedy show on the box. Ray Mears is one guy who I do respect. He really does know what he's doing; his respect for the wilderness is both obvious and genuine.

I love watching movies with hunters in them, though I have had it pointed out to me it's normally because I love to spot the mistakes they made during filming. I watched one of the *Jurassic Park* sequels the other night and a big white hunter had a double gun. This dude is holding the gun with the barrels pointed straight up into the pouring rain. It's like, buddy, you're supposed to be the big white hunter in this movie. For God's sake, don't pull those triggers — you're going to blow the gun up in your face. Not all movies, however, make such clangers. *Avatar* was one of those flicks where they knew what they were doing. This movie got the hunting right. Double tick.

From a young age, girls can be fantastic hunters, even better than boys.

Strangely enough, I'm not the only dad to hunt with his daughter. There are some amazing girls who hunt, and we're not talking butch seven-foot-tall Amazons; these are svelte, young and vibrant girls with a sparkle in their eye who love to party, sing, dance, who enjoy going out with boys, and also doing girly things. Hunting just happens to turn them on and many of them are exceptionally good. From a young age, girls can be fantastic hunters, even better than boys. Once I took Taygen to hunt gemsbok in Africa with another professional hunter, John van der Westhuizen. We soon came across a herd and decided the bull standing at the edge of the herd was the one Taygen should try to shoot.

'That one there,' I whispered to her as she raised her gun. 'The one at the back, shoot him.'

Taygen, at 15, was quite short and couldn't see her target over the scrub. 'I can't see him,' she replied.

I said, '*There*, the one at the back. He's looking at us right now. You need to shoot him fairly soon.'

She squinted through her scope. 'I can't see him clearly,' she said.

'The one at the very back,' said a now-anxious John.

By the time she asked us to repeat which one we'd lined up, the whole herd had spooked and was gone.

I turned to my daughter and said, 'You really need to be quicker. When we say now's the time to shoot, you need to place your shot.'

Taygen gritted her teeth. I knew she wanted to say something, but instead chose to bite her tongue. We kept walking, and it wasn't for another four or five hours that we came across more gemsbok. John and I were eyeing two very nice bulls standing side by side. We started discussing the merits of each.

'The one at the front is pretty big,' I remarked.

'Yeah,' agreed John. 'But the one at the back has a bigger base on his horns.'

As we whispered about which animal we should shoot, this wee girl pushed us both aside and *bang!* Taygen shot the biggest gemsbok right in the neck; pole-axed it. As it went down, she took one step forward and turned to us with a look of steely-eyed determination. 'I fucking saw that one,' she said calmly.

'Ah . . . yeah,' I muttered, amazed. 'Good shot, darling, well done.'

'Tremendous,' said a nervous John, not used to a wee girl being so assertive. The native trackers all smiled. Taygen was their favourite.

'Good shot darling, well done.'

Raindrops on Roses

I confess to being a bit of a gear nut, always searching for kit that is new and innovative, lighter and better — or just plain sexy! Over the years I've tried pretty much everything available in the outdoors market. Here then, in no particular order, is a list of 10 of my favourite things, part of my kit that I've tested, kit that works.

KNIFE

In line with the belief that a man cannot have too many knives, I have a lot of knives. Let me elaborate, a *whole* lot of knives. Many of them are handcrafted by some of the greatest knife makers alive. However, only one gets to travel in my pack into the hills. I'm kind of embarrassed to say it's a small folding knife I picked up years ago in a market in the Russian Far East for 100 roubles. That's about $4.50 New Zealand . . . Yep, I can hear you laugh from here, and I really am more than a little embarrassed to have even admitted it. Let me tell you, though, I've used that knife to dress out a heap of animals both big and small, from 600kg moose through to small rabbits. It works.

BOOTS

I have a plastic bin full of boots I've put to the test over the years; some have failed dismally while others have worked brilliantly.

Here are two I rate highly and use regularly. My Schnees, for use in extreme

cold. They utilise a Thinsulate insulation with an added wool lining in the boot, plus they come with detachable liners made from Thinsulate quilted onto felted wool. I always take a spare set of liners along so I can dry one set while wearing the other. I'll typically use these boots when the mercury looks like dropping below −15°C, and have also worn them at −40°C and still remained warm.

My alpine/bush boot is a Gronell. Made in Italy and incredibly comfortable, they're around five years old and pretty much coming to the end of their life. Five years is pretty darned good, I think! I may trial another boot to replace them, though I admit I'm just not sure which yet. I've heard that Kenetrek out of Montana have designed a great hunting boot, which they get made in Italy. Hmm. They may be worth a punt, Nigel.

RIFLESCOPE

Pretty close competition here between two top German contenders, Schmidt & Bender, and Leica. After some consideration I'm going to give it to Leica. Some things work and some things just work bloody well. My Leica ER scope falls into the latter category. Low light, wet conditions — nothing seems to faze this scope. I particularly like the extra-long eye relief when this scope is mounted on rifles with a little more kick, like my .300 WSM. It adds just a little more insurance against receiving a magnum eyebrow in steep shooting situations!

BINOS

Hands down it's Leica for my choice of binocular. Over the years I have traded my way up through various brands of binos until I could finally get my mitts on a pair of Leica 8x32s. Next step was to trade these for a set of Leica Duovids in 8+12x42, until finally I was able to trade yet again and find myself the extremely happy owner of a pair of 10x42 Geovids. Beautiful, beautiful optics with a laser rangefinder incorporated. Heaven-sent.

PACK

An old Fairydown from back in the day when the best packs in the world were made right here in New Zealand. I can't even remember which model this one is, but it carries a decent load of meat, keeps most of the rain out and, importantly, when it's been dropped down some cliff it bounces really well! If I had one thing to say about the majority of packs on the market nowadays it's that they are over-designed. Too many pockets; far, far too many zips. Kind of makes me believe most pack designers only tramp or hunt when the weather is fine. Mine floats okay in rivers, but again, too many zips means water floods the main compartment from the bottom up. Again a sign that the designer never had to pack-float down through a river gorge. So, I'm still searching for the ultimate pack. May have to build it myself.

TRAIL FOOD

No contest here. Mountain House dehy is so damn good I often eat it at home when I'm too rushed to cook. Yes, I know, quite sad really. My favourite is Turkey Tetrazzini, closely followed by Chili Mac with Beef. Mmm mmm.

TRUCK

For years I'd driven the venerable Hilux 4WD — no doubt about it, a ute made for the New Zealand outdoors. So when Isuzu asked me back in 2010 to test-drive one of their new D-Maxs I promptly said, 'Listen guys, thanks. I'm really flattered, but no thanks.'

Have to give them their dues; they were persistent buggers until finally I relented and took one for a spin (looking back, a pretty harsh spin if I'm being totally honest!) and man, I was really impressed. It's a great truck. A simple beast, to be truthful, but that's what I loved. A truck that the world's biggest truck maker had engineered was always going to be hard to beat. So I swapped to become an Isuzu man and have pulled more than one mate out of bogs and rivers where they've got high-centred.

I love my D-Max. Named him Bodacious, after one of the toughest rodeo bulls ever on the circuit. The name? Well, it just seemed so bloody apt.

WET WEATHER GEAR

The Tahr anorak is my go-to coat when precipitation is likely. The hood is still the best hood anyone makes in the world — though I reckon I can make it better! And the length is there to keep your date from getting wet. Nice and simple, not too many pockets.

COOKING STOVE

Love my wee MSR WhisperLite. I always make sure I carry a wind deflector for alpine use. When you're wet, frozen and crying for your mama, the sound of a cooker rapidly boiling you a brew is like the sound of angels singing on high.

BLACK BILLY TEA

Like Mad Dogs, Englishmen and a few crazy Kiwis, I can't seem to get through the day without a decent brew of tea. Let me tell you, I've had some weird looks from customs officers all around the world when I pull out a packet of Bell's best from my bag.

ABOVE LEFT Lou McNutt, the Wolf Girl from Waipukurau, digs wolves — literally. She's just clambered down a wolf den to grab two cubs as part of an ongoing study into wolf behaviour. Over the years Swazi has taken an active interest in conservation around the planet. Lou is one of a number of highly-skilled and incredibly passionate animal scientists Swazi assists with clothing. Alberta, Canada.

ABOVE RIGHT John Goodrich with a snared Amur leopard about to be collared. Russian Far East.

CENTRE LEFT It's that McNutt girl again, this time in Mongolia with a snow leopard she has trapped to gather data from. In 2011 the Mongolian government was considering opening up hunting for these magnificent animals. At the last moment they pulled the pin on the plan. Wow, that was close. Mongolia.

CENTRE RIGHT James Fraser in his Swazi hi-vis, releases a kiwi in the Rimutakas. This particular bird is called JB and is named for my brother, John, and father, Brian, after they sponsored the release programme. JB has proven to be a thorn in the side of the monitors, as he is always going on huge walkabouts outside the range of his monitoring collar. Yeah, sounds like a Hughes . . . Orongorongo Valley.

BELOW Celebrating Tiger Day in Terney. The tiger you can see in the back of the Swazi ute, yeah, the one holding the flag — he's not real, okay? Russia.

Hunting bears a new way almost gets us killed.

18

BEARS WITH SPEARS

The exact reason I decided I wanted to hunt a bear with a spear is a little hazy, though it seems to have stemmed from my appearance on *60 Minutes* in May 2003. In that programme the final sequence of my grizzly bear hunt on Baranof Island, in south-east Alaska, was shown. I'll admit, I voiced my concern when TV3 first told me of their plans to run the footage. But then they came back with, 'Davey, you hunt bears. Do you want the documentary to be a sanitised version of your life, or would you rather be up front and honest with viewers?'

If you strive to make excellent rain gear, forget about laboratories and 'rainroom tests'. You need to go to south-east Alaska — it's one big unforgiving rainroom. The hood on our rain gear is absolutely the best hood on the market.

Put that way, the only option was the honest approach. And cross your fingers! My concerns were about subjecting viewers to some fairly candid hunting footage — I'm constantly aware of how hunters are regarded. Yet, far from the outrage I'd anticipated, we had an incredible amount of mail saying 'what an adventure!' One letter, however, really stood out: the writer said he could understand and accept hunting a bear — if I had done it with

DANNY ELLIS

Gunsmoke lays up in Lover's Cove, Alaska. This shot, taken by Danny Ellis, is one of my favourites.

a spear! Which got me thinking — what a cool concept.

Now all I needed was to find a hunting guide who was a few sandwiches short of a picnic. Luckily I knew just the bloke. Jim Boyce, who you met in Chapter 1, was a guide based out of Sitka with whom I'd hunted bears, blacktail deer and mountain goats — but was he up to hunting bears with spears? Of course he was. Any man who went through US Navy Seal training camp is going to be a man to ride the river with. When things get sticky, as they can and will do, Jim is a guy I definitely want to have by my side.

ABOVE Quickly gone. Within days the salmon transform from flesh and skin to mere bones on the beach.

BELOW So calm and peaceful. We then walked around the corner to surprise no fewer than three female bears with five cubs in a meadow. It quickly became a huffin' and puffin', chompin' and stompin' affair.

The spear I chose to take to Alaska was made by Cold Steel in the US and is based on the type used by the Samburu warriors of northern Kenya. Its best feature is its ability to be split into three parts: the grip, head and the shoe, all fitting easily in my gun case, making it perfect for travelling. Made from 1055 carbon steel, it's incredibly tough, combining strength and impact resistance admirably. The blade holds a great edge, though in the coastal region of south-east Alaska I noticed you did need to keep an eye on the blade, as it rusted quickly. If you aren't paying attention you'd lose that wonderfully sharp edge.

I figured the best time to hunt bear was the autumn, when the salmon were spawning. As you moved through the forest, the noise of the streams would dampen any approach sounds and make a close stalk more feasible. I practised throwing my spear regularly and fixed my maximum range for accuracy and energy at around the 7-metre mark. But the same question bugged me: could I get in that close? Bowhunters often brag to rifle shooters about the need to get under the 30-metre mark. How did a hunter, used to the luxury of a rifle, feel about getting even closer to something as powerful and dangerous as a bear? I reassured myself that several years earlier on a grizzly bear hunt, I'd fired my first shot from 6 metres. Of course I could do it! Every night for six months I told myself this before I fell asleep. But doubts remained. While hunting bears with spears is not entirely unheard of, there is little in the way of published articles through which a hunter could conduct some research. Still, the whole enterprise was not as crazy as some may consider. Besides, I'd hunted bears maybe a dozen times in the past and was ready to add a little more spice. History

shows that the Athabascan Indians of Alaska would take on bruins with their spears in a tested passage of manhood. I'd never met anyone who had attempted, or for that matter accomplished, such a feat. Like most things in life, sometimes you've got to learn on the job. I would make mistakes, no doubt about that. I just hoped they wouldn't prove costly.

Before I knew it I was on Kuiu Island, south-east Alaska. The rain, which had consistently come down most of the morning, was even more so consistently coming down. Heavily persistent. Persistently persistent. I adjusted the cords on my hood a tad tighter, blew away a trickle of water from the edge of my nose and gazed again into the salmon-choked stream in front of me. I quickly became mesmerised by the scene, as half a dozen salmon fought the swift current. It was only the loud splashing downstream which snapped me out of an almost hypnotic trance.

The sound was unmistakable. I quietly reached to the right for my

'Hey Davey, eight bears in a pack. Wow, way cool!' You're crazy, Boycey.

Sitka, the capital of Alaska when the state was owned by the Russians, still has a strong connection with the old country. St Michael's Russian Orthodox church in the main street.

OPPOSITE 'Tonight? Here? Tonight we are kings.'

spear. Another splash. Closer now. There. Bear! Peering through the thick undergrowth, I could just make out a black shape across the stream about 20 metres out. The bear stepped around a log jam into a small pool, where it expertly snatched and caught one of the humpies. Nice bear. Maybe a six-footer. Not what we were after today. We had set our goals a little higher.

I watched intently as the bear climbed the small bank above the stream, disappearing into the devil's club brush with a salmon dangling from its mouth. A silent sigh relieved some tension. I was tight, way too tight, and on edge. Understandable.

Barely three minutes had passed since the small bear departed when I felt, rather than saw, a slight movement to my left. It was the slightest flicker, the tiniest distraction, yet enough to make me turn my head ever so slowly. There was a bear coming towards me about 10 metres to my left.

Look at his ears. They sit on the side of his head. He's big enough. His gait pigeon-toed, belly low as he swaggers closer. Yes, by God, he's big enough alright. I curl, then uncurl, my grasp on the spear shaft. Loosen your grip. Roll back your thumb. There is no emotion. No fear. No predation. Cleanse your mind. Guide the spear, don't choke it, don't throw it. Move it. Imagine it. It will be. Eight metres. He stops. Looks around. Seven. Let him come. Six — shield your eyes, he must not see your eyes! Now, watch him step. Wait. Wait. Five metres. He will lift his right leg and my spear will be released.

The moment . . . is now.

'Dave! Dave!' Jim's warning hiss ripped through the air. I turned to face the unseen danger that must be lurking nearby. But Jim was not looking my way. He was directing his warning to my cameraman, Dave Abbott, there filming for our planned TV series. Dave was standing 15 metres away on a tree stump.

'Dave, if you stand there a bear will spot you easily.'

Dave didn't answer, or move. He simply took one finger slowly from his camera and pointed beyond Jim to where I stood — right beside a bear now anxiously swaying from side to side as he decided his next move. Fight or flight? Dash or bite? He spun and exploded out of the stream back to where he'd come from. Sonnavabitch! We all fell about laughing. Where had he appeared from? When bears move quietly not even the forest can hear them.

We spent the next eight days throwing spears and chasing bears through streams and valleys. We howled for wolves, travelled through primeval rainforest, caught salmon and halibut. We ate well. Everything was as it should have been. We never speared a bear, although I threw the sharp stick in anger once, only to learn that your stance affects your aim downhill, and the shaft skidded off the back of a huge bear. We'll return.

I remember a day when Jim and I took a moment, just on dark, as we were leaving a stream where it fed into the ocean. The sky had turned a blue so surreal, so stunning, I could not believe my own eyes. It was as if light was flowing through the sky, then refracting itself via a sapphire filled with the brightest stars. Jim spoke. Jim the poet. Jim the dreamer. Jim the Bearman. He looked to those skies and said, 'Elsewhere, Davey, we are but mere men. Tonight? Here? Tonight we are kings.'

For a split second it felt that way, as if nature herself had rolled out a carpet reserved for royalty. Then, as quickly as it had appeared, it vanished. I glanced behind me. It was dark. What a place to test your nerve. This darkened forest. Such a perfect place. Where bears are kings.

LEFT Your blood warms, your senses heighten and you feel incredibly alive. Hunting with a spear in the thick underbrush of a rainforest makes for a bloody exciting experience.
ABOVE RIGHT The salmon spawn is on, and with it the bears congregate in the streams to fill themselves in preparation for oncoming hibernation.
BELOW RIGHT In this part of the world, eagles are as common as seagulls lining the beaches in New Zealand.

Tuna with Thai green curry and sticky rice

INGREDIENTS

1–2 tuna, filleted
2 florets broccoli
1 zucchini
1 onion
1 green capsicum
2 carrots
4 shiitake mushrooms
3 tablespoons olive oil
1 teaspoon soy sauce
1 can coconut cream
1 cup rice
2 sprigs coriander

If ever a fish was chased inexorably across the seas, prized for its high dollar worth, and relentlessly sought for its high food value, then it is the magnificent tuna. Globally, many species of tuna exist, though sadly now many are in decline: so harassed, so senselessly fished almost to commercial extinction, it is doubtful they may recover.

The tuna in my recipe is the southern blue fin. Commercially it, too, has received something of a hiding, though strangely, it is not yet that highly cherished by the Japanese fish markets. (I say 'not yet' with a foreboding sense of doom for the hunter-gatherer and his prey.) Too oily, too bland . . . ya-farkin-hoo! That means for the recreational fisho there remains great fishing, should you wish to brave the wild West Coast. Believe me, for you will fish in mid-winter, and it is wild!

With John Lea, CEO of RD1, and his 300kg bluefin from the Hokitika trench.

Take one, or even perhaps two, fish, depending upon the size of your party, and tag all the others before releasing them back to the sea. They will recover and they'll be there the following year to fish again. It's about sustainability, concern for the fishery and a deep respect for a fish which, in my humble opinion, is quite without peer. The prize? Some of the best-eating meat you'll ever consume. There are so many ways to eat this meat: sashimi, sushi, smoked, baked, fried . . . Here's a favourite one of mine.

Slice up some broccoli, zucchini, onion, green capsicum, carrots and shiitake mushrooms. Julienne the carrots, as they will look much more attractive when cut this way. Well, as attractive as a carrot can possibly look. Now add them all except the mushrooms to the pan for a stir-fry.

The Greymouth bar. On this day we waited a few hours before heading out.

Don't be scared of a few good dollops of a fine olive oil — the aficionados say when you fry oil it always deteriorates, and so you should use a cheap oil, but I reckon *all* ingredients should be the very best and to hell with the experts! Let your tastebuds rule . . .

After a few minutes on the heat and with cooking well under way, add 1 teaspoon of soy sauce. Get hold of some decent Japanese sauce, you won't regret it.

We're frying now, so keep the heat up without scorching the broccoli. Add the mushrooms once you consider you're about three-quarters there. Righto, take the pan off the heat and let's get the fish going.

Cut the 500g of tuna into chunks around 2.5–3cm. Over a medium heat, add 3 tablespoons of olive oil to the pan. Throw in the tuna and keep an eye on it, turning once you see it cooking roughly about a quarter of the way through the meat. What you are trying to do is cook the tuna until it's three-quarters done — no more. I like to eat meat just about raw, while Maggie heads somewhere between medium and well done. It's a chef's nightmare, so, as with the true meaning of life, seek balance.

Once the fish is three-quarters cooked, get a large deep wok-shaped pan or, you know what, just a bloody decent-sized pan with a lid. I often use a heavy cast-iron casserole camp oven. That's the old possum trapper in me coming out.

Empty the veggies back into the pan and now add the fish. Pour in the coconut cream and stir the mixture gently, trying not to crumble the fish. Once you've got it all thoroughly mixed together, bring the heat back up slowly. Now add some green curry paste, stirring it continuously. Bring the heat back up but don't make it a bubbling cauldron. Consistent heat, not a rapid boil. Good and hot? Put the lid on and take it off the heat to allow the fish to slowly finish itself and for the curry flavour to permeate.

Rice. Let's not dick around, we'll use the microwave here. Soak 1 cup of rice for 10 minutes in a bowl of warm water. This is very important. The water level should be just above the rice, a little over 1 cup of water. Use a glass container — you don't want to melt a plastic one in the microwave. Cover the bowl and cook at full throttle for 3 minutes. Stir the rice; you'll notice that some of the rice is still translucent, kind of see-through, or not quite cooked, and some has a white centre, which is cooked, so mix it up well.

Heat the rice up again for a further 3 minutes. To check if it is done, bite some and if it's crunchy, well, it ain't done. If it needs more cooking, heat it up and check every 3 minutes or so, until it's opaque. The cooking time depends on the power of the microwave.

Spread some rice on a plate and pour on the curry. Make sure you give yourself at least two extra pieces of the tuna — because you deserve it! Garnish with some fresh coriander.

Those of you who travelled forth to catch your own tuna may at this point find yourselves reminiscing about the terror of the Greymouth River bar and a small shudder will run down your spine. Taste the tuna. Brother, it was all worthwhile.

LEFT Tony Roache's magnificent boat, the *Cova Rose*. I've fished on her at the Three Kings and in the Hokitika trench.
RIGHT My brother John holds our second landed fish. After this fish we released all our subsequent catches.

Returning to Africa on safari, and tracking the wily buffalo.

19

BUFFALO SOLDIER

Having lived and worked in Africa, the continent was no stranger to me when I eventually went back for two plains-game safaris with Taygen. But I longed to return for a dangerous game hunt. I have always wanted to hunt the Cape buffalo; after talking to many older and more experienced African hunters I could see that the buffalo was placed right up there as one of the most dangerous of the big game — and for good reason.

She can get pretty hot on an African foot safari.

I couldn't wait any longer; it was time to test my mettle. I didn't, however, wish to hunt in the way most modern African safaris are carried out nowadays. The thought of sitting on the back of a jeep travelling down trails, tracks and dirt roads looking to see where herds have crossed the road didn't arouse my juices. On such a trip the trackers will jump out, check the spoor where the animals have crossed and then figure out if any bulls were in the group. If the professional hunter (PH) believes

The cooing of doves, lions in the evening. and sunsets to die for. Africa, whether you know it or not, is deeply rooted in all of our pasts.

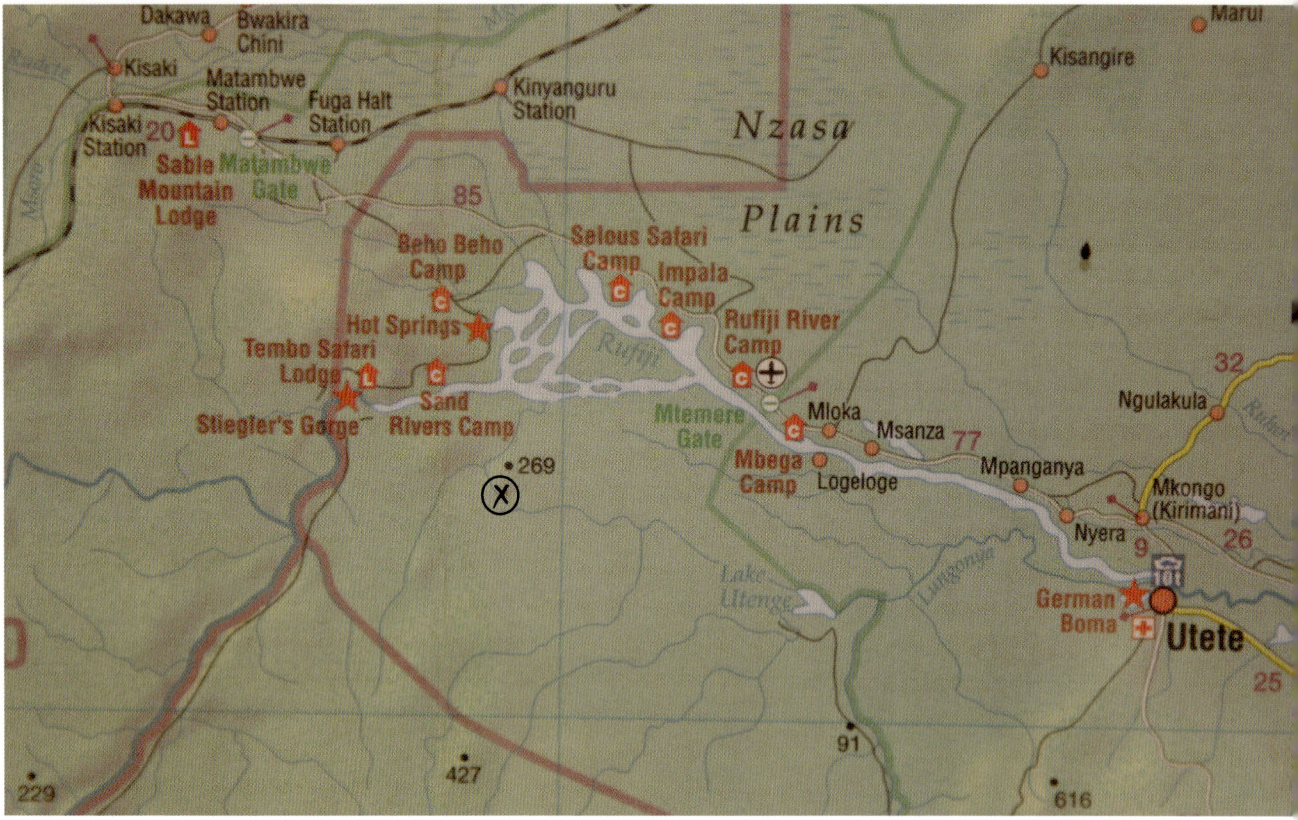

The mighty Rufiji River in the heart of the Selous.

a good bull is with the herd, then you'll alight from the jeep and start tracking. It still augurs for a good hunt, but I was after a *great* hunt. A classic hunt. Beneath Hemingway's green hills of Africa. Safari!

The harsh reality of hunting on foot with porters is actually the cost, which can balloon to four or five times that of a traditional motorised safari. Add African logistics and finding a hunter keen to do it, and the challenge is one many would give up on. As far as local companies are concerned, a motorised hunt can be done and dusted in four to five days. A new hunter aboard means they're making a bit more money from the trip.

It took quite some time before I cracked it, but finally the moment came on a visit to Laurence Frank in Kenya. Laurence is a dear friend and one of the most respected large-carnivore biologists in the world. When I mentioned my dilemma he immediately pointed me in the direction of Richard Bonham, a man who came from a long line of Kenyan hunters and game wardens. As poaching is rife in Kenya — one of the reasons is there is practically no wild game at all left outside the parks — Richard did most of his hunting in Tanzania's Selous Game Reserve, which allows controlled hunting.

'I'm from Whangaparaoa, mate!'

I did some more research, and found Richard came highly recommended by previous clients. We got in touch and he gave me the lowdown on the prices. Initially my response was that the buffalo must be gold-plated, but the lure of attempting the trip in this manner made me itch with excitement. *This is what I want to do*, I thought. So I saved like billy-o, got the money together, paid my deposit, grabbed Dave Abbott, my cameraman, and headed to Dar es Salaam, Tanzania.

Richard picked us up from the airport and gave us a rundown on what to expect, adamant that his every word in the field was to be followed. If we came across poachers, we needed to open fire. If we were charged by an animal in the long grass and he didn't run, Richard expected me to stay put too. If he did run, however, he expected me to get out of his bloody way in a hurry!

Taking a public flight with firearms on board is illegal in Tanzania so we chartered a plane from Dar es Salaam to the Rufiji River. We spotted

animals below, but were too high to pick them out clearly. Besides which, when you're flying countless kilometres over Africa it starts to all look the same. As we were paying for the flight, I had no problem asking the pilot if he wouldn't mind getting down lower. He turned around and said in a distinctly Kiwi twang, 'I recognise that accent. Where are you from, mate?'

'Levin, mate,' I replied.

With that, our pilot from Whangaparaoa took it upon himself to prove he'd missed his calling as a Second World War Spitfire pilot. His antics were pretty amazing, and I almost have no doubt that on one or two occasions we flew under the bellies of elephants. Many a time our wing tips were just barely off the ground. The pilot swore me to secrecy regarding his daredevil behaviour — no worries, mate. Just sharing it with a couple of people, here in my book. Crazy loon.

I was hopefully after some mud-dwelling dugga boy, an old bachelor who no longer found himself part of the herd.

We landed at the Sand River, part of the Rufiji near Beho Beho, and got our gear ready for the trip ahead. Thirty porters carried our supplies on their heads. I wondered whether the wee flat boats we would be riding in would be enough protection from raging hippos. It's common knowledge that hippos take down more people in Africa than lions, elephants, buffalo and crocodiles combined. Yet they're one of those animals we tend to think of as friendly types at the zoo, or stars of the cartoon world. In reality, hippos possess razor-shrarp tusks and razor-sharp tempers. If they think you're in their territory, look out — they're coming.

Our routine was to rise at five, have a decent plate of porridge and head into sand country. Such a breakfast would stand you in good stead for the day, where walking for nine or 10 hours was nothing out of the ordinary. We'd tell the porters basically where we figured we'd be at the end of the day and they'd set up the camp to meet us.

So off we headed to hunt into the wind. With the midday temperature reaching highs of 55°C it was imperative to keep hydrated. For the first few days, Dave and I struggled to come to grips with the heat, yet by day three we had adapted to the extreme heat. I am constantly amazed at how well the human body does acclimatise. I recall hunting mountain lions in Montana during winter in –34°C, then coming home to New Zealand, changing my undies and flying to northern Queensland to hunt chital deer in 44°C with 100 per cent humidity. A temperature range of some 78°C with no side effects and all within a matter of days.

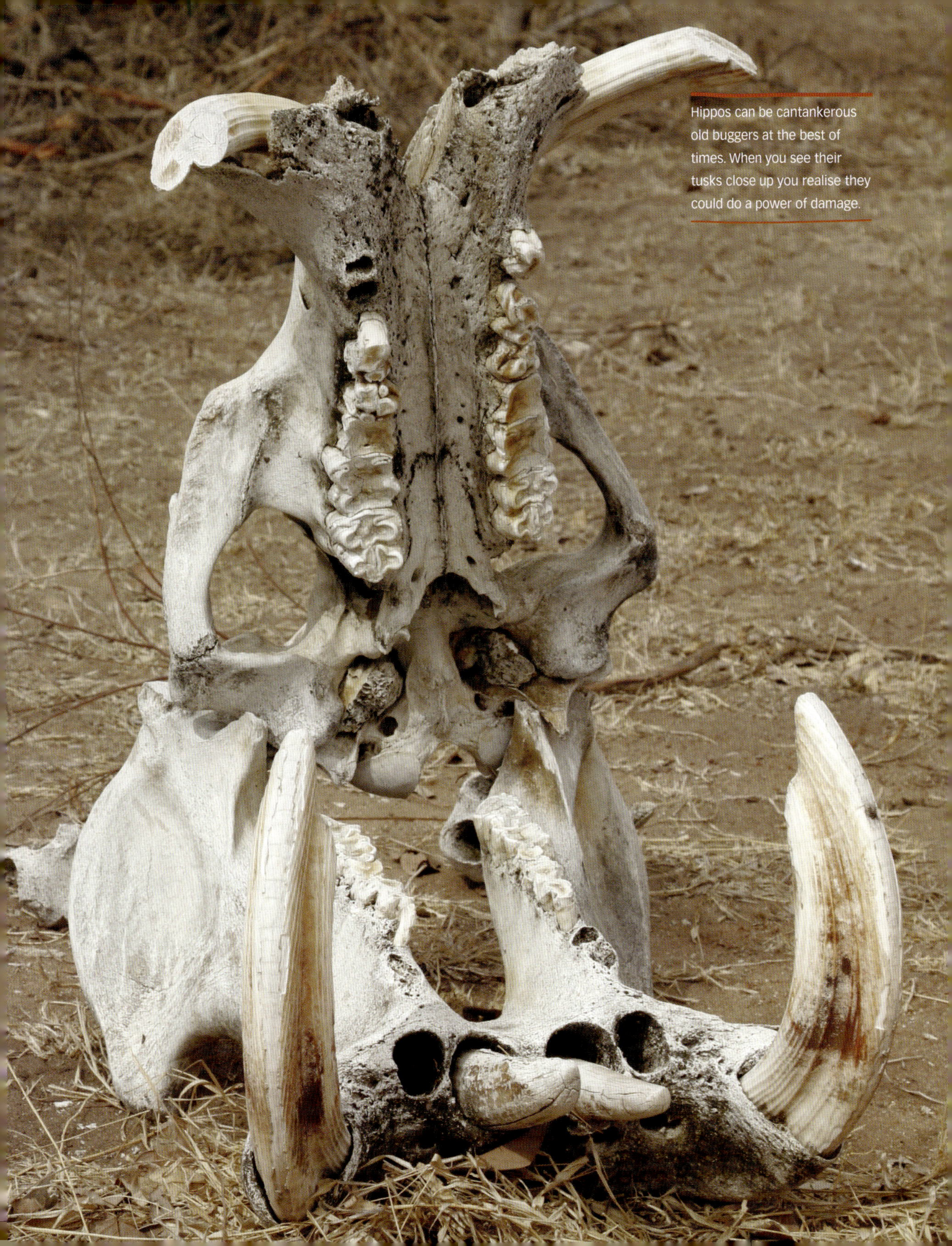

Hippos can be cantankerous old buggers at the best of times. When you see their tusks close up you realise they could do a power of damage.

Every team should have its own mascot. Thunderbox-Man was ours. It had two holes cut out in the back for the porter to look out of as he walked through the bush.

Buffalo. My goal was not necessarily to find the biggest bull. I was hopefully after some mud-dwelling dugga boy, an old bachelor who no longer found himself part of the herd, and the length of his horns was irrelevant. In such a hunt, excitement outweighs nervousness. Jitters or a tiny touch of fear prove you're alert and watching. When I'm travelling through country and looking at the brush ahead, I often visualise what to do if something in there wanted a piece of me. My routine is the same as if I were on a defensive-driving course. When you see a car pull up to an intersection on an open road, you picture what would happen if that car just pulled out. Being prepared on the road is no different to hunting dangerous game. I often run through scenarios in my head. What would happen if a bear, elephant or lion stepped out right now? By no means am I saying every hunter does the same, but I have no scars from animals (well, apart from one an old Danish girlfriend gave me, but that really is quite personal), so it's working for me.

Despite the tension and nerves before a big hunt, I never lose sleep — unless I happen to be in bear country. I defy anyone to fall asleep immediately when out hunting bear, especially if you've ever experienced a huge snout pushing on the other side of a thin nylon tent wall. Nowadays it takes me at least four minutes to doze off in bear country. Generally, falling asleep has never been an issue. Unless I've got a bit of hokey-pokey on my mind, I'm gone in seven seconds. There have been times I've faced major issues and challenges in my business — cash flows, debtors and creditors — when lying awake should have been the only option. But you can't do anything lying in bed, unless a brilliant idea comes along. In that case, I wake up and jot down thoughts in my notepad by the bed. After that, I sleep. I'm not one to stress out, which is not to say stress is not in my life. Why lose sleep over it, man? You need your sleep. In places like Africa and Alaska — where strange noises inhabit the night and animals possess teeth and claws — you do sleep lightly, but strangely very well. I try to focus on the rhythm of the night while I sleep; oh, and have a loaded gun, one in the chamber, safety on — and a torch ready by my side — just in case.

In all my Africa travels I've been lucky enough to have never had malaria or crook guts — and I'm sure luck really has played her part. To put this into perspective, each year there are around 250 million reported cases of malaria, with just under 1 million people dying of the disease.

Tsetse flies are another one of those things that love to bite you in Africa. You'll know when you have been bitten too, little buggers! Again, tsetses, like the mossies, carry diseases which contribute to human deaths, some 300,000 alone last year. To keep malaria at bay, I normally take Doxy tablets. Generally though, touch wood, the only time I've been sick on a hunt is from picking up something on the flight over. Spending two or three weeks in the wilderness having gone in there with a bloody town flu — and sleeping on permafrost — is not the best feeling. I can assure you as well, seven weeks bedridden with viral pneumonia will put the dampener on your hunting success.

With our 30 porters loaded up, we simply turned to the south — and began walking.

Even after years of hunting, I felt like a complete novice next to Richard and the trackers. These hunters read signs the way we read the daily newspaper, scanning the entire time, their senses taking in everything. The way they operated was similar to the way a headline grabs your interest. They looked and looked, before suddenly alerting us that it may be worth pursuing a particular track. They got particularly excited sticking their fingers into a pile of buffalo dung, swirling it around, pulling it out and informing us the animal responsible was not that far off . . .

Kani, Richard's tracker and an old elephant hunter from Kenya, was also part of our group. Good hunters have good stories and Kani was no exception. His skills included taking down elephants with no more than a bow and arrow. It was entirely illegal, but Kani and his tribe did this for meat. His method was to stalk right underneath the elephant and drive a poison arrow straight into its gut. It seemed an incredibly brave thing to do, but one question remained: what do you do once you loosen your arrow?

Kani looked at me through his remaining eye. 'Run like fuck!' he said.

The next obvious question: 'How did you lose your eye?'

Kani went on to explain: 'One day I stick the elephant and then run like fuck, because he's chasing me . . . I was dodging this way, then that way, then I run my eye straight into a stick!'

The park is named for Frederick Courtenay Selous, who was killed here during WW1. His tombstone is to be found in the bush near Beho Beho.

Here was a man, no taller than five foot, who possessed balls of steel. Nay, titanium! I'm always taken by how well Africans know the land, the animals and their behaviour. They can sense buffalo, yet even when they locate a herd, know not to push it until everything is right. They may decide not to follow the herd but instead suggest we go to a spot out of the way because the buffalo will be making their way, in a big circle, to that place. Sure enough, that's exactly what happens. They know exactly what the animals are up to, absolutely nail it! We don't know we're alive. Their tracking skills had us in awe.

The big thing when hunting buffalo is to be certain you've got enough gun. You'll kill a buffalo with a .308 pretty easily if you put it in the right place. While the .375 H&H is popular, I favour a .416 Rigby, as things often don't always work out the way you'd like. With a decent bullet — say a Swift A-Frame and Woodleigh solids — the Rigby is a good buff stopper. Again, be sure to carry enough gun to stop the animal. A small calibre will kill, but what if the bullet hits a twig or a branch, something previously unseen to the shooter? Trust me, even big heavy bullets fly awry when they hit a branch, and then you have a wounded animal on your hands. Out of respect for the buffalo — or any other creature for that matter — you need to be able to stop it. If unsuccessful, you now have a hairy moment on your hands. Your world, my friend, is about to slow down.

Any wounded animal is a dangerous animal.

Early on, we came across a few buffalo but weren't in a great position to shoot. In long elephant grass things can happen in a great big hurry. Without warning, a buffalo can be steaming past, just metres away in the long stuff, and you have to hope like hell it's not peed off with you. You must always concentrate. Never take your eye off the prize. The biggest lesson I learnt in Africa is that everything bites. *Every single thing bites.*

On about the ninth day we left camp early as we'd struck sign of a herd. After three hours of tracking we came upon them — literally finding ourselves in the middle of a herd. At such times you can use the wind to your advantage, giving you a chance to take a good look at the animal. When the moment finally arrives, it's amazing how it is never as you visualised. Having hunted in thick country with limited visibility for so long, I'd imagined I'd be shooting from up close. Suddenly, here they were

OPPOSITE ABOVE LEFT Another job was to provide meat for the porters. 'Looks like it's impala for dinner boys!' ABOVE RIGHT Kani and me with captured ivory, bound for the government bond. What the officials did with it I cannot say BELOW LEFT Richard Bonham. A bastard, but a good bastard nonetheless. BELOW RIGHT M'bogo. It was with a relief I heard his death-bellow from the long grass.

— up close, but in the open. They'd emerged through a gap in the trees and across from a dried-up waterhole. For me, it proved a beautiful moment.

Times like these are zen-like for a hunter. I've learnt to chill out, lose all predation thoughts and any lurking fear.

Make like the sand.

So we did. Sat perfectly still in the open on the hot sand 30 metres away from the herd and watched as a few hundred buff walked past and every time they did, Richard, who sat alongside me, whispered, 'No . . . no . . . no.' By now, I was a reasonable judge of buffalo and could tell when a herd was thinning out.

I was in the middle of reciting my mantra: 'Money shot. Money shot. Boomfah!'

Buffalo are dangerous animals and aggressive when feeling . . . well, actually, they're aggressive most of the time! Meanwhile, Richard still hadn't found one I could shoot. Just before the decision came to move on, the second-to-last bull piqued Richard's interest.

'No,' he said, then just as quickly, *'Yes!'*

In a split second he'd changed his mind. As I heard his affirmative I was in the middle of reciting my mantra: 'Money shot. Money shot. Boomfah!'

'Full stroke! Full stroke!'

(Okay, my mantra. With the animal in sight and within range my finger hovers right beside the trigger, exerting no pressure whatsoever until that exact moment when the kill zone is centred in my scope — that's the money shot. Close in, you don't need to worry about 'squeezing off the shot'; in fact, you can pull as hard as you like. And as the kill zone appears I shoot, right then, without hesitation. The second part of my mantra, 'full stroke', reminds me to stroke the bolt *all the way* back, especially in Magnum rifles with their long actions and cases, hence there is no chance of a jam. And as we all know, jams quickly become pickles.)

Roughly where you should shoot a buffalo humanely and quickly: smack in the heart.

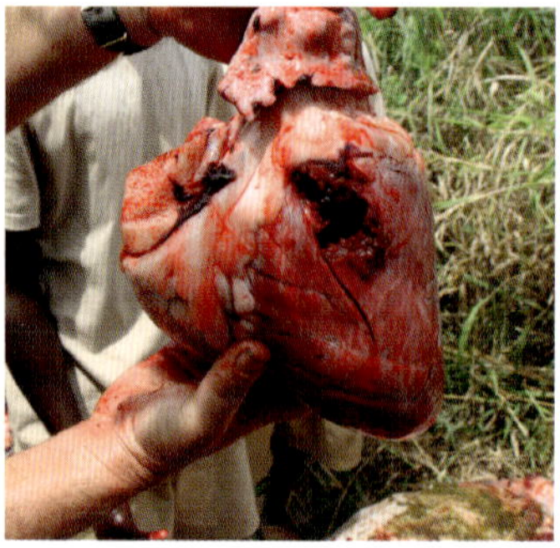

I probably shouldn't say this, but I will because he's such a good mate: Richard's follow-up shot went straight through the buffalo's ear. The poor bugger had a .470 hole as an earring. Richard will no doubt give me all seven colours of grief when he reads this, but really, come on, a back-up shot in the ear: that's slick shooting, bro!

When my bullet hit, the buffalo took off in a huge hurry and I didn't have time to get a second shot in. The buffalo hoofed it into a whole pile of thick stuff, and Richard called, 'Wait!' Two or three seconds later, we heard the death bellow of the bull. I knew I had shot him in the heart by the way he had hunched his shoulders forward. When we reached the animal it was dead — with the back-up shot through its ear making this absolutely certain. I shot that particular animal because it was right; it looked different to the others. He wasn't a really old bull, but just looked right, so I had no hesitation whatsoever pulling the trigger.

That night we had buffalo tongue for dinner. Our cook, with nothing more than an open fire in the African bush, would put many European Michelin-rated chefs to shame. Each night began with soup. Cream of mushroom soup, asparagus soup . . . just the most beautiful soup, with freshly baked bread rolls, followed by the most amazing impala steaks or, in my case, buffalo tongue with an assortment of relishes. How this guy could conjure up such delights in the middle of nowhere was anyone's guess, but it was stunning fare.

A lot of the porters ate meat only once or twice a year. For them, it was heaven. To be able to feed the guys as much meat as they could eat, as well as drying meat to take home to their villages, was a personal highlight. For water each night, we dug a deep hole in the sand, similar to elephants, who burrow down until they hit gold. Elephants, however, don't have the luxury of water purifier tablets. It was great water; we never got sick and we lived like kings. We carried a shower and dunny around with us. What more could you want? We had a beautiful table, not a big table, but a beautiful table to eat our dinner on and mosquito nets to sleep under each night. The only downside was the warm gin, but you can't have everything, especially when you're supposed to be roughing it.

Kani had been blessed by a local witchdoctor and thus protected from the sting of the scorpion. He would dump three or four scorpions in my boots each night to literally keep me on my toes.

Filming our final minutes in Africa, convinced that I was dying.

20

THE DAY A HUNTER DIED

No doubt about it, I have had several scrapes that have nearly seen the end of my days on this particular planet. When that happens, I want to go screaming, the same way I arrived. Run-ins with terrorists, animals, planes, vehicles and swollen rivers spring to mind, but the day I resigned myself to the fact my life was over, was in the Selous Game Reserve in Tanzania, on that buffalo hunt with Richard Bonham.

It was indeed a fantastic hunt, perhaps the most memorable I have ever been on, but it also held some poignant moments. Easily the saddest part of the hunt during the course of our safari was finding so many dead elephants. Over the short span of the two weeks we were walking, we counted 30 carcasses. Gangs of Somali poachers were working the park, killing seemingly at will any and all animals which would gain them financial reward. These men were mean, ruthless killers — of people and elephants.

We were on safari in the Selous for a total of two weeks, and in that time we counted the carcasses of over 30 elephants, slaughtered for their ivory. Some were mere calves, their ivory weighing less than a kilo, yet on the Asian market that kilo represented a months' wages for the poachers. When will it end? Who will end it?

Just where then was the money coming from? According to Nindi, our government game scout, up above the Selous Game Reserve a new road was being built by the Chinese. The fine gentlemen running the construction of the road had placed standing orders for rhino horn, elephant tusks and ivory. The contraband was being shipped in containers supposedly packed with compressors and machinery heading back east for maintenance, but there were no machines inside the casings, just ivory and rhino tusks. To find the carcasses was devastating. First you'd spot the vultures, and after closer inspection, elephants with their heads hacked off. The trunk would be sliced off, then the bastards simply hacked the face clean in half and pulled the tusks out. Bastards, bastards, bastards.

Richard was adamant at each daily breakfast that if we spotted these poachers we were to open fire. Be the first to shoot. Don't hold back. No warning shots. Shoot to kill. At one stage Kani our tracker stopped, looked around then informed us we were barely five minutes behind these guys, and one thing kept playing and replaying in my mind: if we do not shoot first, they will and we will die.

As well as poaching elephants and rhinos, the Somalis were also poisoning crocodiles in the river. The crocs would take the bait, crawl out from the river and die on the banks. Then the Somalis would skin them, leaving the carcasses for hyenas and vultures. Often we came across acres of bleached bones. The carnage was incredible, like something from a movie.

Poisoning was also part of their MO. What made this even more abhorrent is the fact the poison is so easily procurable in East Africa. The poachers all use a product called Furadan, made by the FMC Corporation in the States. Get this. Furadan is banned in America yet available over the counter in Kenya. It's not only used by poachers for their ill-gotten gains, it is also used to lace meat and kill lions, leopards, people . . . it's a pretty evil practice. Melons and other fruit were injected with the poison and left where the elephants would find them. Once eaten, the Somalis would surmise where the melon was taken from and follow the tracks of the dying animal. Within an hour they would come across dead

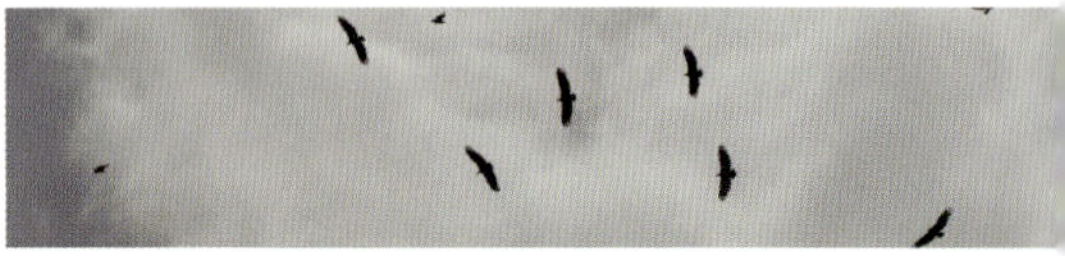

elephants. These guys weren't fussy. The animals needn't be freshly dead. Hack their faces off, rip out the tusks and away with the ivory.

One day near the end of our hunt, as we snuck along a dry riverbed, we discovered we were close to where the poachers were operating. We stopped to rest under the shade of a large acacia tree and using our binoculars glassed the terrain all around.

Richard soon found a pile of pomegranates and said, 'Hey, Davey, you've got to try these! They're delicious!'

So he cut one open, gave me half, which I ate, while he devoured the remainder. A few minutes later Richard asked, 'What do you think, old boy?'

'You know what, Richard?' I replied. 'It actually tastes a bit off.'

'Oh,' he scoffed, 'mine was fine.'

Richard cut open another half-dozen and we ate them all. For the next while we sat there munching on pomegranates when suddenly Nindi tore out of the bush and in broken Swahili screamed, 'Stop! What are you doing, Bwana, what are you doing?'

Richard replied, 'What does it look like we're doing, eating pomegranates, would you like some?'

Nindi gave us both a blank look. 'Richard, these pomegranates don't grow here. These are fruits that Somalis use to kill the elephants.'

'Richard . . . These are fruits that Somalis use to kill the elephants.'

I'll never forget the panicked look on Richard's face: *Fuck. What have I done? I have killed the both of us.*

And I was thinking, no way . . . Perhaps it wouldn't have been so bad if we hadn't seen so many dead elephants that day. I was carrying a vivid and immediate picture of just how powerful the poison was.

'Well, we're not just going to die here,' I said. 'We're going to do something about it. Let's drink a whole lot of water and make ourselves sick.' (I have since discovered, in our case anyway, this was the worst thing we could have done.)

Richard and I proceeded to try to make ourselves sick, but failed miserably. We put our hands, fists and sticks down our throats; nothing worked.

I have to be sick to get rid of this poison.

I poured sand down my throat. It proved to me that, even if you want to, sometimes you can't physically make yourself sick. With my life utterly depending upon it, I couldn't manage it. By this point, Richard had turned to me and asked how I was doing.

'Well, you know, um, not too bad at the moment,' I replied.

His next words made me shiver. 'I'm going, Davey, I'm going fast. My heart feels like it's doing 150–160. I've lost the feeling in my fingertips. I can't feel my toes.' With that, he slumped to the ground. He then turned to Dave, the cameraman, and said, 'You need to film this. I need to say something to my family before I go. I need to pass on a message.'

Dave, a placid, gentle type from Whangarei, was in tears. 'Fuck,' was all he managed. Like all good cameraman he filmed everything. Richard, head now slumped on chest, hunched beside him.

'Come on man,' I said, 'You've got to say something to your family, to your wife. You need to talk to Tara.' In minutes I would be doing the same for Maggie and the kids.

With the energy draining from his being, Richard looked at the camera and said, 'Tara, what a wonderful, wonderful life I have led, doing all the things that I have wanted to do. Meeting you and having our children was

Our porters dry buffalo meat over the fire to take home to their villages. Many only eat meat twice a year.

the best thing I have ever done. I am so sorry that it has to end like this.'

Then his head slumped down once more.

I shook him. 'Come on, Richard! You need to say a couple more things.' All the time I'm thinking, *I need to talk to Maggie. I need to say something to the kids. I need to say something to the boys and Taygen, one last piece of advice for my children before I go.* So I said, 'Come on, Richard, come on . . . you need to finish this.'

Richard looked up. I was right. He had more to say. He wasn't finished yet, thank goodness. I'll never forget the way he looked into the camera. 'I need to tell you something, Tara,' he said. 'Something that's always . . . well, something that I desperately . . . how do I say this?' He glanced once more at the camera, before looking at me, tears now in his eyes, before finishing with, 'Tara . . . I'm the guy that spoofed Davey Hughes!'

LEFT Nindi, the Tanzanian government game scout who accompanied our safari. He was a cool guy and, as I was to find out, he had a wicked sense of humour.

RIGHT We gathered our water in the same manner as the elephants, by digging a hole in the sand.

'You bastard!' I yelled. 'You bastard! You bastard! You prick-faced son of a bitch, Kenyan bastard!'

Everyone reckons Africans are pretty fast runners, but I caught every single one of those trackers, all of whom must have been in on it, and planted the biggest kiss you could ever imagine on their heads. I chased that bastard Bonham around until I could rugby-tackle him. When successful, I kissed him, then licked his face with all the drool and sand that still filled my mouth and whispered in his ear, 'We're going to live!'

I had thought I was dead, yet it was the most amazing feeling to realise I would live. It's nothing like being charged by a grizzly, or getting hit by a train. With those scenarios, there is always a chance of survival, a glimmer of hope and a chance to act. When you have been poisoned with Furadan deep in the African bush, there is no antidote. You are going to die.

That day in Africa I had accepted I was dead. I remember looking back with no regrets. I was happy and thought, *what a fantastic fucking life I have lived. What wonderful people I have met and loved.*

Every day, no matter where I am, I wake up and say to myself, 'Today is a good day to die.' You have to, or else it means you have not lived life as you ought to have. I have had the best life.

And that was it. The day I died. The best practical joke ever.

Quite the haute couture on safaris nowadays. I only wish I had a photo of the porters' and trackers' faces when I walked into their camp that morning.

R.COATS

Survival tips

There are many mishaps that can befall the tyro heading into the bush. I'm going to touch on just two, as in my opinion all the other stuff is either common sense, or things you will have figured out for yourself well before you set foot in the scrub. So I'm not going to tell you how to start a fire, set a bone, build a shelter that keeps out the rain or become an instant hunter-gatherer with just a knife. You'll have ample fire-lighting gear in your first-aid bag and you'll know how to make a lean-to or cover yourself in leaves, ferns and moss, as well as where and when to do it, i.e., not in a valley floor where you'll freeze your nuts off.

1 | GETTING LOST

What kills most folk when they get lost is panic. Raw, blind, uncontrollable panic. So here's my first tip. Sit down. Tell yourself you are not lost, merely confused. By a stream? Hey, make a brew. Personally I have never been lost. I've been confused for a day or two at a time perhaps — but never lost. Start talking to yourself if it eases your mind. Don't berate yourself or begin arguing. You'll need to try to get over the initial panic quickly, because the next symptom to come down the pipe is despair. It is despair that takes away the will to live, despair that eliminates the reason you will pull through your ordeal.

Here's the second tip. Focus on a bloody good reason to live. Kids, family or loved one? *Yeah!* Now you have something to be positive about. Someone to live for. Damn, it's actually fun being lost! According to experts, the drive to get home is the number-one factor in successful survival stories.

Okay. Let's get un-lost. What was your last known location? Was it a high ridge, a creek crossing or track? Can you backtrack to that spot? Most people get lost in the bush within a kilometre of a track or hut. Shut your eyes. Was the last track to the east? The west? Can you travel in a set direction with or even without a compass? You can? Good, head that way. Not feeling too confident? Okay. Sit back down. Think again about the last location that you knew where you were. If you're not positive about getting back to that point it's time to start building as comfortable a shelter as you can. Stay put. You will be rescued. Enjoy yourself; most people will be getting up in the morning and going to work, while you'll be living the life of Riley.

Plenty of hunters get lost when close to their camp or hut when returning from their day's hunting. As dusk approaches they speed up, take shortcuts, get bluffed! Same deal. Sit down. Once you are certain you are completely stuffed up with direction, make your camp for the night and gather firewood while it's still light. Be positive, a night out is an adventure. Say that out loud five times, counting on your fingers. 'A night out is an adventure.' Once it has been dark for an hour (thus allowing your mates time to return to camp) fire three rapid shots to alert your hunting companions to your plight. No answer? Wait half an hour and repeat the shots. Hunting on your own? Stay put and have a comfortable night out; you'll have it all figured by the morning and if not, well, settle in and wait to be rescued.

Remember, nowadays there's no bloody excuse for not carrying a lightweight global positioning system (GPS) as well as a personal location beacon (PLB). Both items are pretty cheap to hire as well, a handy fact should you seldom visit the back country. I carry a McMurdo Fastfind 211 PLB. It weighs a mere 170gm and operates on two frequencies, the 406MHz international distress frequency plus a 121.5MHz frequency, accurate to within 60 metres, for search teams to home in on your actual position. What is more, it works in just about every place on the planet.

Lastly, for goodness' sake, take a map of the area you are travelling through.

2 | GETTING INJURED IN THE HILLS

Rule 1. Sit an accredited first-aid course and carry a first-aid kit.

So, what should you carry in your first-aid kit? The reality is that essentially you need only two items: something to stop the bleeding and something to stop the pain. Of course, those are the basics; we tend to fill up the rest of the kit with all manner of just-in-case extras. I've just emptied mine on the table in front of me and here's a list of what I carry in my small bag:

- 4 x crêpe bandages
- absorbent wound dressings
- wound closure strips
- antimicrobial wipes
- painkillers (Tramadol)
- anti-inflammatories (Arcoxia-Etoricoxib)
- EpiPen (adrenaline injection syringe)
- antiseptic ointment (Betadine)
- electrical tape (to bind bandages)
- 2 x blister pack
- knife and small diamond sharpener
- tweezers
- lighter
- fuel tablet
- candle
- 10-metre-long parachute cord
- small back-up torch
- magnesium fire stick
- loo paper
- 2 extra bombs for whatever rifle I'm using that day

That's my basic kit. Some of the items are not for my personal use. I have never had a blister, for example, and do not generally have bad allergic reactions that would require an adrenaline stab. (The EpiPen delivers a single intramuscular dose of adrenaline into your patient. At around $250 it's an expensive piece of kit, especially considering it has a short life of a little over 12 months. I carry it because of the many isolated and far-flung destinations to which I travel. In essence, it saves lives.)

Of course, if I am going anywhere where there's a likelihood of contracting tropical diseases such as malaria or yellow fever, then I make sure I have all my shots well in advance, plus I carry all the necessary tablets and definitely some Viaderm cream. Ask your travel doctor to prepare you a list of medications to take.

The best thing you can ever do for any injury or medical emergency is ensure that Rule 1 has been followed.

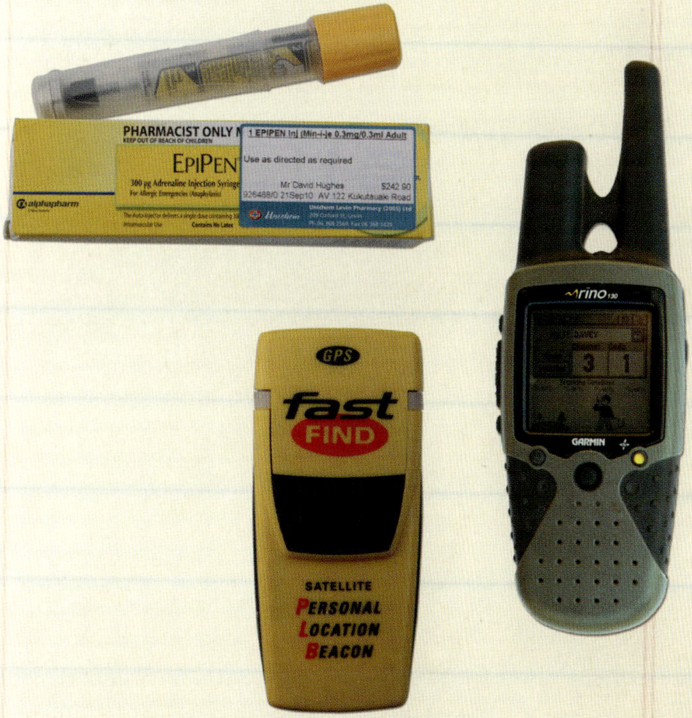

Travelling to China to help save tigers from extinction.

21

TIGER! TIGER!

Tavis, my youngest son, at a market in China. Behind him were both Amur tiger, and even more rare, leopard skins for sale.

When we first picked up the army contract, my son Tavis and I travelled to China to view new machinery that would seal waterproof boot-liners. While there we had a few adventures, one of which was horse riding on the grasslands out of Beijing. It was mid-winter, and it was damn freezing. Afterwards, at a nearby market, we found locals selling tiger and leopard skins, and tiger parts. My shock was evident.

'Dad, how can they do that? It's just so bloody wrong,' was all Tavis could say.

I agreed, though I confessed there was not a lot we could do about it.

Six months later I was in the States with a bunch of guys, one of whom was Laurence Frank, the world-renowned carnivore biologist from Chapter 20, who was at that time living in Kenya. Another was John Banovich, a world-class wildlife artist, wildlife conservationist and

LEFT Given that majority of our crew was American, the reception at Vladivostok was surprisingly friendly.
RIGHT The Vlad Air jet at Platsun.

hunter. Both were just as shocked when I revealed what Tavis and I had recently seen in China, though John admitted the bigger problem was Russia — a place he had recently visited and where, more than likely, many of the skins would have originally come from.

John first visited Russia in 2002 and quickly immersed himself in the study of tigers. A hunter himself, he preaches sustainable hunting and the importance of the tiger in the ecosystem. 'Even though hunting has proven to be one of the most effective tools in wildlife management,' he says, 'few groups are willing to work with hunters. Being a hunter as well as a wildlife artist gives me great access to both sides.'

With such experienced heads all in one place, talk around the dinner table soon turned to how we could aid the tiger's plight. But first let's get something straight. The animals in question are not, as everyone tends to call them, Siberian, but rather *Amur* tigers. A river of the same name runs through the far eastern area of Russia, all the way to the ocean. These incredible beasts have been part of this remote wilderness for thousands of years, and the forests of the Sikhote-Alin Nature Reserve are among their last refuge. In the shadow of towering mountains and cliffs as steep as a hen's beak lies one of the most beautiful places on earth: Khunta Mi. There in the Russian Far East, on a sandy beach at the edge of the Sea of Japan, tigers still roam.

Their numbers have plummeted to around 450, which, although depressing, is at least an improvement on where things stood in 1947, when the hunting of tigers was initially outlawed. Back then, a mere

ABOVE Hunting Amur tigers was outlawed in 1947, when the population was down to 30. BELOW Lenin shows us the way.

30 Amur tigers existed. In recent years, demand for tiger parts, which are used in Chinese medicine, has accelerated poaching. Today, to the surprise of some, one of the tiger's greatest allies is hunters, which is how the Khunta Mi initiative came about.

Primarily, this was John's idea but he needed the help of others to get it going. The plan was to travel to the Far East and help set up a hunting conservation project, where locals could take international hunters on trips to shoot wild boar, sika deer and roe deer. Each punter would pay around US$8000 for the privilege, and would be allowed to hunt where the tigers and leopards lived.

Promoted as 'tiger friendly', each 10-day hunt would collect $40,000 (presuming 4–5 hunters took part), a worthwhile sum when one considers a poached tiger may now be worth up to $50,000.

To say it was freezing when we arrived in Vladivostok in November 2006 would be an understatement. Despite being only autumn, it was brass-monkey stuff. Everyone wants to be known for something; I can tell my grandkids that our group was the first, for the best part of a century, to legally travel through Vladivostok with firearms from another country. We expected a bit of trouble at the border with the Russian guards when we pulled weapons from our bags, especially after we were made to assemble the rifles.

Most surprisingly, this procedure took place in the airport's main foyer and a huge crowd gathered. Imagine being surrounded by gruff, steely-eyed guys with AK47s and being asked through an interpreter to assemble your rifle, put the scope on, put the bolt in and lay out all of your ammunition. Add to this the cops and border guards asking all manner of questions: what calibre we were using; type of scope; how good was the ammunition and did it ever fail? As the crowd pressed closer it began to feel like we were in a turkeys in a barrel, and I wasn't the only one who thought we may not get out alive.

We needn't have worried. Even the ladies at the customs' pillboxes, who at first came across as super staunch-sounding, became friendly. To gain entrance to the country, the method involved placing your passport through a tiny slot in a concrete pillbox, while the woman on the other side asked a bunch of loud questions via an interpreter. Then bang! Passport stamped and you're in. *Spasibo*.

We spent the first few days in Vladivostok finding our feet. It's an interesting place with fascinating architecture and, from a military perspective, was an important port for the Russians. Swazi had provided everyone with an amazing down jacket — complete with a Gore-Tex outer shell. I'd handed out the garments in Seoul, where I first met up the team who had flown in from the States. It was pretty warm there, and most people looked at me sideways, clearly thinking they'd never get the chance to wear what we'd provided. Things changed as soon as we hit Vladivostok. They couldn't get those jackets on fast enough!

ABOVE Vladimir ran the camp and kept us up to date with tiger spotting.
BELOW Outside the Neshinkoe hunting reserve.

One of my favourite shots, a
young male deep in thought.

BANOVICH 2005
To My Friend Davey - In support of "Khunta Mi" Thank you for helping Tigers!
JB

ABOVE The question is, will the species survive? Man alone will determine the fate of the tiger. Vladimir Schetinin, chief of the agency, Inspection Tiger, once commented that the surest bet for the species would be widespread AIDS among humans. Sketch by John Banovich.

OPPOSITE The Russian Far East is a long way from Moscow. Life here is tough, and so are the people.

We took a flight on Vlad Air from Vladivostok to a place called Platsun. I enjoyed the novelty of carrying my own luggage on board and entering the plane from the back. You just shove your gear on the racks above and tie it down. With no seat allocations, you just find a spare and away you go. The runway at Vladivostok Airport appeared to be nothing more than a mass of cracks joined together by patches of concrete, and when those cracks are filled with ice it makes for pretty hairy landings and takeoffs. Kind of reminded me of that Paul Simon song, 'Slip Slidin' Away'.

On reaching Platsun, we headed north in vehicles to Terney, a small town on the Sea of Japan where we met the Russian directors of the tiger project. Also in Terney is the Wildlife Conservation Society, an American group funded by a couple of zoos in the US. Two of the American biologists present, Dale Miquelle and John Goodrich, had spent many years in the area studying the Amur tiger. We arrived as they were in the midst of building a brand-new headquarters. The boys were fairly animated, as fresh tiger tracks had been found that very day around the new compound. It seemed they wouldn't have to go far to conduct their research, in fact, maybe they could simply roll out of bed and gaze out the window . . .

Clearly not everyone shared my enthusiasm for tigers living in such close proximity to the community. And who could blame them? While poachers are justifiably vilified, some country types grow tired of waking to find a tiger has taken two or three of their favourite dogs. In the end, many locals, unable to cope with the disappearance of another pet, take matters into their own hands. As human habitation encroaches on that of the tiger, things can only get worse. Urban spread dictates that the tiger's range is decreasing, so the idea of setting aside more land as reserves is a sound one.

The hospitality of the locals in Terney blew me away. Seeing Westerners was clearly a novelty. The language barrier is always there, but a smile is universal. Look into someone's eyes and you're well over halfway to communicating.

These hardy types welcomed us into their homes and fed us. If you loved vodka this was the place to be. Do I love vodka? Well, I was definitely in the right place! Yet it was the simple things that meant the most: walking into a small Russian grocery shop and seeing Anchor butter in the fridge. I had to buy some and admit it felt good to be supporting the dairy farmers back home. No doubt the presence of Ladas on New Zealand roads is thanks to selling butter to these dudes. To be in Russia was to see dichotomy in action; here were shopkeepers using digital scales to weigh what they were

selling, yet they added everything up on an abacus.

But we were in Russia to track tigers, not shop. We left Terney in a brand-new Land Rover and headed for the boondocks, yet despite the vehicle being pretty much fresh out of the yard, it kept dying on us. We were tearing along a rough Russian road when suddenly there was a huge bang. Engine parts spewed upwards, one making a large hole right through the bonnet. Curious as to what we'd disgorged across the countryside, I walked back down the road to retrieve the part. Not being that mechanically minded I wasn't overly sure exactly what part I now held in my hand, but given the fact the vehicle had now come to a complete halt I'd wager a bet it was a reasonably important one. Thankfully, we had other vehicles with which to discover the Khunta Mi.

John Goodrich and Dale Miquelle take measurements from a captured Amur tiger.

Within the reserve were several tigers that Dale and the WCS boys had captured and placed tracking collars on. Locating and tracking the tigers, however, took a fair bit of telemetry as many of the collars were reasonably antiquated affairs. Our method was to take three bearings on the radio collar — a reading that remained static for some time would suggest the tiger was on a kill and stalking them could be possible.

There is nothing like the thrill of seeing fresh tiger tracks in the morning. Dale and John got even more excited upon discovering tiger scat.

'Wow!' Dale would comment.

'Oh man!' John would reply.

'Yip, sure looks like cat shit to me,' I'd chip in.

At one stage they became so animated I was sure they were going to eat it! John was particularly skilled in tracking and trapping. If a tiger sprayed a tree to mark its territory, he could smell it, then decipher the sex of the animal. Granted, it's a little weird watching a guy sucking and licking a tree, but he knew his job.

Once the whereabouts of a tiger are known, soft snares are set up which don't harm the animal in any way when it is trapped. When you come across the tiger, it is shot with a tranquiliser dart, knocked out, and ropes tied around its feet in case the anaesthetic wears off prematurely. Just the other month a tiger actually managed to get out of a snare and mauled one of the guys badly. John himself has been mauled, so everyone gets very slick and professional around a snared tiger. While you're doing your best for the tigers, the tigers actually don't understand that; you're a threat and when they do the hissy-roary thing, as big cats do, the sound reverberates right through you.

Having your wits about you on a hunt like this can mean the difference between losing a limb and keeping it, or worse. One of our guides had been back-tracking a female, the preferred method to track tigers, especially in the snow — at least that way you're not going to run into it and have a disagreement. My new mate had been conducting a faecal survey and wanted to take the tiger scat for analysis. Unbeknown to the hunter, a male tiger was also tracking the female, but *forwards*. When they ran into each other in a wee gully, both were shocked. The tiger, taken by surprise, attacked and chewed his victim up pretty bad. To prove to you how tough these guys are, he somehow managed to make his way back to his vehicle and into hospital. He kept his leg, but now has a false knee. He's still out there, still loves tigers and claims the whole incident was just a big mistake on the tiger's behalf.

Tigers are huge, magnificent beasts; the sheer size of their heads and paws is mind-boggling. As our mate who nearly lost his leg discovered, such a creature is not to be fooled with. Ask if someone has been injured recently in the Terney area and answers will be forthcoming. A few months before our arrival a guy poaching was killed by a tiger. Another poacher was shot by a cop.

John Goodrich sniffs a tree a tiger has sprayed. 'Yep. Female, thought as much.'

One of the hunting blocks we stayed at was run by a bloke named Vladimir, an ex-commander of a Russian nuclear submarine based out of Kamchatka.

One night after two or three bottles of vodka I mustered the courage to ask a fairly sensitive question. 'Now, Vladimir,' I said, 'you need to tell me truthfully. If the balloon had gone up, would you have pushed the red button?'

He didn't answer. The next morning at breakfast, however, he asked to speak to me outside.

'Du-VEED, I would not have pushed the button

unless we were being attacked,' Vladmir confessed.

It was pretty cool to find that humanity. Not everyone is a warmonger, even people running nuclear submarine fleets.

Dale Miquelle and Sergei Petruenko with the 4WD paid for by Swazi and Manawatu Toyota fundraising in New Zealand.

One of the aims of the Khunta Mi initiative was to provide vehicles for the scientists. When we thought about what these biologists really needed, it was transport to get from block to block. Sadly, it took the best part of 13 months to negotiate with the Russian mafia and local customs to get a new 4WD truck to Dale and his team in Terney. Despite being a *gift*, the Russians wanted a tax of US$30,000. With some stiff negotiating we got that down to US$5000. Leaving aside the red tape, I believe the trip to set up the initiative was a success.

The initiative started advertising hunting trips in the US and, already, Russ Smith, a good dude from Montana who runs a hunting outfitter company, is taking groups of full-paying hunters to the region.

Kiwis are great ones for mucking in, a trait I focused on when thinking about how we could help the Terney area. When I returned to New Zealand, we set up the Siberian Tiger Trust and from various events raised enough money to buy the aforementioned 4WD. According to Dale, having a reliable vehicle to transport staff is already making their jobs that much easier. Practical stuff.

People often ask how I can hunt predators one minute and save tigers the next. The latter is undoubtedly one of the greatest predators to walk the face of the earth, yet there are so few left. As a hunter, it feels like my kin or brother. If I can do something to ensure this species survives, then I will do it. Generally, people question my integrity for taking this position, again because it encompasses two totally divergent views. My question to them is: 'What are you doing on your comfortable lounge suite?' Get off your arse if you're really that keen about saving wildlife, about doing meaningful things. Up! Up and simply go and do it. It is too easy to just be a critic.

There is not another animal on earth that knows more about the soul of man than the Amur tiger.

LOU MCNUTT

ABOVE All animals are amazing, but every now and then you come across one which has a real sit down and take notice wow factor. I reckon this Namibian Rock Agama fits into the latter category. Etosha, Namibia.
CENTRE There are times when the hunter must place his rifle upon the ground and take up his camera. He who hesitates to do so is neither a hunter nor a human.
BELOW LEFT AND RIGHT In both instances the bear and the elephant went from seemingly docile feeders to very large and capable animals once they noticed me — a curse on noisy cameras! Okay boys, whose turn is it now?

Have you known the Great White Silence? . . .

Have you broken trail on snowshoes? mushed your huskies up the river,
Dared the unknown, led the way, and clutched the prize? . . .

Have you suffered, starved and triumphed,
grovelled down, yet grasped at glory,
Grown bigger in the bigness of the whole?
'Done things' just for the doing, letting babblers tell the story . . .

Have you seen . . .
The simple things, the true things, the silent men who do things —
Then listen to the Wild — it's calling you.

Let us probe the silent places, let us seek what luck betide us;
Let us journey to a lonely land I know.
There's a whisper on the night-wind,
there's a star agleam to guide us,
And the Wild is calling, calling . . . let us go.

adapted from The Call of the Wild *by Robert Service*

Most sports require only one ball.

My gun safe

Over the years I've bought quite a few guns and promised myself, this gun is the very last gun in the safe. Suffice to say, after a period of time they invariably have been sold or replaced! Why is that? Well, I have a rule: if I buy a gun, say for a specific hunt, then I sell a gun as well. That way I only need one gun safe.

Here's a list of the not-for-sale large-calibre guns I'm currently shooting with. These guns will never ever be sold. Unless of course I happen to sell them to make way for my next very last gun in the gun safe!

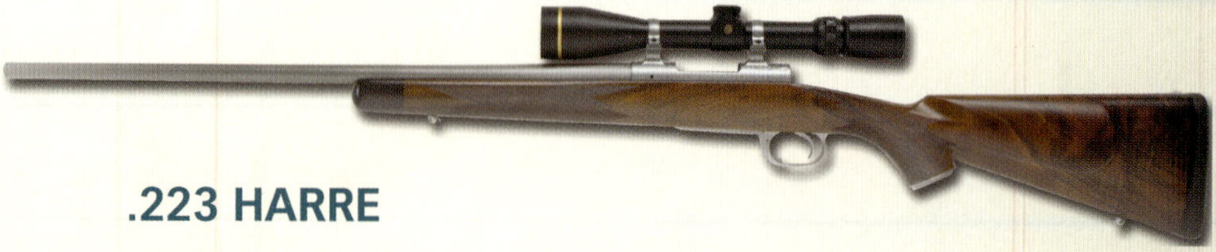

.223 HARRE

This gun is a honey. The only female gun in my cabinet, she is just so bloody cute! Custom made for me by Brian Harre, an Auckland gunsmith, she features some incredible technology not seen on other guns, whether they be custom-made or manufactured. Brian's integral work on the trigger, the receiver and the unique way he milled my bases and rings out of the same billet of steel make this gun a delight to shoot. The wood is New Zealand walnut, from a tree he cut in Blenheim in 1971. Accurate? Oh my God.

.38-55 WINCHESTER LEVER ACTION

I've always had a thing for lever-ies! This gun is a Winchester Centennial grade, model 1894. The wood is outstanding for a Winchester and I had the sight made by Montana Vintage Arms of Manhattan, Montana. I called into their shop with my gun and asked if they had ever made a Vernier sight for a lever action.

'No we haven't,' came their reply.

'Well, you're about to!' I answered.

I love to fire up the kiln and melt down a 20:1 lead–antimony mix for my cast bullets. These projectiles, pre-swaging and lubing, weigh 252 grain and I load the cases with 44 grain of FF black powder. *Kaboomfah!*

.416 RIGBY

The .416 Rigby is a great African calibre. While by no means the largest, for the international hunter it represents a most excellent choice of calibre to take down large game, such as buffalo and lion. If you wish to hunt elephant it's also a good choice, but should it ever be required, I'd be wanting my PH to back up with something a little heavier.

My rifle is a Dakota Model 76 African with a Schmidt and Bender 1.4 to 4x20 scope — plenty of field of view and awesome for close work. Weighing in at 9.5lb undressed without scope or ammo — yes, it's heavier than your average deer rifle — that weight is needed to help absorb the 5000+ ft/lbs of energy. When hunting dangerous game my favourite mix is two rounds of Swift A-Frame 400 grain up first, with two Woodleigh 410 grain solids backing up in the magazine. Some guys use only one soft round followed by solids, but I prefer two very reliable softs, then my solids for any heavy work. I'm driving these at close to 2400 feet per second. The Dakota is reliability plus, a real workhorse of a gun with the legendary pre-64 model 70 Winchester-style action and Mauser-based extractor. For a big cannon it is surprisingly accurate and an absolute pleasure to hunt with.

.300 WSM KIMBER

My travel gun. The Kimber 8400 Montana in .300 WSM is light, robust and not a bad calibre to boot. I've shot large animals such as moose, tough animals like tahr and mountain goats, as well as black bear, all with great results. In bear country, the fact that I am able to load and accurately shoot 200 grain ammo gives me an all-round better sense of security. Of late I've been loading Woodleigh Weldcores, an Australian-made projectile, and man, I am impressed, not only with their excellent ballistic coefficient but also their stopping power. A bullet you can trust certainly gives you heaps of confidence.

I've topped my Kimber with a Leica ER 2.5–10x42 scope. I've always believed you can generally get away with a fairly average rifle, but if you're after continued success in the field, here's my take: if you can afford to don't scrimp on the optics. The Leica, in my opinion, is without doubt the finest rifle scope I own.

.60 CAL FLINTLOCK

Ahhh! The pure romance of black powder. I'm certain this whole smokeless-powder phase we are witnessing is no more than a fad and that sooner or later we'll go back to the joy of firing black powder weapons . . . Okay, maybe not!

Everyone who shoots my .60 cal smoothbore falls in love with it. Even Cathy Dunne, our accountant at work, has a soft spot for shooting this baby. Cath is not the tallest of people and the gun kind of towers over her, but the balance of this Wyatt Earl-made flinter is superb, making holding it on target pretty darn easy. Wyatt, a Kiwi gunsmith from Upper Hutt, has made quite a few flinters over the years. I feel incredibly privileged to be looking after this particularly handsome one for the next generation of black powder shooters.

MY BLASER

Over the years perhaps one of my most recognised hunting guns was my Blaser R93. Having made an appearance on the TV show *Border Patrol*, here in New Zealand plus over the ditch in Australia as well as in Europe, this gun is the one that blew up in my face on a trip to Alaska. Still to this day I'm asked at various talks around the country just how the hell I did that! Here's what happened.

I'd bought the Blaster in their Luxus Model — that's the one with a premium stock and engraved receiver. Initially I had two barrels, a .243 and .375 H&H, with both performing very well on hunts here and abroad. My troubles began, however, after I bought a third barrel in .300 Weatherby calibre.

OPPOSITE My Alaskan guide Bobby Warren.

Right from day one that barrel gave me gip. I could only fire three to four shots before the bolt would lock solid, the only method to eject the empty case was to place the butt on the ground and with a well-aimed boot, kick the bolt open. Hmmm. Not too good in a $7000 gun, I thought. Not too good for a back-up shot on a charging bear either, come to think of it! I asked the New Zealand agent, Hugh Bradley of Stager Sports, what he thought could be the problem. Hugh assured me it was a teething problem with a new barrel and as a suggestion said I could moly-coat (molybdenum) projectiles — with luck the barrel would come right. It came right okay, right apart in my face.

I'd booked an Alaskan hunt with Johnnie Laird of Muskeg Excursions to hunt mountain goats in the Misty Fjords National Monument. High up on the mountain with my guide Bobby Warren, we spent days lying about in one-man tents on an ice shelf, waiting for the mist to clear so we could go hunt.

Finally the morning came when we decided we had enough visibility to safely traverse a mountain pass to where we hoped to find some animals. Bobby and I scoffed down a quick breakfast, checked our weapons, running a pull-through down each barrel before taping the muzzles in yellow electrical tape. Time to go. We'd only just crested the pass when we spied a damn good goat at less than 200 metres.

'Take him, Davey.'

We had time. These goats are going nowhere, I thought to myself as I made a comfortable rest to shoot from. Lining up on the goat I squeezed off.

'You're a foot high and three feet back!' reported Bobby, his eye still stuck in the spotting scope.

Damn. That is pretty shit shooting to say the least. Okay. Breathe, line up. Money shot. BANG! I remember a huge explosion, suddenly I couldn't see, or feel my hands. I do remember hearing Bobby yelling, 'Shoot again! Shoot again!'

It was so evident the barrel had been poked from the day I bought it. I had all manner of gunsmiths look at it, including one chap who was the chief weapons technician on the US Air Force's

stealth bombers. The barrel went back to Germany where the Blaser techos tried to tell me the first bullet down the barrel, a Swift A-Frame projectile, had shed its bonded jacket and my subsequent shot had blown up the barrel. Yep. I asked Randy Brooks of Barnes Bullets what he thought of that, knowing I'd get an independent point of view.

'Davey,' he said, 'as much as Swift are my competition and I'd love to say that it's a genuine possibility, a Swift bullet is just *not* going to behave that badly. Sounds more like a barrel problem to me.'

Good news was Blaser offered me a new barrel at cost less 20 per cent . . . that was 400 Deutschmarks (around NZ$400). Okay, I guess I could live with that. Problem was, by the time it got here, incurred the local agent's mark-up, had a few more expenses added on . . . well, the cost had now escalated to $1600! Stick it!

Not long after the *Border Patrol* TV shows aired and people all round the world started commenting on the internet about my blown-up barrel, I heard rumblings Blaser were considering taking legal action . . . The shows kept airing . . . and airing, until finally in exasperation the managing director of Blaser in Germany (the previous MD, Gerhard Blenk, had been a Swazi fan and I'm sure a man who would have sorted the problem prior to my gun blowing up), asked how he could just make this sorry state of affairs go away. I told him it was really up to Blaser. After all, I'd paid return fares to Ketchikan, hired a guide, paid tags and licences, taken a couple weeks off work, with a probable all-up cost, including fixing my rifle, of around NZ$18,000. I suggested perhaps Blaser should figure out what they thought was fair compensation.

Finally Blaser sent me something to ease my despair and take all the pain away. At long last there was real closure for both parties, the final chapter in this long saga had come to an end.

In a magnanimous gesture, taking into account all I had lost, the MD of Blaser sent me a bottle of schnapps . . .

Hunting elk, drinking airag with nomads and following a wolf into a cave.

22

ANTIPODEANS IN MONGOLIA

About the only Mongolian I can remember offhand, though I can't spell it, goes: *'Ich nera chagoya, ounce namuk shan.'* When I arrived home from a hunting trip, Maggie asked if I had picked up any of the native tongue. I repeated the above and she damn near slapped me. Guess I can understand given the direct translation is: 'My dear, you are so pretty, kiss me quickly tonight.' I was just talking to my camel . . .

There were four of us (two Aussies and two Kiwis) travelling to Mongolia to hunt elk, or maral stags as they're known there, and I knew only one of them. A few months earlier, I had met an Aussie, Gordon Alford, at a hunting show in Sydney. Gordon was hell bent on organising a trip to Mongolia. Mongolia is divided in two, Outer and Inner, the latter being a part of China. Outer Mongolia opened up to the West as recently as the early 1990s. Until then, the Russians had been running the show. Having been closed off for so long made it an incredibly exciting place to visit, let alone hunt.

As a child I'd read so many stories about nomads sweeping across the steppes in hordes, charging towards the Great Wall, following Genghis Khan, a leader who'd managed through the force of his personality to join the various tribes and factions into one great army. It sounded like pure adventure! And of course, due to a lack of hairdressers, everyone got to grow their hair long. Gotta love that.

The Aussies turned up in practical winter gear, namely cotton shirts, T-shirts, KingGee pants and nylon windcheaters. As we slid across an icy runway in Ulan Bator, it occurred to the Aussies they'd gone a little light in the garment department. Fortunately, I'd packed some gear I wanted to test in Mongolia, so I distributed a fair bit of it to our trans-Tasman cousins. I still believe in the ANZAC code of brotherhood, as you can see.

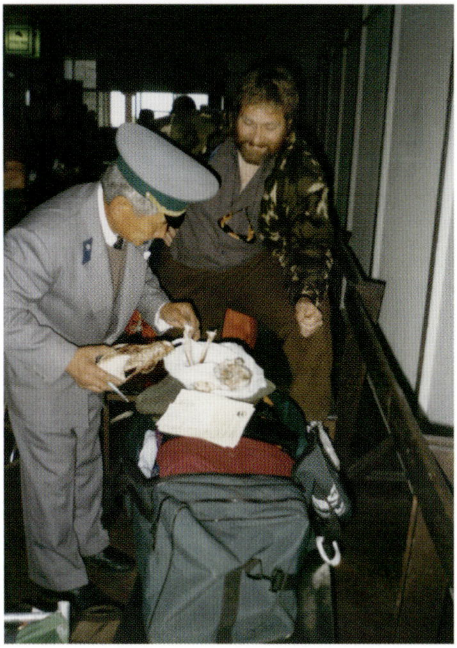

A precursor to *Border Patrol*? Leaving Ulan Bator I am questioned by a Mongolian customs officer on the contents of my bag.

The capital city of Ulan Bator is where we spent our first few days, gathering permits and learning the art of bribery, known in other cultures as taxes. Travel to places like the US or the UK and you don't really feel like a foreigner. There will always be *something* you recognise. A soft-drink can, or the name of a bank, or a chain of restaurants. In Mongolia *everything* is foreign. People stare. And stare. And stare. Mind you, this was the 1990s, nowadays they probably sell Coke and . . . No. I can't bring myself to mention it. You know, the burger franchise.

In our case, their curiosity was heightened upon seeing a bunch of Antipodean hunters loading and unloading weapons. We may as well have been from the moon. I loved it! Travel for me is not about museums and cathedrals. It's about sitting in a *ger* (a felt-lined tent most Mongolians call home) with someone who can't speak English, discussing nothing and everything in the greatest detail.

After a couple of days we boarded a biplane bound for the Khentii Mountains. Chris Graham, an archetypal Aussie and a guy I'd get to know and like, decided to team up with me for the hunt. Chris exemplifies everything that a good Aussie hunter is: resourceful, a pretty damn good poacher and an incredibly likeable dude. Thinking on it, maybe I should

I do believe I could have written a whole book on this one plane journey! The frozen engine took four hours to start, black oil spray covered the windows during flight, a tethered goat in the back got loose and ran amok, the pilots drank a whole bottle of vodka — I kid you not . . . *and* they had me sitting next to an Aussie.

Chris Graham steps across the steppes with his maral stag trophy.

have just said 'everything a good Aussie should be.'

The first morning we found ourselves high on a snow-covered ridge, with a decent-looking bull bugling away on an open face opposite us. The sound is instantly recognisable to a hunter; the bull in question is proclaiming his dominance: 'Hey, cows, this is my harem. I'm the boss.' When you hear them bugle it really gets your heart pumping; this is bloody exciting stuff. Other bulls will often try to steal his girlfriends, so the lead bull must keep his wits about him. I've never regretted forking out a small fortune on my Leica binos, believing the investment of carrying good glass always pays itself off tenfold. I pulled them out. Hmmm. It definitely looked worth our while to get a closer appraisal of this bull.

An hour later we had worked our way in on the bull and suddenly his bugling sounded very close. There! He stepped into a clearing less than 400 metres above us on the face. My guide burst into life: 'Shoot, shoot, shoot!'

Through an interpreter, I informed him there was no need for any long-distance shooting. 'I'm here to hunt,' I said, letting him know of my plan to sneak up and have a good look at the animal before I made any decisions.

I proceeded to weave my way up a side spur, one that provided substantial cover — this was going to work well, I remember thinking. The wind was perfect. I knew I could get close to the elk. Slowly, slowly, sneaks the monkey.

When stalking any animal during the rut, it's best to remember the cows — or the hinds in his harem — will invariably be the ones to get spooked. The old fella, meanwhile, is interested in only one thing: sex. As a result, he's pretty oblivious to most danger at that time of year. I had good cover and a solid plan of attack, all of which was ruined by my guide, who simply walked straight into the open and blew the whole thing out. The Mongolian guide was livid I hadn't shot — long distance or not — as doing so would mean the hunt was over, he'd get a decent tip and could take an early lunch. But it wasn't to be. I realised I would probably have to replace him or guide myself for the remainder of the trip.

We tramped around for the rest of the day, keeping an ear open for any more bugling, but things had gone silent and for the next six hours we played the role of armed trampers. Strangely enough, I particularly enjoy this part of any hunt, almost as much as actually stalking an animal. You get the chance to immerse yourself in the local flora and fauna, as well as shake off any travel weariness.

That evening Chris and I spent the last hour before dusk glassing the valley around the camp, taking a liking to a far-off, lengthy and somewhat narrow ridge with a wide, lazy saddle. There was a strong wind blowing and during a brief respite we could just make out elk bugling in the distance. Perfect.

Long before first light, we decided, bugger it, let's leave the local guides behind and head out on our own. Three hours into the morning we found ourselves, by our reckoning, to be just below the saddle we'd spotted the previous night. Twice now we'd heard an elk bugle ahead of us on the ridge. As we waited for the dawn to make our final approach, we leaned our rifles against a nearby tree and opted to take a leak. I was busy doing what you do when Chris let rip with the loudest fart I've ever heard.

You dirty bastard, I thought. That should be in *The Guinness Book of World Records*. I wasn't exaggerating; it was a ripper, something even a Swazi garment wouldn't withstand. As I busied myself with my own concerns, Chris did it again! Only the second time was louder than the first! Enough. I was about to give him a serve, but when I turned around — still holding my old fellow — I saw the biggest goddamn bear I've ever seen. Just metres away from this clawed killer two grown men stood, mouths open wide, holding onto their penises. When I heard that sound again, it suddenly dawned on me: they weren't farts — they were growls!

The bear stood on his hind legs glaring at us. He looked at me, then turned to give Chris the once-over. If that bear could have spoken I'm dead certain he would have said something

Our felt-lined *ger* was a warm and comfortable home.

along the lines of, 'You going to shoot me with those little peckers, boys?' Then, with a sudden huff, it disappeared off the side of the hill. Chris and I glanced over to our guns, still leaning against the tree, still 10 metres away.

Chris breathed a huge sigh of relief. 'Fuck me, Koiwoi, that was close. I was going to yell at 'im to bugger off . . . but I don't reckon he spoke any English.'

I was still mesmerised, watching the bush move down in the valley where the bear had disappeared.

'I dunno about English-speaking bears, Chris, but what I do know is this: I'm going to hunt bears one day.'

ABOVE The armies of Mongolia changed the way of mankind forever, and in more ways than one.
BELOW 'Today we will be very brave hunters Koi-wee.'

We didn't get on to an elk that morning but we had a few other adventures, including bumping into nomads. It's the Mongolian people I remember so vividly; so pleasant and incredibly bright. In fact, if you had to rate their intelligence I'd say Mongolian nomads would outsmart the average New Zealander. Not too hard, Aussie Chris would probably reckon. They're a friendly people, but they'd be a pretty dour enemy. Chris and I found ourselves sitting in a *ger* with a local family, the mother of whom brought out some *airag*, or fresh fermented mare's milk. Luckily, I had film to change in my camera, so left Chris with the honours. Clearly apprehensive, Chris looked down at this huge bowl of drink. Take one for the team, Aussie, I thought.

He took a sip, turned to me and said something which sent shivers down my spine: 'Davey, today we will be brave hunters.'

It was then I realised what he was drinking must have tasted like the proverbial.

Now I had to drink my bowl. Being a death-or-glory kind of guy, the only way to attack it was to gulp it down in one go. So I did, proud of my acting ability. Despite the contents making me want to reach for a bucket, I sculled it, rubbed my belly and said, 'Ha. Good!' I breathed a sigh of relief, put the bowl down and quietly thanked the gods it was over. My only challenge now was keeping the gunk in my belly without throwing it up.

No sooner had I finished than the bowl was refilled, only this time to the top! By then I'd had a chance to gauge the actual taste: a mixture of vinegar, warm milk and curdled bits of yoghurt. Now I had to go back for seconds. They say if you drink enough pints of Guinness — even if you despise the taste — you'll eventually find one you like. The drink in front of me was no different. That second bowl tasted like the nectar of the gods and, despite supposedly having come from an animal's udder, its light alcoholic content gave me a pretty quick buzz.

It was here that I first heard the story of Genghis Khan being buried beside a baby camel. In Mongolian tradition, the grave of the mighty ruler had to be in a secret location. According to Marco Polo, 20,000 people were killed in order to keep Khan's grave hidden. The slaves who dug the grave was killed by soldiers once they'd finished the job. Then the soldiers were bopped off, and so on it went. But they soon realised they were in danger of killing everyone who knew where the grave was. Someone had the bright idea of killing a baby camel in front of its mother, by the grave. Then they took the mother away and buried the camel next to Genghis Khan. Because camels have long memories, the mother camel would return to the grave every year. The only flaw in the plan was when the mother died; since then, the site of the grave has remained unknown. Perhaps a touch of *Ripley's Believe it or Not* . . . As an eternal romantic, however, I choose to believe. I'm forever being reminded that over half my lies are true.

As an eternal romantic, however, I choose to believe. I'm forever being reminded that over half my lies are true.

Meanwhile, the *Boy's-Own* adventure continued. The next morning I bit the bullet, grabbed my guide (who'd sulked for days after Chris and I had left camp to hunt on our own) and took off in the direction of bugling elks I heard on a dome-shaped hill. We worked our way up slowly, ever so slowly; again the wind was perfect. As we started getting closer to the top we began bumping into lesser bulls circling the dome. My guide looked at me. *Why not shoot one of them?* he pleaded with his eyes. I put my forefinger to my lips and shook my head. The clear option was to patiently work my way through and sneak past the lesser bulls. Once we reached the dome we spotted cows, lots of them. Down on your belly you go. Snake your way in the snow and get as close as you can without giving yourself away. I managed to get about 30 to 40 metres away from the bull, who was lying down bugling. It became a waiting game.

The stalk had already taken a good three hours in freezing cold conditions. I continued to wait for the bull to stand, so I could get a shot in. I couldn't get any closer. I became a log. Watching, watching. At last he stood. Through a tiny gap in the trees I determined he need only take one more single step to show his shoulder. Forty metres. Broadside shot. I brimmed with confidence. Ahhh. Such is the folly of man.

'Stay here!' I yelled, calling him an absolute dick in English, something he apparently understood.

For at that very moment my guide decided he'd scramble about on his hands and knees to finally dig out his old binoculars. Doing so caused one of the cows to bark. Certain my bull would still have to walk through the gap in the trees, I was dumbfounded as he began walking *backwards*. Through the thick stuff he back-pedalled, unaware of where the danger was coming from, but heeding the warning bark. I had seconds before I'd lose him. The bull continued to back up. All I could see now was his neck. Money shot! Full stroke. Down he went.

The bull is down and still, my scope is on him, and close by I can hear animals running in all directions. I concentrate totally on the bull, prepared to give him a minute before I walk up. My guide, as you can probably tell by now, is anything but conventional. Up he jumps, running through the snow straight for the bull, yelling and screaming like an excitable toddler. Unbelievably, the goddamn bull jumps up! He's in bad shape. During the mating season, the bulls' necks grow to a massive size, and I'd obviously missed the spine due to his now super-sized neck. He isn't in a good way at all, walking very slowly, yet I can't get a follow-up shot, because of this crazy bloody Mongol acting like a kid the night before Christmas.

The guide pulled his AK-47 off his shoulder and decided to end things for the bull. He fired the whole mag at 40 metres — and missed every shot except for two, one of which happened to blow a hole in the bull's antler. Another blew a tine clean in half. Miraculously, the bull was still walking. By now my Mongolian friend was out of ammunition. I soon caught up, grabbed him and dumped him in the snow.

'Stay here!' I yelled, calling him an absolute dick in English, something he apparently understood. I followed up on the bull and finally put him down.

No animal needs to go through that. It was the last time I'd ever use

Nosler Partitions. Nosler make some pretty good projectiles, but in my opinion the Partition is not one of them.

The guide fired off the whole mag, blowing one of the antler's tines clean in half . . .

Things loosen up in a camp when an animal has been shot. People relax. There is meat to hang; the headskin needs caping out; you've got antlers to boil to get rid of excess flesh and brains; the cape will also take some extra work, then needs to be salted and dried as much as possible for the journey home. That feeling of achievement and relief, when hunters tell stories of how they prepared for the hunt, how they stalked the animal and finally pulled the trigger, is tens of thousands of years old. Sitting by the fire, the hunter animatedly goes through every detail, sharing the emotions with those in camp.

I'm glad Kiwis have finally learnt it's okay to share emotions with mates rather than continuing that stoic attitude of yesteryear. It's refreshing to be candid and honest with our feelings. Hell's teeth! I've even got used to All Blacks congratulating each other after scoring nowadays. Of course, in this instance I get to graphically tell my mates of the rat-a-tat-tat chase to finally reach the bull and we all fall about laughing with each telling.

Over the next couple of days my hands were full with my Mongolian maral stag, while the others continued to hunt. No sooner had I finished, than a group of nomads from a nearby village rode by, informing us that packs of wolves were sweeping down from the Siberian plains and killing their camels. In Mongolia, when winter temperatures can plummet to –60°C, camels are responsible for pulling wagons laden with *ger* out of winter's way. It's a tough life. If you can't get to warmer pastures where horses, goats and sheep can graze, you're going to lose your home and your herd. Your wealth. These wolves were decimating the camels and sheep of the concerned villagers. When they asked if there was a hunter who could help, I didn't hesitate. I had my maral stag and was looking for a bit of adventure.

I joined the mad Mongolians, astride little horses with tiny wooden saddles, and we tore across the famous steppes. As I looked around me — standing, because the saddle was too small for my arse — I stole a

There was not much left on a sheep the wolves killed the previous night.

glance at these dudes dressed in *drab deel* (like a big bathrobe made from heavy fabric), long hair and black moustaches and thought, I'm riding with Genghis Khan's descendants! I must confess, I'm not a great horse rider and here I was with some of the best in the world. Patient people the Mongols!

I shot a lot of wolves that day, maybe 20-odd. One was an alpha male, which I knew I'd shot a little far back in the body. He'd crawled into a cave and when we pulled up, my Mongolian friends made a move, pulling a knife across their throat meaning, 'He's dead.'

I jumped off my horse and said, 'No boys, in New Zealand we finish what we start.'

I cranked one into the chamber, fixed my Petzl lamp on my head and ventured inside. At first the cave appeared small, but on closer inspection I realised it was cavernous.

All I could hear from the rear of the cave was a deathly growl. I could just make out the wolf as he cast shadows as he ran around me. I tried to get a fix on him with my gun, moving to the side of the cave, wanting to get my silhouette away from the opening, when all of a sudden my Petzl lantern went out. I remember thinking, *That's not fair*. It didn't fade to yellow or give any warning sign, it just went *pvitt*. Bright light one second and out the next. The rules had changed as an enraged wolf, who could see in the dark, realised he now had the upper hand.

I poked my rifle out in front of me, feeling him brush past the back of my legs several times. As I did so, I reached for my tiny one-cell, back-up Maglite torch. By this stage, things should have gone from bad to worse, but the reality is that the wolf just went quiet. I shone the torch around the cave and found him lying on his side. He'd died. I didn't have to shoot him. If he hadn't, however, my final moments may well have been gripping a torch between my teeth, squinting into the darkness of a cave 11,000 kilometres from home.

The reception you get heading back to any village post-hunt is great, but these guys — seeing how many wolves we had shot — carried us in on their shoulders. We were escorted into the headman's *ger* and told

to sit in the best seat in the house, by the fire. Pretty much like entering a North American Indian *teepee*, there's a standard protocol: move to the left. Women then arrived bearing platters of meat, watched by what seemed the entire village, all sitting on their haunches. As the esteemed guest, I was to have first choice of whatever meat I desired.

As usual, the one thing you crave when hunting is a bit of fat, so I reached for some sausages. Good choice, they all said by nodding their heads in unison. But then I realised *they don't make sausages*. What I was looking at was a pile of sheep intestines. On the edge of the platter were a couple of sheep's hearts. I quickly changed my mind, grabbed a heart, jumped up, stood tall while whipping out my knife, cut a piece off, poured it down my throat and went 'Arrrggh!' Everyone inside the *ger*, 30 or 40 strong, replied in the appropriate way: 'Arrrggh!' It was a goddamned cool evening.

As I have found in so many isolated and wild places, while men may openly preen and postulate, it is indeed the women who hold everything together.

Camels are used to pull the *ger*-laden wagons out of winter's way. With packs of wolves devouring the camels, the Mongolians had a big problem.

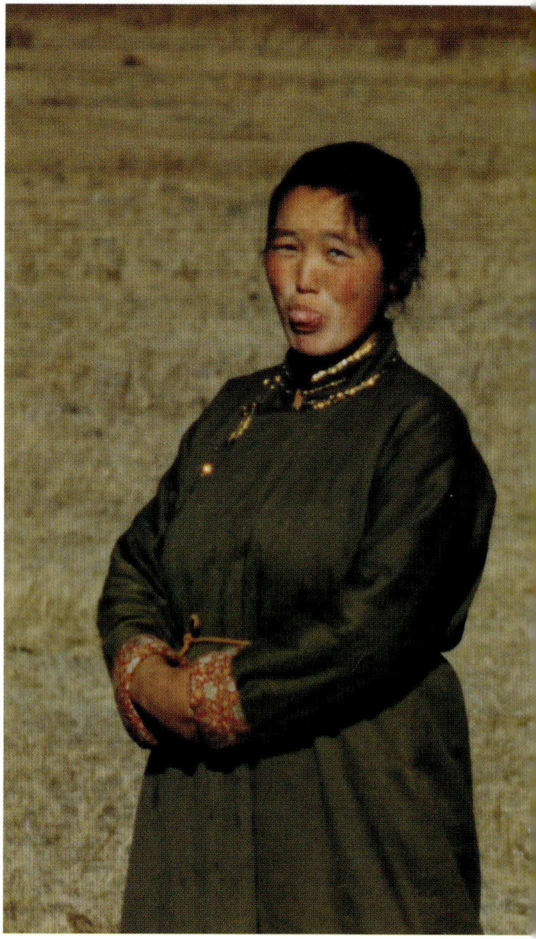

ABOVE Not exactly the kind of horse that would win the Melbourne Cup. Nope. No, that's kind of more like the horse that would conquer half the world.
BELOW A marmot, drilled through the head and awaiting roasting on an open fire. The Mongol army travelled with marmots, which were eaten as special treats on their campaigns. Which is interesting when one considers the marmot is at times host to the flea that carries the bubonic plague.

It would be remiss not to explain that the animal I *won't* eat is wolf. I've shot a number over the years in different countries. No animal will eat a wolf on the first day, or even the second. Another wolf may, but ravens, wolverines, even bears, wait two or three days before they eat the carcass. This is my own personal observation, by the way. I guess not many wolf researchers get to see this firsthand as they don't shoot their subjects. I don't know why they don't get eaten quickly; perhaps it's the smell that puts other animals off. Wolves really stink. I think the reason I won't eat wolf relates to something in the back of my mind which is still present, I believe, in most humans. Think about this: thousands of years ago we used to take our old and weak out of the village and leave them to the wolves. In the back of my mind the wolf is part of me, is part of my ancestry, and I won't eat wolf for that reason.

Hanging out with Mongolian villagers was a highlight of the trip.

Hunting was almost secondary. Maybe, as a Kiwi, you have an affinity with all kinds of people; could be we really are a friendly lot. I just wanted to meet as many people as possible. My new wolf-hunting mates took me to a place called Khokh Nuur of Kahr Zurkh (Blue Lake of Black Heart) where Genghis Khan (my new friends pronounced his name *Chingis Han*) arrived as a guy called Temujin. There he met the armies and tribes of Mongolia, who crowned him Genghis Khan, universal king.

I was secreted away on a journey to a sacred spring where Genghis was said to have drunk. To Mongolians it was a most sacred place and none would drink from it. Can I truly say I indeed drank from the spring of the great Genghis Khan? I believe so. I have no reason not to believe my fellow hunters. I even pulled a few rocks from the bottom of the spring, one of which I'm sure was knocked in by Genghis himself. Today, when I lift that rock at home, I'm taken to a windswept place. I glance to my left, then to my right. I see you men of the steppe, warriors with the blood of Genghis in your veins. If I listen very closely I can still hear our voices as we scream in unison, hooves pounding, hearts racing. We drive our enemy before us! We shall steal his horses — ha! We will hear the lamentation of his womenfolk. This is our way of life.

When I come back home from these sorts of trips, I feel nine-foot tall and primaeval. Then I sit in my office, back straight, chin up and Sharee — who started out as a machinist, later became my PA and is now GM — will put five-and-a-half-weeks' worth of paperwork in front of me and start: 'You'll need to sign this GST return. You need to do this. You need to do that.'

I look up at her and I say with my iron face, 'Woman, do you not know who I am? Do you not know where I have been? The things I have seen? The things I have done?'

And she sweetly says, 'Fuck up, Dave. Sit down and get on with it. You're in Levin now.'

OPPOSITE You know how I mentioned that whole thing about proud Mongolian women holding the place together? I take it back.

I look up at her and I say with my iron face, 'Woman, do you not know who I am?'

A small monument dedicated to Genghis Khan near the Blue Lake of the Black Heart. As one can see by the horse hair and other small offerings, Genghis is still revered.

Never-fail camp-oven bread

INGREDIENTS

6 handfuls plain flour
6 cupped hands sugar
2 cupped hands yeast
1 cupped hands salt
water

Fresh hot camp-oven bread. It is, quite simply, to die for.

Straight out of the campie, with great lashings of butter, cheese and good old piccalilli. Mmm mmm! A word of caution is needed here as this recipe is double-yeasted: it may pay to be careful around company you wish to impress, for it does tend to induce gas. Copious amounts thereof.

Now, all this mucking around with raising the yeast, preparing the dough separately — forget it. Into it and on to it, I say. The following ingredients are based on cooking in a 12" campie. I'm not a baker and I'm not a Michelin-starred chef, so the way I prepare and the way I bake are purely based on my own experience. This long-guarded recipe is an old bushman's secret, handed on to me by Rob Adams, the Mad Trapper of Pohangina Valley. Rob himself received instruction from a crotchety old rabbit-board trapper, who in turn picked up this fine cuisine recipe from an red-headed Irish whore he'd met in the Coromandel goldfields. As you see, the pedigree is impeccable.

Light the fire. You should have enough wood handy to keep a small fire going for around, say, two hours. Remember, you're after coals, not a blazing beacon big enough to warn of an imminent Viking attack.

In a large basin add in 6 handfuls of plain flour. Six handfuls are just that, about as much flour as you can fit in your hand. If you're a Sam Whitelock sort of a bloke, with tennis rackets for hands, you'll simply need to adjust. Add 6 cupped hands of sugar, 2 of yeast and 1 of salt. (To gauge a cupped hand, make your hand tight, — *toight as a toiger* — as if you were using it to hold water to drink, filling it to the first crease of your fingers. For those in New Zealand, this is about the same capacity as the lid of your DYC yeast container.) Mix the ingredients thoroughly. Now make a well in the centre and add the warm — first crucial point, *warm*, not hot — water, enough to start binding the dough.

Everything should now be either too dry or too wet. Too dry, add more water; too sticky, sprinkle a little flour on the dough as you mix. I forgot to tell you, you should probably have cut your fingernails before playing with this mix. Now we're kneading the dough. Folding it and rolling it. If you've been on your own in

Gregg's

the bush for the last few months this can be quite an erotic moment, depending upon how creative your folding and rolling gets . . .

Five minutes of kneading. That's 300 seconds if you don't have a clock. Knead too long and you'll end up with a cracked crust; not enough and you'll have large air bubbles in your bread — unless you're a snowboarder, big air is a pain in the loaf. Shape the dough into a circle to fit the bottom of the campie with, say, a 1cm gap clear all around the edge. Put the lid on the campie and lay it about 15cm away from your fire. We'll give the campie a quarter-turn every 10 minutes for 40 minutes total.

Keep the fire going to build the coals; remember, round wood that has not been split will make the best coals. I prefer beech over totara, the latter giving too hot a coal for my liking. Okay, this is where you'll need to show some faith in me — and the following instruction! Don't make any noise while waiting for the mix to come to life. Definitely don't split any wood, bang pots — Cajun stomps-from-the-swamps dancing is also a no-no. Guess what I'm trying to get across is, don't scare the yeast while it is awakening or you'll end up with scones or, worse still, psychologically damaged bread. Crumbs.

Now grab some Bell Tea tea leaves to make yourself a decent brew of black billy bam-a-lam while you sit back and spend the next 40 minutes, while your loaf rises, in quiet contemplation of the world and all its glory or of the state of your navel, or simply getting all the dough mix out from underneath your fingernails.

Time to have a squiz at the mix. Has it risen? Great, put the lid back on gently and prepare to bake! Hang the campie about 20cm from the top of the coals at approximately 150°C heat — 150°? I hear you splutter — how do you figure that out, pilgrim? Put your hand under the campie and start counting. Seven seconds before it gets unbearable is 150°. Less is too hot, more not hot enough. With a shovel or spade cover the lid of the campie in 5 cm of coals from the edge of the firebed. Leave it to bake now for 45 minutes until it becomes a beautiful, crisp-crusted creation.

Righto! Dust off the top coals nice and gently, lift the lid and, yes, there it is. Give the campie a few swift spins in each direction, while firmly holding the handle, to free the bread from the edge of the pot. Place the loaf on a bench.

Two, four, six, eight, there ain't no need to wait. Never-fail bread.

LOU McNUTT '10

Caught by a speed camera just outside of Shannon. Over the 12 months of gruelling training (okay, the few months leading up to the race) this was the only day it didn't rain or blow like 40 bastards.

Tackling the epic Coast to Coast, hurting like hell and then nailing it.

23

FIT AND FIFTY

If you've always wanted to compete in the Coast to Coast but have never got around to it, I recommend making the first payment of $1133.00. After that investment there's no way out. It's quite a chunk of money to throw away on a whim. The Coast to Coast was something that had always appealed to me. Throughout my forties I had this dream that next year I would train and compete, but it never eventuated. Perhaps time and having the purpose of mind eluded me. And then I went on my first major kayak trip.

Along with a group of good mates, including the indomitable Andy McBeth and the unflaggable Bob Foster, we embarked on a 60-odd-km trip down the Hollyford River to Martins Bay. My companions were world-class racers, filling my ears with stories of great adventures, rivers with killer snags and murderous logs

My fellow trainees after our first day on the Rangitikei River at 340 cumecs. None of us slept that night; we all knew what day two held for us.

and whirlpools — I was hooked. I told them how much I'd enjoyed it and their response was 'Great Davey, because we thought we'd finish this trip by kayaking those 60km back upriver!' Me and my big mouth. After the long slog back up the Hollyford the boys again challenged me.

'If you enjoyed it that much, why don't you do the Coast to Coast, Davey?' they asked. 'You'd love it.'

I thought, *You know what? I think I bloody well will.* So I psyched myself up and gave my money to organiser, Robin Judkins.

I started to train, knowing there were three aspects I'd have to school up on. The first was kayaking, for which I'd need a grade-two certificate. For cycling, I needed a bike (obviously) and for running, I needed new legs. Living in the bush all these years hasn't been kind to my knees. Carrying heavy loads of venison resulted in a bunch of knee operations when I was younger. In those days they used to open you up, rip the cartilage out and leave bone on bone. I can't run. I really can't. I can run from the cops and have been known to make good a few escapes from hippos and grizzlies — and that's about it. But it was the kayaking that truly scared the crap out of me, especially as I've never really been able to swim. Hard to believe, especially for a Kiwi, but such a disability hasn't

I had my taxidermist Mark Walker fashion my bike helmet out of a possum. Juddy ruled it out at the Kumeroa gear check, saying it could too easily hide an iPod.

always been a bad thing: turning up at a river and deciding to set up camp instead of swimming to the other side has saved my life more than once.

The Rangitikei River was running 340 cumecs bank to bank on my first attempt with instructors. A cumec, for those who will be paying $1133.00 at the end of the chapter, is a ton of water. Literally that means each additional cumec is an extra ton of water passing you by every second. Hard to visualise? Let's imagine an average elephant, weighing approximately 5 tons. Put that way, you can now start to visualise elephants running past, not water. Three hundred and forty cumecs, put simply, would be around 68 elephants running past you every second. Every second! That's wild. Add to the mix dark water throwing up logs, falling out and having absolutely nowhere to go, and you have a hunter who would rather face a raging bear than a raging river.

However, if I were to compete I'd have to discover some sort of technique. On that first ride on the Rangitikei, I tipped out four times. By the final time, I was beginning to seriously doubt I had the energy to get back in the bloody thing. Sadly your only alternative is to let go and float down river without a boat. Mad Dog Mike, my instructor, screamed at me over the incredible noise the river was making. So you get back in, and then you fall out again. Then, when upside down, you have a dire need to get out for something called air, something you're fast running out of. Now you're upside down having to pull the pin on your skirt, get out of the cockpit right side up and hang onto your paddle — don't ever let go of the paddle.

During this Houdini act, 68 elephants are throwing you against the cliff. *Every second*, you'll recall. Now try to get your kayak alongside your mate's at a 90-degree angle, and push it onto theirs so you can drain it out. Turn it over, pull up alongside them, go to the back of the kayak and push yourself up onto the boat, all the while fighting a bloody raging river. Now squirm your way along a long skinny piece of plastic, back into the cockpit, swing your feet up, over and around, get inside, put your skirt back on, get back inside, regain some composure and control. Here come the frickin' elephants again. Allow yourself to be smashed against rocks and hurtled through waves.

'Ahh, Davey, you don't know how lucky you are to be able to kayak this river so full,' says Mad Dog. No points given for guessing why he got his nickname.

For the cycling leg I resurrected a bike I'd bought when I was 15. It was six years old then, yet here I was 35 years later using it for the most arduous race in the land. A 41-year-old bike ridden by a 50-year-old man. Compare the carbon-fibre racing bikes of today to a piece of steel dating back to the late 1960s and you have to laugh. Using my second-hand bike in the race wasn't a joke, it was nostalgia — it added another dimension and I do believe nostalgia is becoming a thing of the past. I love stories, so the yarn of riding my old Carlton in a race where technology has become a big factor was a major thing. I was going to compete with an old body, an old bike but, thankfully, a new Hurricane from Q Kayaks in Ashhurst. People from the latter had turned up at work one day having heard about my crazy plan to take part in the event. So they gave me a kayak, as well as many encouraging words and much-needed advice.

Everyone who competes in the Coast to Coast needs a team. Mine included Maggie, Taygen, a top mate Mike King (no, not the comedian) and, for the first section, Mike Bygate and his wife Helen. Dave Abbott was filming for our TV show, *Adventures in Wild Places*. Of the 800 people who competed in 2010, 799 were serious. For me, it wasn't a race, but more about competing with myself and meeting the challenge of getting across the finish line at Sumner. If I could do that, shake Juddy's hand and grab my medal, my goal would be achieved.

Another challenge was juggling training with the dramas of filming our TV series. *Adventures in Wild Places* had taken us all over the globe that year, but being away for a month at a time in places with snow, ice, sand and rivers meant keeping fit was possible, but running and kayaking were not. The other sacrifice you make — business aside — is family. Poor Maggie, the winter was a harsh one that year and every time the sun shone I put in a long day's training. If the rivers were up, I would never kayak on my own, which usually meant jumping on the bike and battling headwinds, gales and torrential rain. You'd better grit your teeth because if you can't do it on training day, there's no way in hell you'll be able to do it on race day.

Come race day, particularly for newbies, fear of the Waimakariri River looms large. Everyone has read so much about the Rock Garden, the Hamilton Rapids, and the crazy bluff system. It's the equivalent of a ride on a roller coaster when your harness has come undone and you've slipped off the seat, leaving you hanging on to the outside for dear life. The fear of kayaking those bluffs and walls — thankfully I'd managed two practice runs on the Waimak — were very real for someone who can't swim.

On one run I'd been tipped upside down in a whirlpool and found my personal flotation device wasn't working at all well. Too much air was circulating in the pool so it didn't provide enough flotation to get me up above the water. You try to fight it and get back up to the tantalisingly close sunlight, to the now much-needed air, until you realise there's no way you'll manage it. So in the back of your mind you recall a conversation about going down to get up. You relax, get sucked down and pop out. Easy, huh? Give me the elephants.

You are told falling out in the Waimak will drain the energy from your being. The first time you fall out it takes around five minutes to empty your boat. The second time takes 10, the third time 20. By the fifth time it will take an hour as the river has sapped whatever energy you may have left. So stay in the boat! What a novel idea. As a newbie, each time you dance with the river you change. Surprisingly you learn to like it. You learn to love those rapids. The Rock Garden is a very cool slalom to enjoy, and I wish it were longer. Riding big pressure waves gets you screaming, hooting and hollering.

In kayaking terms this is called 'reading your lines' and if these aren't bang on bad things can happen. So you crave to read them well, to be able to enjoy the exhilaration of the river's life blood. Flow. If you try taking the easy calm-looking water — or chicken route — to the side of the rapids in the wall, it will often tip you from your boat so quickly you won't even get out the 'Arf' of 'Ah fark'. The gentle eddy awaits to spin you around and grab you to her bosom. Despite appearing easy, the chicken route is often a disaster waiting to happen. If you can, try to nail what appears to be the hardest part of the river.

Which is easier said than done when the chicken route looks so inviting . . .

OPPOSITE
ABOVE AND BELOW LEFT We're out of here! I clip in my pedals and try to dodge Dave and his ever-present camera.
BELOW RIGHT Dave Abbott shows it's not all beer and skittles for an adventure cameraman.

SPEIGHT'S
394
SWAZI
THULE

SPEIGHT'S
394
SWAZI
Genoese

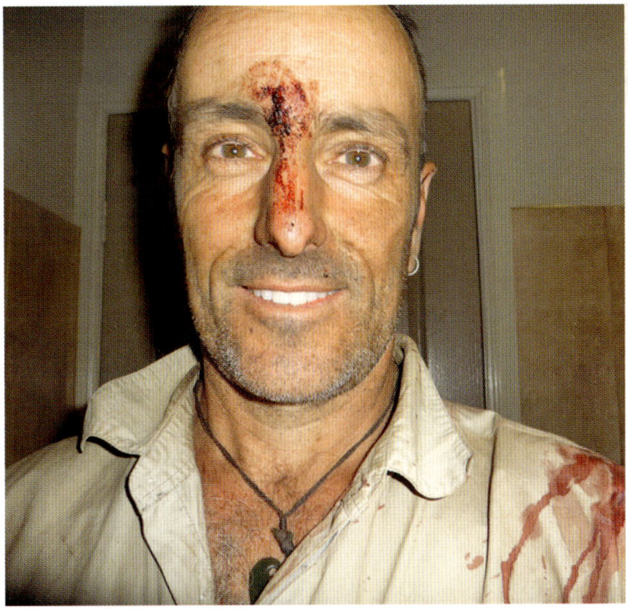

PAUL'S CAMERA SHOP, CHRISTCHURCH

The running and cycling race looks a little like this: 3km from Kumara Beach to Kumara township, where you jump on your bike. From there you ride to Aickens Corner, 55km of stunning West Coast native bush, not too many steep hills. There's a bit of gradient, some great little downhills, and along that part of the course, you encounter incredible West Coast hospitality in the form of people on the road playing bagpipes, the piano accordion, banging pots and pans and cheering you on. Ma and Pa Kettle are there with their umbrellas. From Aickens Corner, you've got a 33km run up the Deception, over Goat Pass, then down the Mingha to Klondyke.

ABOVE Quick! Hurry! Taygen and Maggie drag me through the transition at Aickens. OPPOSITE Well into the 33km mountain run section and my knees want a divorce. However, everyone smiles going over Dudleys Knob. It's mandatory.

I was piss poor right from the start. I knocked three minutes off my fastest 3km run time, but still turned up at the bike transition horribly down the field. My knees weren't great. No excuses though; there are some tough bastards out there with knees worse than mine and they're not whining. One guy had a compound fracture to his thumb; the bone was actually sticking out.

'Mate,' I said as we ran. 'You'd better see the St John's people when you get to Klondyke.'

He replied, 'No way, they'll want to pull me out of the race. I'll wrap it up and get it seen to in Christchurch.'

I persisted. 'That's a compound fracture you've got there. You could lose your thumb.'

Without hesitation he said, 'It's worth it.'

Worth it? Of course it's worth it! You realise there are people out there with a lot more resolve than you, so you keep going, digging deeper than you ever thought you could. You're a Coast-to-Coaster, matey.

Steve Gurney breathed a sigh of relief as he realised his mantle of Coast-to-Coast guru was not under threat from the Dark Horse from Levin, particularly as I ended up doing the run three times over. This was mainly due to Dave the cameraman wanting to reshoot scenes. Rather

wisely, he knew the best footage would not come from running beside me, so he often asked me to stay where I was while he perched on a riverbank in the distance.

Once there, barely audible, he'd yell, 'Davey, I want you to come across the river, run past the camera as close as you can. Make a decent splash in the river, I reckon that'll be pretty good footage!'

As other runners whipped past me I waited for the thumbs up from Dave, before following his directions. As even more runners loped past, Dave would then say, 'Yeah, that was good, but I think if you go back and hit the river a metre or two further down, it'll make for a better splash. We want splash, buddy!'

I turned around, headed back up the hill and waited for the thumbs up once more. After the second attempt, Dave would say, 'I'm sorry, that splash was perfect but you'll have to do it again; that bloody second runner coming through blocked my view.'

I'll give you splash, matey.

The Coast to Coast winds its way through and across some of the most amazing country in the world. Many competitors looked at Dave and me as if we were a bit odd, clearly thinking we weren't super keen on finishing well up in the field. We were hell bent on the journey, not the destination. The problem was that Dave would find some stunning flowering rata or a spectacular waterfall on the side of a hill and we'd stop to film it. Most other runners were heads down, tails up, going for broke, but they'd just missed a stunning cascade.

Dave is actually an amazing athlete in his own right, having competed in the Coast to Coast, Southern Traverse and a host of other multisport events such as the Xerox Challenge. This time it was different, and I know we were both lapping it up. Way cool!

We spent time at Goat Pass, stopping to yack to the locals and other competitors. The greatest part of this particular journey is not what you discover about your own depth of steel and resolve, but about the people you meet. Thank goodness there are enough brave hearts to pull you through, to egg you on and to get you back in the kayak when in reality you'd rather just bloody die.

Klondyke Corner! Great, at long last a chance to sit down, and not on a bike seat. As a two-day eventer, I'd rest here the night. Around 300 people were lined up to cheer me as I crossed the stage finish. I shed a tear and thought emotionally, *This is unbelievable, what support for us lesser beings*. The truth was Juddy had just organised a briefing and it was taking place as I ran over the line. A long-awaited massage took some of the stiffness out of my legs. I was pooped and needed a good lie down. The news Juddy was giving, however, was that a weather bomb was due to hit and all campers should make sure their tents were well pegged down. If the river came up too quick, well, there could be a change of plan for the next day. Hey, the event has always gone ahead. She'll be right. How wrong.

Mike Bygate had parked up his luxury caravan in the camp area and we sat outside it eating venison sausage sammies, ice-cream, steaks,

OPPOSITE 'Hang on Davey, get back up that rock slide and then come motoring down like you're on some great big scree — bit more urgency this time though, okay?' Righto, Dave.

The 'old bastard' catching him up was riding an ancient bike, gritting his teeth and wishing he was hunting in Alaska.

anything I bloody well wanted! We gave heaps of shit to our neighbours about everything under the sun and they gave it back twice as hard. Everyone was in a jovial mood. Then one of our neighbours got up and casually took two kayaks off the roof of his 4WD SUV before heading off to the loo. His wife jumped straight into the wagon and proceeded to drive towards the kayaks. We jumped up yelling and gesticulating. 'Look out, lady!' we all screamed. She smiled out the car window, then gave us the bird as she drove over the top of the kayaks. Not good. Realising her mistake she panicked, shoved the vehicle in reverse and backed over both boats. Ohhh. Definitely not good now.

The weather bomb was coming big time. Juddy announced that he was pulling the Waimak River section . . . But, but . . . but, Juddy, I'd drowned a dozen small deaths to get ready to race the Waimak. Some things are the way they are. Move on. So we did. We took the entire Team Swazi crew 40km down the road to Castle Hill Station where Chrissie Fernyhough and Johnny Bougen wonderfully allowed us to crash in the shearing quarters. (If you are struggling with this book, then John Bougen is to blame, by the way — he put me up to it!) I slept so well that night. God, I hurt next day, though. Toughen up boy, I told myself as I walked around in a doubled-over zombie-like state at 4 am. We had to get back to Klondyke for the start of Day Two.

Rain? This wasn't rain, this was merely West Coast mist. The water running down the road was 5cm deep, making cycling the downhills a fairly interesting proposition. The newly added section was around 140km of cycling. The good thing was that over half of the ride would be downhill! You can kind of guess what the bad thing was . . .

Some punters had pulled the pin. Perhaps they felt that the weather was too bad. Maybe they didn't think their gear was up to it. Maybe they didn't think *they* were up to it. Whatever the reason, who was I to judge? It was their decision. The conditions, however, reminded me of training in Horowhenua in springtime! On some of the descents I reached speeds of 80kph, but with so much water on the road I found myself literally aquaplaning down the hill. Far out, I thought, this is cool. I started to enjoy myself. Everyone who passed me — hmmm, I guess around 799 riders — yelled 'Go for it, Swazi!' What a buzz.

A big problem that arose on the bike leg was finding a like-minded

OPPOSITE
ABOVE The rejigged bike section added a 140km leg, but hey! At least half of that was downhill . . . can't be feeling too bad, just passed a big bunch going over Porters Pass. BELOW Yeehah! The other side of Porters.

PORTERS
SKI AREA

bunch to share the load. Every group I entered was either too fast or too slow. I never hit that happy medium. Failing to do so meant I rode virtually the entire section on my own, a tough ask with no let-up. I looked forward to the part of the ride where I could cruise at the back of a good bunch while those in the engine room did the leg work and sucked me along the road. When you're on your own, however, it's your power, your pedals and no slipstream.

Such drama would have been fine, if it hadn't ended up on national TV. Ex-cricketer turned broadcaster Mark Richardson and Olympic gold medallist Ian Ferguson had entered as a team, and Mark was being interviewed by Prime TV as he did the cycle leg. He noted that he wasn't doing too well and feeling it.

'Even that old bastard behind me looks like he is catching up,' he added.

With that, the camera panned beyond Mark to reveal that the 'old bastard' catching him up was riding an ancient bike, gritting his teeth and wishing he was hunting in Alaska.

I was as surprised as anyone my old bike was doing so well. My family and support team were there to egg me on.

'Come on, Dad, you're nearly there!'

'Nearly where?' I'd joke back.

ABOVE I'd been dreaming about mincemeat and cheese pies and when I turned up at the 85km mark to grab more food and drink I caught Mike and Taygen having a health snack.

BELOW By the time we'd reached Castle Hill Station on Day Two, the weather decidedly brightened up, so I stopped to strip off my long pants and raingear.

Once more the steely resolve of Coast-to-Coasters burst through. Who cares if this section was now longer? Who cares if there are more roadworks than first envisaged? Multiple punctures resulted, yet not once did I see a person on the side of the road fixing a wheel on their own. Another competitor would always pull clear of the bunch to help see them right. 'I'll hold your back wheel up, mate, you get the tyre on.' This selfless humanity — in a competitive atmosphere — blew me away and was something I never thought I'd see in a race. Coast-to-Coasters are special people. Obviously such a scene is reserved for two-day competitors. Those who complete the Coast to Coast in a day are elite athletes with one thing on their minds, to beat everyone and get across the line as quickly possible.

My heart and soul was in that bike leg, and I managed to correct time lost from the first day. The hardest part was thinking a transition was coming at the 65km mark as Juddy had mentioned — along with bottles of electrolyte and lollies — only to find that once the distance had been covered there was no respite. Ah well, I thought, must be at 70km. That, too, came and went. At 75km, nothing. The transition ended up being at 85km, during which time the voice in my head repeated and repeated, 'It's not fair!' As I struggled through Springfield all I could smell was mince and cheese pies. My mind continued to taunt me. The transition finally arrived and my team rushed out, grabbed me and my bike, started rubbing me, and generally going about things in a great big fat hurry. They were super-hyped, so much so I had to slow them down.

'How are you guys going?' I asked. 'Are *you* having a good day?'

They'd pause and smile. 'Oh yeah, actually we're having a marvellous day!'

End of the kayak section down the Avon. If I'd have known it was going to be race in a river of molasses I would have opted for my fast Hurricane race boat instead of the Skua sea kayak.

My toes were so sore they felt as if someone was smashing them with a hammer with each pedalling revolution.

Support crews are the life and blood of the Coast to Coast, most having been duped in by some athlete to take two or three days off work and be constantly yelled at. Endorphins run high for many athletes, yet at times tempers fray in others. At the transition stage it's not uncommon to hear conversations like this: 'Where are my sunglasses? Where are my bike glasses! What have you done with them? You know I need them! They're on the sheet, for God's sake! Have you guys even *read the fucking sheet?*'

Meanwhile, the support crew sit back and take the flak, although some are as bad as the competitors. 'You arseholes, where's my fucking team member? Where's my goddamned drink?'

It's laughable how serious some people are. As if five seconds is going to make a difference.

I still had a 60km ride into Christchurch, battling a fairly decent headwind. For cycling purists a 140km race is not actually all that far. But coming off the top of a 33km mountain run and with a long kayak section in front of you it's still a fairly demanding distance! By this stage I felt like utter shit and for some reason my toes were so sore they felt as if someone was smashing them with a hammer with each pedalling revolution.

Then as we entered the Christchurch perimeter roads we began to hit more traffic. The intersections had a half a dozen police holding up the traffic as we drew near. Having seen the traffic pull up and stop specifically for you — the motorists in turn expecting to witness elite athleticism — it would be remiss to disappoint. I dug deep and pedalled as fast as possible through each intersection. Drivers beeped their horns and yelled, 'Well done, Swazi, keep going!'

Out of the view of motorists, it was time to suck in some big ones and relax. Alas, 200 metres down the road was another set of lights and more cops stopping traffic. Oh God, time to perform again.

My support team only beat me by three or four minutes as I rode into Hagley Park. I thought I'd made good time, pleased to hear from Maggie that I'd nailed the previous leg and that the team hadn't expected to see me for another half-hour. They were building me up, I'm sure, but it was good to hear nonetheless. They knew which buttons to push. For the first time in the event I was about to jump into a kayak, looking forward to a change from wheels and legs.

Months earlier, the guys at Q Kayaks had given me three kayaks to test, and I'd chosen a beautiful racing boat called a Hurricane, though I'd shied away from it at the very last moment, feeling I wasn't skilled enough to use it on the Waimak. So they built me a brand-new super-fast sea kayak, one suitable for a river like the Waimak.

In reality, I should have taken my Hurricane down the Avon as sea kayaks are pretty heavy and draught a lot more. The Avon was so shallow I ran aground six times. Having prepared for the thunderous, angry Waimak, it was bizarre to be parked behind Japanese and American tourists punting their way through the Garden City, snapping photos as they went. It was a big day for them, too, so it would have been rude not to give them a little splash with my paddle on the way through. Just on their legs, mind, not their cameras.

'Sorry, er, so sorry, Coast-to-Coaster coming through.'

The Avon River really was like kayaking in molasses. It couldn't have been more different to the river we were supposed to race on. White water and dangerous currents were replaced by weaving through all manner of weeds. As we were negotiating an entirely new course, anticipating how far to go was near impossible. Your head, however, needed it. How far until we hit the bay? When would we reach deep water? The only thing to do was ask someone on the riverbank.

'How far to the rowing club?'

Not far, was the response. Three-quarters of an hour later and still no boat sheds. Better ask someone else.

'How far to the rowing club, mate?'

'Oh, a wee way yet!' came the reply.

Oh God.

'Oh, a wee way yet!' came the reply. Oh God.

The beloved rowing club was finally in sight. No longer did I have to wade through the Avon's shallow water. Drag was no longer an issue and speed was now possible. It had been a slow, arduous ride through Christchurch, made more difficult by expectant motorists! The great news was we had hit the sea; the bad news was the tide was going against us. The wondrous feeling of escaping shallow water was short-lived. Now I felt as if I were going backwards. But at least I could see the finish of the kayaking section. Hundreds of people waited. It was time to really put it in. All the while your body is complaining that it's hardly had time to recover from the cycle ride. None of it matters. You are now going to finish the race. That is your total focus.

Mike King and Taygen were there to rip me out of the boat when I landed, something made more difficult given the kayak's specially designed hip braces. Unbeknown to them, the only way to exit was one leg at a time. Mike — a strong, strapping high-country farmer — reached behind me, put his arms under my shoulders and pulled. I thought my knees were going to come off!

'Mike,' I managed. 'Do me a favour and let me get out by myself, man.'

Which he did. Once free, they pulled me out of the water and sprinted me up the ramp. I'm sure Mike just about carried me! Hey, I'm supposed to be doing the racing. I only had one thing on my mind: this transition needs to be quick. Straight from the kayak into bike shoes, bike helmet and go!

Last section. I'm yelled at by an official: 'Six kilometres to the finish!' Okay, 6km. An individual pursuit. I hammer it and catch a lot of competitors, some of whom had overtaken me during the morning ride. I am now catching them! People are out of energy, but I've scored some from I don't know where. I glance at the speedo on Old Faithful. Should be 5km left. 4km. 2km. Dig it in, dig it in! The mind starts playing tricks again. This is it. The last 1000 metres. *Allez allez allez!* When is this going to end? Soon, you hope, when the speedo says you've actually just passed the 9km mark.

Some things no one can take away from you.

You can't sprint much further. You've been doing it too long. When you look up you see orange cones in the distance. Somehow you find something extra. You can sprint once more. One of the Coast to Coast officials grabs your bike. You float down a couple of small steps and onto a big sandy stretch only 60m long, and there you see the most amazing word in the entire English language: 'Finish.'

A huge crowd is gathered at the finish line. My family is here. As I run down the finishing chute I spot a sea of Swazi people. Our team has been in the South Island for the Waimumu Agricultural Show in Gore and they'd driven all night to get back up to Christchurch for the finish of the race. My mates Jan and Wain and Flick are there. There's Tavis jumping up and down as I run the last 20 metres, yelling, 'Dad! Go

If ever you wanted a high in your life, cross the finish line on the Coast to Coast. There's not much else comes close. Juddy, mate, you're a fricken' legend.

Dad!' He'd had no trouble spotting the crazy guy with long blond hair looking like death.

Once past the tape I run into Maggie, Dave my cameraman, Mike King and Taygen. I am close to tears. Juddy is there to meet me and gives me a hug and a can of Speights. I don't drink beer, but pop the top and guzzle that thing in one gulp. It is the best bloody drink I've ever had. I hobble down to the water with my pebble from the Tasman Sea and, as tradition dictates, throw it into the Pacific Ocean. Alongside me, fellow competitors are utterly buggered. Totally satisfied.

The Coast to Coast is a yearly event where elite athletes test themselves and hackers give it a crack. The latter includes fat guys, weedy guys and old women. When you see these everyday Kiwis — and the pain on their faces — you realise that for many of them finishing demands more effort than it does of those who are in contention to win. For the hackers, training for, then competing in, the race requires supreme sacrifices on every level. . . the training, the gear, the time, not to mention the pain they go through. You have to take your hat off to them and say, 'Wow, that shows depth of character.'

When I threw my pebble into the ocean, people were walking into the waves casting out their demons. I saw competitors I knew were suffering from cancer. Completing this race was their way of saying, 'Get out of my body, I've beaten you, this is where you finish.' *He tangata*.

That night the team took me out for dinner. We went to a Mexican restaurant in Christchurch and I ordered the biggest steak you can imagine. When it turned up in front of me, my head drooped more and more as the minutes passed, then I collapsed face first into my meal and fell fast asleep. You're a bloody Coast-to-Coaster, mate.

R COATS 011

A few parting words of wisdom.

24

THE CALL OF THE WILD

When I look back on my life it seems a crazy old ride. I guess I'd like to be remembered as a businessman, father and hunter. I'd love to think my kids are proud of what I do.

I'd like to be thought of as a person who always tried to do the right thing for other people. I don't want a huge tombstone. In actual fact — and Maggie is a little spooked by this — when I die I want to be sewn up in a burlap sack, thrown in the back of a helicopter, flown into the Ruahines and propped beside some young totara tree. There, whatever's left of my body will help that tree grow.

There are many things I don't know, but here's something I do: life is not about building empires. Life is about getting off your arse and doing the things you really want to do. It's not a dress rehearsal. You get one stab at it. If you don't do it now, you never will.

I love the saying 'The best time to plant a tree is 20 years ago and the second best time to plant a tree is right now'. In other words, if you didn't do it 20 years ago because of family, business or whatever else, do it now. To make it happen, sell something, for God's sake. Sell the flash 4WD, drive around in an old car, and go and have an adventure. You will never forget it. You will never regret it.

I don't want to be the 75-year-old who goes on a cruise and dies of a heart attack having never travelled. I know people who have run companies, retired, gone on cruises to Fiji and died of heart attacks. And they weren't 75; they were in their goddamned fifties. People say, 'You're so lucky, you get to travel around the world.' Hey, I've made sacrifices to do that — and as long as you're not sacrificing friends or family, everything else is up for grabs.

But it's not over yet. I'm hoping for many more years roaming the hills — both here and overseas — hunting, fishing, adventuring. It's hard not to feel at times that you are part of a long, long line, reaching back into the Stone Age, of hunters, trappers, scouts, explorers . . . and sometimes even bullshitters.

I guess I'll see you out there — in your Swazi gear.

Baboomfa!

A fitting end to our journey, an Arab dhow off the coast of Zanzibar.

THE SECRET LURE

He caught up with me in the carpark of the Upok Pub
An old bloke in dirty clothes, looked like he'd just crawled from the scrub
He winked at me once and quickly glanced from side to side
His hand was in his jacket with something he wanted to hide

'I heard you were a trapper son, that much I've already seen
Your truck smells like a possum and desperately needs a clean.'
Well, I reckon it wasn't my ute but his body that needed the soap
As he pulled out a sack full of flour all tied up with rope

'This here, this here is my magic jacko potion,'
And he eyed that bag with a kind of loving devotion
'It's my own secret recipe mind,' he said
'A secret recipe I keep locked up in me head'

'I promised I'd share it with no one, but I'll be a little rash
You see son, it's my last personal possession and I'm in need of the cash.'
Now I'd sold a line of plews at auction that very same day
If he thought I'd part with that money for his lure he had it the wrong way

'Listen here old-timer; a new lure really is the last thing I need
But if you join me inside I'll shout you a beer and buy you a feed.'
So we drunk a few beers and we spun a few lies
Me and the trapper with the rheumy hands and clear, clear, bright eyes

You'll say I'm a mug and sure it's more than likely true
But I slipped him a couple of fifties just to see him through
One day an old trapper with arthritis I'll probably be
And maybe, well just maybe, some young bloke will do the same for me

I left the pub feeling good though a hundred bucks fewer
Got 40 miles down the road before I discovered his lure
He must have slipped it in my bag when I went to the dunny
An honest bloke at least, for in that bag was all me money

Next week I was back out on my block laying out a line
High up on a ridge that was just covered in sign
I'd been going at it for a while when I stopped for a fag
That's when I noticed the remaining lure had leaked from my bag

Cursing I started back to camp when suddenly I had a notion
Reached to the very bottom of the bag, 'This here son, is my magic jacko potion.'
I laughed loudly and the echoes bounced from hill to hill
It's only discoloured flour; I doubt even one possum I'll kill

That night a storm broke to end the long hard drought
The sort of storm that washes all of your baits clean out
Next day I went round my line dejected, not a darn jacko in sight
Well what did you expect mate, she had rained all bloody night

Then I came across ten possums all on the same bait
Say, wasn't this where I'd laid the old man's lure — sure was mate
I counted over three hundred skins in the space of an hour
Me dead sure it was only discoloured flour

I've been back to the Upok Pub, of that you can be sure
More than once tried to find the old man and his secret lure
Today I asked the barman if he knew the bloke I wished to seek
'Why yes mate. Hell! I was at his funeral — it was only last week . . .'

I yelled, then I cried and the whole pub hushed to turn my way
I'll get that secret recipe alright, but she'll have to wait for Judgement Day

The following people were Clan Swazi members as at 1 March 2011. Their names appear in acknowledgement of their contribution to the Swazi brand. A brand in fact ow by these people, we here at Swazi HQ being merely the guardians they have entrusted to look after Swazi. Thanks for making this journey possible, guys.

Jarrod Abbot. Graeme Abbot. Kurt Abbot. Dave Abbott. John Abbott. Wayne Abel. Peter Abel. Simon Abel. William Abel. Willie Abel. Blake Abernethy. Scott Abery. Marty Abraham. Tom Abraham. Trish Abrahamson. Ruslan Abramov. Phil Abra
Absolom. Gary Aburn. Bellamy Acker. Arthur Acland. Jack Acland. Tammy Acton-Adams. Kelvin Acutt. Aleisha Adam. Joshua Adam. Robert Adam. John Adam. Daniel Adam. Justin Adams. Jonathan Adams. Don Adams. Carol Adams. John Adam
Adams. Douglas Adams. Richard Adams. Barbara Adams. Lisa Adams. Trevor Adamson. Anita Adamson. Stewart Addenbrooke. Richard Addis. Dayne Addison. Mark Adie. Grant Adkins. Marcus Adlam. Kevin Adolph. Grant Adolph. Cara Adrai
Afanasyev. Anna Affleck. Jim Affleck. Lindsay Affleck. Anita Afitu. Czarina Faye Ocampo Agajona. Brent Agnew. Roxanne Agnew. Annette Ah Chee. Andrew Ahlers. Mark Ahlers. Rachel Ahtila. Tony Ainsworth. David Aitken. Graeme Aitken. Grar
Kyle Aitken. Russ Aiton. Mark Akehurst. Bev Akers. Simon Akers. Baden Alber. Bruce Albon. Geoff Alderton. Daniel Aldridge. Simon Alefosio-Tuck. Novikov Aleksey. Martin Alexander. Denise Alexander. Anna Alexander. Greig Alexander. John A
Daniel Alexander. Waiotu Farms Ltd Alexander. David Alexandrakis. Igor Alexandrov. Kathie Alford. Stephen Alford. James Alford. Eddie Alford. Christine Algie. James Aliferis. John Alker. Jodi Allan. Chris Allan. Nick Allan. Andrew Allan. Jan
Richard Allen. Matt Allen. Hamish Allen. James Allen. David Allen. Roger Allen. Steve Allen. Lisa Allen. Sidney Allen. Helen Allen. Russell Allen. Pauline Allen-Hunter. Stephen Allerby. Philip Allerby. Joshua Alley. Joe Allison. Brett Allison. Shau
Hayden Allison. Pedro Allison. Brian Allison. Karl Allpress. Bryce Alsemgeest. Liz Alston. Alexander Altuhov. Charles Amblard. Kris Ambrozkiewicz. Paul Amey. Yash Amin. Kane Amohanga. Justin Amor. Chrystal Amos. Matt Amos. Hylton Amos
Ander. Ryan Andersen. Deb Andersen. Ross Anderson. Blair Anderson. Mark Anderson. Chris Anderson. Richard Anderson. Stuart Anderson. Caroline Anderson. Dave Anderson. Tania Anderson. Kurt Anderson. Jacob Anderson. Monique Anderson
Anderson. Guy Anderson. Jason Anderson. Juliet Anderson. Craig Anderson. Garry Anderson. Kirsty Anderson. Sue Anderson. Brian Anderson. Joshua Anderson. Grant Anderson. Kieran Anderson. Mike Anderson. John Anderson. Sandra Ander
Anderson. Brenden Anderson. Simon Anderson. Fraser Anderson. Brian Anderton. Robert Andrã©N. Richard Andrell. R D Andrell. Wayne And Lois Andrewes. Chloe Andrews. Sally Andrews. Doug Andrews. Tom Andrews. Nicole Andrews. Wendy
Jeffrey and Anne-Marie Andrews. Wayne Andrews. Henrik Anesen. Lina Ang. Christine Angland. Jeff Angus. Hamish Angus. Lynley Annals. Bruce Annan. Adrian Annan. Sloan Annand. Simon Annear. Gus Anning. Alexander Anokhyn. Dawn
Michael Anselmi. Trevor Ansley. Steve Anslow. John Anso. John Anstice. Grant Anthony. Clayton Apihai-Paget. Viv Aplin. Swazi Apparel. Mike Appleby. Brian Apps. Campbell Apthorp. Geoffrey Archer. Felicity Archer. Jarad Archer. Lyndsay Arc
Archer. Christine Archer. Darryn Ardern. Shahrir Ariff. John Arlidge. Dave Armistead. Paul Armit. Vicky Armit. Cam Armitage. Suzanne Armitage. Dave Armitstead. Mike Armour. Chris Armstrong. Nathan Armstrong. Kirsty Armstrong. Joy Armstr
Armstrong. Shane Armstrong. John Arnot. Steven Arnott. German Artamonov. Valentin Artemenko. Phil Arthur. Shane Arthur. Blair Arthur. Lucas Arthur. Ross Arthur. Dann Arthur. Steve Arthur. Jon Artz. Akhmetov Rustem Ashatovich. Dave
Graeme Ashby. Dean Ashby. Marty Ashby. Mike Ashby. Dan Asher. Glen Ashford. Shane Ashforth. Sam Ashley. Neville Ashley. Steve Ashley. Meirion Ashton. Regan Ashton. Damon Ashworth. Julie Ashworth. Kaydee Ashworth. Venkateshn Asiria
Askes. Olav E Aslaksen. Darryn Astill. Matthew Aston. Margo Astwood. Jon Astwood. Sue Atkins. Sara Atkins. Rick Atkinson. Jeff Atkinson. Bill Atkinson. Suzanne Atkinson. Dave Attwell. Mark Attwood. Bill Aubrey. Rob Aubrey. Shawn Auck. Serg
Maurice Aukett. Demelza Aukett. John Auld. Michelle Aulding. Tim Ausherman. Bob Austin. Raewyn Austin. Adam Austin. Brad Austin. Julie Anne Avery. Frank Avery. Ray Avery. Eric and Louella Axon. Mark Ayres. Mark Ayson. Peter Ayson. Tom I
Anneti Bacica. Debbie Back. Tracey Badger. Paul Badger. Ryan Badger. William Baghoomian. Aaron Baigent. Paul Baikie. Sarah Bailey. Brant Bailey. Ray Bailey. Bernard Bailey. Ross Bailey. Roy Bailey. Chris Bailey. Glen Bailey. Jack Bailey. Craig Ba
Bailey. Terry Bailey. Wendy Bailey. Brendon Bain. Stewart Bain. Iain Bain. Barbara Bain. Justin Bain. Dave Bain. David Bain. Sandy Bain. Peter Bainbridge. Scott Baistow. Caleb Baker. Nick Baker. Sven Baker. Derek Baker. Brent Baker. Peter Baker. Cor
Geoff Baker. Carol Baker. Dave Baker. Errol Baker. Mark Baker. Maureen Bakulich. Roman Balakin. Rajiv Balbharan. Nigel Baldock. Susan Baldock. Glenn Baldock. Tony Baldwin. Yvette Baldwin. Peter Ball. TJ Ball. Jim Ball. Gillian Ball. Tricia Ball. Andy
Jon Ballantine. Debra Ballard. Graham Ballard. Cathyanne Ballard. Alistair Balsom. Kerry Balsom. Linley Balvert. Jessica Banfield. Krystine Banicevich. Bruce Bankier-Perry. Tim Banks. Sam Banks. Jay Banner. Mark Bannister. Damian Baptiste. Ihar
Lawrence Baraniuk. Tony Barber. Katrina Barber. James Barbour. Hoz Barclay. Donna Barclay. Nick Barclay. Cam Barclay. Dave James Barclay. Nicholas Mcgregor Barclay. Simon Bardon. Laurence Barea. Robin Barefield. Michael Baring. James Barke
Barker. Mike Barker. Kaylea Barker. Paul and Rachel Barker and Morrison. Murray Barkman. Seth Barlow. Allister Barlow. Karl Barlow. Murray Barltrop. Phil Barnard. Ian Barnes. Howie Barnes. Lorraine Barnes. Ryan Barnes. Gabrielle Barnett. Deanne
Finn Barnett. Matt Barnett. Phil Barnett. Callum Barr. Tom Barr. Sherri Barr. Gloria Barr. Ian Barraclough. Richard Barraclough. Andrew Barrell. Graham Keith Barrell. Les Barrett. Pat Barrett. Caitlin Barriball. Andrew Barrie. Mark Barringer. Lloyc
Russ Barron. Sarah Barron. Clive Barrow. Louise Barry. Shane Barry. Jack Barry. Richard Barry. Suzanne Bartholomew. John Bartholomew. Rex Bartholomew. Tom Bartle. Selwyn Bartlett. Brenda Bartlett. Ben Bartlett. Joe Bartley. Tony Barton. Roge
Matthew Barton. Mike Barton. Adrian Barwick. Mavis Barwick. Hereward Basher. Dave Bashford. Cate Basingthwaighte. Inna Baskakova. Samuel Bassett. Francis Bastiaansen. Warren Batchelar. Linda Batchelor. Mike Batchelor. Kate Bateman. Bri
Sheryl Bates. Graham Bates. Peter Bates. Kristy Bates. Laurie Bates. Diane Bates. Nick Batkin. Bruce Batory. Jasper Bats. Bryan Batt. Nathan Batts. Pete Batty. Eric Bauchau. Roger Bawden. Mathew Bax. Duncan Baxter. Dave Baxter. Peter Baxte
Bayazitov. Rod Bayer. Mary Jo Bayles. Stephen Bayley. Angus Bayley. Aleksei Baylin. Corey Bayliss. Hylton Bayliss. Kevin Bayliss. Paul Bayly. Charlotte Bayly. Tim Bayne. Peter Bayne. Colin Baynes. Storm Baynes-Ryan. Eric Baynton. Nigel Bayto
Bazarbaeva. Justin Beadle. Ben Beadle. Kevin Beadle. Andrew Bealing. Glen Beals. Sheridan Beams. Tony Bean. Warwick Bean. Chris Beard. Dierdre Beard. Fleur Bearda. John Bearsley. Darren Beaton. Mickey Beatson. Ryan Beatson. Robin Beattie. Jo
John Beaufill. Richard Beaufort. Sean Beausang. Winton Bebbington. Richard Beck. Nigel Beck. Elliott Becker. Nick Beckers. Denis Beckett. Nathaniel Beckett. Nat Beckett. Mark Beckett. Stephen Bedford. Chris Bedford. Darin Bedggood. Robert Be
Ben Beech. Stefan Beeching. Robert Beeching. Shane Beeching. Andrew Beer. Kelvin Beere. Chris Beere. Edward Beetham. Belinda Beets. Haze Begbie. John Begg. Wayne Beggs. Mike Begley. Alistair Beissel. Kelly Beker. Jason Belcher. Karina Belfiel
Belfield. Bruce Belfield. Stanislav Belikov. Sam Bell. Frances Bell. Crystal Bell. Emma Bell. Peter Bell. Alan Bell. Murray Bell. Dominic Bell. "Chris Bell. Craig Bell. Shelley Bell. Mark Bell. Kaye Bell. Ian Bell. Catherine Bell. Cameron Bell. Nathan Bella
Bellamy. Marian Bellamy. Steve Beller. Trent Bellingham. Don Belliss. Marina Belozertseva. Gary Belt. Craig Benbow. Rob Benden. Peter Benders. Phil Benefield. Jerome Benefield. Diana Benfell. Micheal Benfell. Tarek Benjemaa. Mark Bennett.
Bennett. Kevin Bennett. Veronica Bennett. Neil Bennett. Tom Bennett. Matt Bennett. Robert Bennett. William Bennett. Nathan Bennetto. Michael Bennie. James Bennie. Kathryn Bennie. Brad Benning. Lorraine Benning. Mark Benns. Lynette Benn
Benseman. Jo Bensemann. Nathan Bensemann. Caleb Benson. Blair Benson. Pierre Benson. Robby Benson-Cooper. Margaret Benton. Inessa Berezovskaya. Donna Bergersen. Michael Bergin. Thomas Bergin. Ben Bergman. Dirk Bergman. Willie Berke
Berkett. Ashton Bernhard. Karl Berquist. Luke Berquist. Mark Berrett. Lawrence Berry. John Berry. Nick Berry. David Berry. Simon Bertenshaw. David Bertram. Jeff Bess. Mitchell Best. Kaitlin Best. Olivia Bester. Amy Beswarick. Justin Bet. Clint Beth
Bethell. Donna Bevan. Maiotaki Bevan. James Beveridge. Anthony Beveridge. Heaysman Beverley. Cees Bevers. Rick Beviins. Warren Bevin. Gary Bevins. Mark Bewley. Lyall Bezett. Manjori Bhattacharya. Aidan Bichan. Peter Bichan. Shane Bich
Bickerton. Bryan Bickley. Barry Bicknell. Rodger Biddington. Jonathon Bidois. Sandy Bidwill. Paul Biggar. Ian Biggs. Cheryl Bigham. Rob Bigwood. Simon Bilderbeck. Grant Bill. Mike Billett. Dan Billing. Wayne Billing. Ken Billing. Mike Billinghu
Billings. Rob Billington. Edmund Billington. Steve Billington. Ken Binion-Cooper. Mark Binney. Derek Binnie. Helen Binnie. Chris Birch. Patrick Birch. Sam Bircham. Terry Bircham. Chris Bird. Stephanie Bird. Alistair Bird. Nick Bird. Cameron Bi
Bird. Keith Birkett. Nigel Birt. Paul Birtwistle. John Bishara. Dion Bishell. Scott Bishell. Jarvis Bishop. Samuel Bishop. Marcus Bishop. Daniel Wayne Bishop. Barry Bishop. Lawrence Bishop. Lois Bishop. John Bishop. Patrick Bishop. John Bissell. Ch
John Bjork. Rafe Bjork. Logan Black. Cale Black. Sam Black. Robert Black. Jo Black. Grant Blackburn. Paul Blackburn-Elliot. Ruth Blackett. Paul Blackham. Graeme Blackler. Eddie Blackman. Daniel Blackman. Carl Blackman. Shane Blackwell. Ross B
Brian Blackwell. Curtis Blackwell. Dan Blair. Allan Blair. John Blair. Bruce Blair. Daniel Blair. Donald Blair. Michael Blake. Mike Blake. Ken Blake. Kim Blake. Len Blake. Brian Blakeley. James Blakely. Lisa Blaker. Richard Blanc. Penny Blanc. Nicky Bl
Mark Blanchard. Bernard Blanchard. Jim Blanche. Peter Blanken. Robbie Blankenstein. Dave Blanks. Andrew Blanshard. John Blatchford. John Blattler. Simon Blaydes. Tomas Blazek. John Blenkhorn. Russell Blick. Anton Blick. Petr Blinov. Kevin Bli
Bloch. Frederik Blontrock. Sean Bloomfield. Rob Bloomfield. Ian Blowers. Barry Bloxham. Andrew Blue. Shane Blumenthal. Kevin Bly. Grant Blyth. Pip Blyth. Henry Blyth. Kathryn Blythe. Jan Blythe. Matt Boast. Yura Bochuliak. Colin Boddie. Bradley
Mitch Bodman. Wolf Boehme. Diane Boenders. Koos Boers. Alexey Bogachkin. Don Bogie. Aidan Bognuda. Bruce Bogun. Quinn Bohan. Ewa Bohm. Jim Boivin. Josh Bokser. Robyn Boler. Rory Boleyn. Wayne Bolt. Jen Bolt. Steve Bolton. Ben Bolton.
Bolton. Katie Bolton. Michael Bolton. Dennis Bomford. Phillip Bond. Mark Bond. Neil Bond. Murray Bond. David Bond. Irina Bondareva. Volodimir Bondartsev. Jason Bone. Robyn Bonenkamp. Wayne Boness. Jean Boniface. Harry Bonifant. Pat Bon
Bonis. Karen Bonisch. Marlene Bonner. Andrew Bonnor. Jo Boocock. Max Booker. Mark Boomer. Karl Boomsma. Jo Booth. Peter Booth. John Booth. Barry Boothby. Ken Boothroyd. Steve Borcherding. Rebeca Borger. Helena Borisyuk. Maurice Borla
Boros. Shane Borrell. Peter Charles Borrie. Ashlea Borst. Wayne Borst. James Boschma. Marty Bothmann. Murray Bott. Daryl Botting. Jono Botting. Stephen Botting. Jane Bougen. Scott Bougen. Gloria Boult. James Bourke. Ryan Bourke. Duncan
Andew Boustridge. Jason Bovey. Grant Bowd. Roger Bowden. John Bowditch. Glenn Bowditch. Lyndal Bowen. Paul Bowen. Maurice Bowen. Tom Bowen. Gareth Bowen. Cameron Bowen. Sue Bower. Jeff Bower. Johnnie Bowers. Dinah Bowie. Steve I
Brooke Bowmar. Keith Bowness. James Boyce. Steve Boyce. Bwana Boyce. Paul Boyce. Nigel Boyce. Quintin Boyd. Lyn Boyd. Melany Boyden. Tim Boyer. Mark Boykin. Jonathon Boyle. Ann Boyle. Jo Brabyn. Julian Bracegirdle. Ross Brackebu
Brackenbury. Paul Bradbury. Matthew Bradbury. Steve Bradbury. Phil Bradfield. Tane Bradley. Tracey Bradley. Patrick Bradley. Robert Bradley. Josh Bradnock. Mike Bradnock. Rena Bradshaw. Diane Bradstreet. Theresa Brady. Brian Brady. Aaron Brad
Brady. Kara Braggins. David Brailsford. Craig Brain. Trev Brain. Tony Brake. Graeme Brake. Noel Brake. Shannon Brake. Paul Brake. Steve Bramley. Lance Bramley. Dakin Bramwell. Jerry Brandford. Christopher Brankin. Robbie Brannen. Andrew
David E Branson. Dene Branthwaite. J.Robert Brash. Jane Brash. Gwen Brasington. Jerry Braven. David Bray. Helen Bray. Donald Bray. Phillip Bray. John Brazao. Dave Breach. Alexander Breading. Stephen Breakwell. Graeme Brear. Quentin Barne
Kathleen Brebner. Trevor Breen. Mike Breen. Sarah Bregmen. Blair Bregmen. George Bremner. Jacqui Bremner. Annabelle Bremner. Nic Bremner. Warwick Bremner. Roy Brenchley. Mike Brennan. Dean Brenssell. Megan Brett. Phillip Brett. Bill Brewer.
Brewer. Alec Brewis. Aaron Brewis. Aleksej Brezhnev. Jamie Brice. Digby Brice. Susanna Brice. Kurt Brice. Dan Brice. Sean Aka Shamus Brickland. Garrick Bridges. Lucy Bridgman. Peter Bridson. Stuart Bridson. Lyn Bridson. Justin Brien. Mike Briggs.
Brighouse. Danny Bright. Adam Bright. Andrew Bright. Anthony Bright. Jo Brightwell. Rachelle Brightwell. John Brimble. Ollie Brind. Carl Brininstool. David Briscoe. Wade Briscoe. Andy Brittain. Karen Broad. Alex Broad. Michael Broad. Rachael Bro
William John Broadley. Matthew Broadmore. Flynn Brock. Kaylene Brock. Sarah Brock. Erin Brock. Jamie Brocklehurst. Tahl Brodie. James Brogan. Paul Brogden. Alex Bromham. Josh Bromilow. Damien Bromwich. Andy Brooke. Andrew Brook
Brooker. Martin Brookes. Caro Brooking. Nyall Brookland. Tom Brookman. Dean Brooks. Greg Brooks. Gary Brooks. Sarah Brooks. Rex Broomhall. Gene Broomhall. Erica Brophy. Marty Brophy. Deryn Brophy. Vaughn Brophy. Darren Brothwell. Hilton
Jessica Brough. Tom Brough. Judah Broughton. Jane Broughton. Steve Broughton. Josh Broughton. Kim Broughton. Ron Brouwer. Gary Brown. Fletcher Brown. Tim Brown. Ken Brown. Kane Brown. Steve Brown. Cathy Brown. Grant Brown. Natash
Andrew Brown. Kerryn Brown. Terry Brown. Craig Brown. Joseph Brown. Mitch Brown. Billy Brown. William Brown. Terence Brown. Ian Brown. Collins Brown. Ossie Brown. Duncan Brown. Nathan Brown. Chris Brown. Neil Brown. Pete Brown. Adriar
Peter Brown. Robin Brown. Antony Brown. Travis Brown. Graeme Brown. Greg Brown. Ricky Brown. Dale Brown. Evan Brown. Rory Brown. Cole Brown. Justin Brown. Noel Brown. Regan Brown. Alan Browne. Ross Browne. Jeff Browne. Noel Brow
Browne. Nigel Brownie. Michael Browning. Richard Brownlee. Lisa Brownless. Tom Brownlie. Bryan Brownlie. Jason Bruce. Shaughan Bruce. Matt Bruce. Allan Bruce. Callum Bruce. Bevan Bruce. Scott Bruce. John Bruce. Michael Bruce. Darrin Bruc
Bruhns. Col Brumley. Barry Brungar. John Brunsden. Brendon Brunt. Jonathan Brunton. Leonie Brunton. Jennie Brunton. Grant Brunton. Josh Bruton. Thomas Bruun. Colin Bryan. Karl Bryant. Hamish Bryant. Malcolm Bryant. Barry Bryant. Nina
Aimee Bryce. Graeme Bryce. Andrew Brydon. Kevin Bryson. Rob Bryson. Carey Bryson. Andrew Buchanan. Ian Buchanan. Mike Buchanan. Simon Buchanan. Geoff Buchanan. Mark Buchanan. Rob Buck. Allan Buck. Cliff Buckeridge. Shorty Buck
Kate Buckingham. David Buckley. Mike Buckley. Jenny Buckley. Isaac Buckman. Garry Buckman. Delwyn Buckton. Natali Budanov. Simon Budd. Mike Budd. Connor Budge. Scott Budge. Irina Budko. Vladimir Budko. Ivan Bugakov. Menahem Bul
Buick. Ed Buie. Ali Buist. Arnel Bulanhagui. Egor Bulatov. Merrick Bull. Jamie Bull. Brendan Bulliff. Kit Bullivant. Lindsay Bullivant. Jeremy Bullock. John Bullock. Tim Buma. Rodney Bungard. Lewis Bunker. Clayton Bunker. Curtis Bunker. Bill Bur
Bunting. Aleksandr Burakov. Mike Burbank-Clayton. Kris Burbery. Fred Burd. Anne Burdon. Barry Burger. Andrew Burgess. Simon Burgess. Sandi Burgess. Kevin Burgess. Dave Burgess. Robyn Burgess. Bryce Burgess. Gerald Burgess. Kay Burges
Burke. Olly Burke. Richard Burke. Rachel Burke. Cameron Burke. Liz Burke. Mike Burkett. Rex Burkin. Danny Burn. Sue Burn. James Burnby. Grant Burnett. Michael Burnett. Kathee Burnett. Steve Burnett. Trish Burnette. John Burnip. Angela Burr
Burr. Paul Burrell. Rob Burrows. Rebbecca Burrows. Storm Burrows. Wayne Burrows. Nigel Burson. Ashley Burt. Roger Burt. Karl Burt. F.M. Burt. Anton Burtina. Steve Burton. Warwick Burton. Garry Burton. Gregory Gordon Burton. Maria Burton. Jo
Burtt. Lynda Burtt. Stephanie Bury. Teresa Bury. Robert Bury. Thomas Busch. Rodger Buschl. Robin Bush. Christian Busse. Tim Bustard. Ken Butcher. Michael Butcher. Wayne Butcher. Tim Butcher. Maree Butcher. Les Butchers. Mark Butler. Pete
Graeme Butler. Tracey Butler. Natalie Butler. Daniel Butler. Maurice Butler. Katrina Butler. Ian Butler. Anne Butler. Matthew Butler. Charly Butler. David Butter. Paul Butterfield. Keith Butters. Brian Butterworth. Brian Butts. Jake Butts. Ivan Byko
Byrd. Barry Byres. Damian Byrne. Richard Byrne. Michael Byrne. Adela Byrski. Michael Cable. Jowell Cabrera. Duncan Cachemaille-Bayne. Andrew Cade. Dennis Cadigan. Wendy Cadigan. Leonie Cadman. Lucy Cahill. Anthony Cahill. Logan Cai. Ste
Darla Cain. Laurie Cain. Hamish Caird. Richard Caird. Hayden Cairncross. Christine Cairns. Liz Cairns. Josh Cairns. Mark Cairns. Jim Cairns-Nelson. Allenia Calder. Jason Calder. Ali Calder. Lindsay Caldwell. Rebekah Caldwell. Brad Caldwell. Brian C
David Caldwell. Mark Caldwell. Daryl Callaghan. Gavin Callaghan. Callie Callahan. Paul Callinan. Rod Calver. Jeremy Cameron. Zane Cameron. Paul Cameron. Jason Cameron. Lindsey Cameron. Murray Cameron. Stephen Cameron. Sam Camero
Cammock. Christopher Campagna. Alan Campbell. Aaron Campbell. Ricky Campbell. Anthony Campbell. Eleanor Campbell. Grant Campbell. Ewan Campbell. Todd Campbell. Andrew Campbell. Gareth Campbell. Cody Campbell. Mark Campbe
Campbell. Allen Campbell. Jo Campbell. Byron Campbell. Brian Campbell. Greg Campbell. John Campbell. Ross Campbell. Peter Campbell. George Campbell. Simon Campbell. Christine Candy. Lyn Candy. Allan Candy. Scott Candy. Andy Cane. Ron C
Kevin Cannell. Bob Cannell. Corin Canning. Peter Cantrick. Jacob Capper. Stephen Carbines. Chris Cardno. Craig Carey. Jamie (Mountainman) Carle. Paul Carline. Josh Carlson. Brett Carlyle. Ryan Carlyle. Wayne Carmichael. Shane Carnie. Max Ca
Ian Carppe. Mike Carr. Catherine Carr. Rodger Carr. Mitch Carr. Steve Carr. Noeline Carran. Natalie Carran. Andy Carrie. Ben Carrington. George Carrington. Sandra Carrington. Boyd Carroll. Shane Carroll. Stephanie Carroll. Glenn Carroll. Robyn Car
Mark Carruthers. Chris Carson. Bill Carson. Hamish Carswell. Brent Carswell. Jane Carter. Chris Carter. Neil Carter. Rodney Carter. Gabriel Carter. Greg Carter. Travis Carter. Marc Carter. Gordon Carter. Simon Carter. Reuben Carter. Karen Carter.
Cartman. Josh Cartwright. Darwin Cary. Martin Caseley. Victoria Caseley. Colin Caskey. Roxanne And Dean Caskey. Kelly Cassin. Nicole Castle. Liz Castle. Red Castro. Steve Caswell. Doug Catherman. Gavin Cattermole. Merril Catto. Todd Cavanag
Cavanagh. Chris Cave. Will Cawkwell. Andrew Cawood. Mark Caywood. Daniel Chadwick. Richard Chalecki. Ross Challies. Hayden Chalmers. Peter Chalmers. Kent Chalmers. Craig Chalmers. Kevin Chalmers. Alastair Chalmers. William Chaloner.
Chamberlain. Bruce Chamberlain. Pete Chamberlain. Sue Chamberlain. Matthew Chamberlain. Trevor Chambers. Johnny Chambers. Davinia Chambers. Jan Chammen. Phil Champion. Lissa Chandler. Wayne Chandler. Simon Channing. Jason Cha
Chaplin. Mike Chapman. Frank Chapman. Peter Chapman. Wayne Chapman. Nigel Chapman. Glen Chapman. Lloyd Chapman. James Chapman. Richard Chapman. Warren Chappell. Gill Charlick. Max Charlton. Joel Charlton. Doug Charmley. Bruce Cl
John Charpentier. S Chatterjee. Patrick John Chave. Sergey Chayka. Al Check. Mark Cheesman. Paul Cheetham. Bart Cheetham. Marie Chegar. Anatoliy Chekmarev. Maxim Cheremnykh. Evgeniy Chernetskyy. Robinson Cheryl. Jenny Chesterman.
Cheyne. Daniel Chick. Stephen Chickonoski. Nik Chiew. Michail Chikmarev. Rick Chilcott. Heather Child. Mike Child. Ricky Childs. Alan Chilton. Dave Chilton. Andrew Chinn. Henry Chiong. Irina Chirik. Andrew Chisholm. Aaron Chisholm. Karl Cl
Mark Chittick. Lyn Chittock. Justin Chittock. Joshua Chrisohoou. Tony Christensen. Jason Christensen. Karl Christensen. Bonnie Christey. Nathan Christian. Spencer Christiansen. Jay Christie. Dave Christie. Cathryn Christie. Matt Christie. Lee C
Mark (Chook) Christieson. Laurence Christini. Hira Christy. Mike Christy. Clark Chrystal. Andre Chudzik. Brendon Church. Brian Churchouse. Roy Claassen. Tony Clapperton. Sam Clark. Robert Clark. John Clark. Ian Clark. Raewyn Clark. David Clark
Clark. Suzanne Clark. Alice Clark. Andy Clark. Craig Clark. Chris Clark. Kevin Clark. Kara-Lee Clark. Estelle Clark. Adam Clark. Matt Clark. Rob (Weta) Clark. Garry Clark. Blair Clark. Roger Clarke. Jeff Clarke. Susan Clarke. Sam Clarke. Greg Clarke.
Clarke. Josh Clarke. Ken Clarke. Helen Clarke. Jason Clarke. Ben Clarke. Anna Clarke. Wayne Clarke. John Clarke. Gary Clarke. Gavin Clarke. Bruce Clarkson. Sarah Clarkson. Greg Clarkson. Cathy Clarkson. Rebecca Clay. Jan Clayton. Lois Clayton. Bill C
Adrian Clayton. Katrina Clayton. Simon Cleary. Shane Cleary. Garry Cleave. Owen Clegg. Alasdair Cleland. Adrienne Cleland. Andy Cleland. Jared Clement. Paul Clement. Maria Clement. Kerran Clements. Sam Clements-Stewart. Jason Clemett
Cleverley. Derek Clifford. Glenn Climo. Daniel Climo. Neville Climo. Mick Climpson. Blake Clinch. Paul Clinker. Jerry Cloninger. Geoff Close. Bill Clough. Deborah Clough. Jane Clouston. Ian Clow. Jonathan Clow. Richard Clucas. Mike Clucas. Barr
Callum Coates. Ted Coats. Rob Coats. Pam Cobb. William Cobham. Graeme Coburn. Alan Coburn. Paul Cochran. Adam Cochrane. Chris Cochrane. Frank Cochrane. Bruce Cochrane. Mitchell Cochrane. Lawrence Cocker. Michael Codd. Alan Codc
Brendan Coe. Barry Coe. Mark Coetzee. Flip Coetzer. Trish Coggan. Benjamin Colbert. Doug Cole. John Cole. Peter Cole. David Cole. Karen Cole. Mark Cole. John Coleman. Jeremy Coleman. Maureen Coleman. Khan Coleman. Mrs Wesley Colema
Coleman. Ric Coleman. Brian Coleman. Philip Coles. Ethan Coles. Brian Coley. Adam Coley. Carl Coley. Chris Coll. John Coll. Grant Colledge. Dick Collett. Mathew Collett. Ross Collier. Matt Colling. Graeme Collinge. Andrea Collings. Brett Collin
Collins. Brenda Collins. Brad Collins. Michael Collins. Todd Collins. Stephen Collins. Simon Collins. Alan Collins. Sonny Collins. Chris Collins. Pat Collins. Dean Collins. Brian Collins. Brady Collinson. Emily Collis. Tony Collis. John Colmer. Murray
David Colville. David Comber. Rodney Comer. Fiona Comer. Paul Comeskey. Loyal Comins. Matt Compton. Pat Conard. Paula Conder. Scott Conder. Lee Coneglan. Gay Congdon. Phil Conlan. Vicki Conlan. Kylie Connell. Pat Connell. Clare Connol
Connor. Stuart Connor. Glenn Connor. Pete Connor. Brian Connors. Richard Conolly. Deanne Conroy. Nicola Conroy. Tom Considine. Glen Constable. Coral Conway. Natasha Coogan. Mark Cook. Stuart Cook. Chris Cook. Adrian Cook. Dale Cook. Joh
Andrew Cook. Bill Cook. Brendon Cook. Helen Cook. Malcolm Cooke. Danielle Cooke. Marlene Cooksey. Marcus Cooksley. Craig Cookson. Garth Coombe. Andrew Coombe. Steve Coombes. Dave Cooney. Mike Cooney. Daniel Coop. Dan Coope. Nigel
Hugh Cooper. Demi Cooper. Peter Cooper. Tony Cooper. Stafford Cooper. Nathan Cooper. Matt Cooper. Sam Cooper. Anton Cooper. Andy Cooper. Lance Cooper. Raewyn Cooper. Fraser Cooper. Lamorna Cooper. Darryl Cooper. Ray Cooper. Chris Coo
Coote. Chris Copeland. Keith Copland. Brad Coppock. Ben Copson. Rodney Corbett. Greg Corbett. Lawrence Corbett. Nathan Corbett. Suzie Corboy. Daniel Corbtt. Rob Corden. Steven Cording. Mark Cordy. Rob Corkill. Jimmy Corkran. Daniel Cornege.
Cornelissen. Phil Cornelius. Andrew Corner. Sam Corney. Jonathan Corr. Benjamin Corrigan. Josh Corrigan. Brian Cossar. Daryl Costar. Nigel Coster. Kerry Costley. Vern Cotter. Larry Cotter. Jeremy Cotter. Paddy Cotter. Linda Cottle. Craig Cottr
Coubray. Bob Couch. Linda Couchman. Stewart Couchman. Aaron Couchman. Andrea Couldrey. Braden Coulter. Ben Coulter. Grant Coulter. Des Coulter. Henry Coulter. Hamish Coulter. Matt Counihan. Martin Coup. Diana Couper. Jayde Couper.
Court. Mason Court. Janet Court. Matthew Courtis. Michael-Brian Courtney. Kelly Courtney-Smith. Andrew Cousins. Bruce Cousins. Rachael Cousins. Aaron Couvee. Stephen Covell. Russell Coventry. Kyla Cover. Scott Cowan. Blair Cowan. Alex Cowa
Cowan. Andy Cowan. Darrell Cowan. Wayne Cowan. Louise Cowan. Hunter Cowan. Peter Cowdell. Dean Cowell. Mark Cowen. Steven Cowie. Ron Cowles. Damian Cowley. Elliot Cowley. Chris Cox. John Cox. Ian Cox. Paul Cox. Lionel Cox. Wayne Cox
Cox. Alan Cox. Brian Cox. Jeremy Cox. William Cox. Paula Coxhead. Linda Coxson. Arthur Cozens. Richard Crabb. Mitchell Crafar. Sarah Craig. Giles Craig. Geoff and Katey Craig. Al Craig. Jordan Craig. Mark Craig. Martin Cramp. Neil Cran. Murray
Jason Crane. Shayne Cranfield. Colin Crann. Vera Craven. Dusty Craven. Rodney Crawford. Jason Crawford. Andy Crawford. Bill Crawford. Loncey Crawford. Bob Crawford. Mikaire Crawford. Donald Crawford. Warren Crawley. Jody Creane. Den
Michael Creed. Cathy Cresswell. Terry Crichton. Mike Crichton. John Crichton. Robbie Crickett. Alisha Crighton. Nico Cripps. Ian Critchell. Tony Crnjac. Brent Croad. Linzi Crocker. Paul Crocker. Zane Crofskey. Ian Croft. Sam Crombie. Andrew Crom
Crompton. Jordan Cronin. Matthew Crook. Jonathan Crook. Simon Crook. Peter Crook. Alan Cropp. Lyn Cropp. Jake Crosby. Sean Crosby. Phillip Crosland. Mark Crosland. Ben Cross. Tony Cross. Cameron Cross. Joe Cross. Thomas Crosse. Mark Cross
Crossland. David Crosswell. Jason Crowe. Colin Crowe. Simon Crowe. Ian Crowle. Matthew Crowther. Kitty Croxson. Guy Cruickshank. Bob Cruickshank. Timothy Cruickshank. Clifton Crump. Graeme Crutchley. Lyndon Cuaresma. Lisa Cubitt. Maree
Jordon Cudmore. Johnny Cullen. David Cullen. Warner Cullen. Blair Culling. Allan Culpan. Peter Cumming. Anne Cumming. Ian Cumming. Kathy Cummings. Larry (Bant) Cummings. Jock Cummings. Chris Cummins. Dion Cunnigham. Neville Cunni
Steve Cunningham. Sam Cunningham. Hugh Cunningham. Sally Jo Cunningham. Lois Curd. Greg Curd. Carlton Currie. Bob Currie. Joe Currie. Warner Currie. Grant Currie. Kevin Curtin. Paddy Curtin. Michael Curtis. Tom Curtis. Dean Curtis. Steven C
Gary Cuthbert. Craig Cuthbert. Charlie Cuthbertson. Steve Cutler. Chris Cuttance. Peter Cutten. Vanessa Cvitanovich. Luciana Da Silva. Karina Dã¸Lerud. Kyle Dackers. Lisa Daglish. Leon Dale. Kris Dale. John Dale. Cameron Dallas. Melissa Dalla
Dallas. Martin Dalley. Ryan Dalley. Laura Dalley. Pania Dalley. Thomas Dalley. Bridget Dallinger. Logan James Dally. Myles Dally. Josh Daly. Damian Daly. Vince Daly. Katarina Daly. Luke Daly. Tad Daly. Bruce Dalzell. Xavier Dalziel. Jeremy Damgaar
Dampier-Crossley. Marcus Damsteegt. Martin Dance. Rance Danell. Marella Dangen. Boustridge Daniel. D'Ostilio Daniel. Roy Daniel. Michael Danks. Brett Dann. Roman Danshin. Dianne Darbyshire. David Darker. Simon Darling. Greg Daulto
Daumann. Levi Davey. Callum Davey. Brian Davey. Beau Davidson. Anthony Davidson. Adam Davidson. Jill Davidson. Chris Davidson. Lisa Davidson. Lorraine Davidson. Donald Davidson. Bevan Davidson. Jim Davidson. Kelly Davidson. Robin Dav
Davie. John Davie. Grant Davie. Elizabeth Davie-Martin. Jewel Davies. Craig Davies. Bill Davies. Mitch Davies. Thomas Davies. Steve Davies. Mark Davies. Joe Davies. Simon Davies. Jesse Davies. Alan Davies. Gareth Davies. Benjamin Davis. Sara Da
Davis. Eugene Davis. Mark Davis. Danny Davis. Andy Davis. Brodie Davis. Scott Davis. Jamie Davis. Stuart Davison. Emma Davison. Grace Davison. Warrick Davison. Sandy Davison. Greg Dawber. Martyn Dawes. Phil Dawson. Charlie Dawson. Paul D
Daniel Dawson. Lindsay Dawson. Sara Dawson. Julie Dawson. Neville Day. Damian Day. Howard Day. Brandon Day. Paul Daysh. Mike Daysht. Tony De Cent. Mineek De Crom. John De Denne. Eric De Graaf. Richard De Graaf. Colin De Jager. Luis F De
Remco De Ket. Suzy De Lange. Hamish De Pass. Denis De Pass. Mike De Ruyter. Kasper De Schepper. Tony De Vorms. Joel De Vries. Ben De Vries. Sarah De Vries. Jason De Vries. Luke Deadman. Michael Deadman. John Deadman. Bryce Deal. Robi
Grant Dean. Kathryn Dean. Calum Dean. Logan Dean. Rod Dean. Linda Deane. Marty Deans. Vaughan Dearlove. Glenn Debenham. Zach Decker. Paul Dee. Peter Dee. Cliff Deery. Steve Deihl. Leo Dekker. Bughaw Cielo Dela Concepcion. Peter Delamar
Delaney. Grant Delaney. Eric Delfosse. Frans Dellebeke. Matt Dellit. Simon Demaine. Jennysic Demolo. John Dempsey. Mark Dempsey. Richie Dempster. Scott Dempster. Stephen Demuth. Johnny Dench. Roy Dench. Charles Austin Denherder. Chris De
James Denholm. Alex Denholm. Jim Denholm. Newton Denise. John Denize. Michael Dennis. Nick Dennis. Kaye Dennison. Troy Dennison. Louise Denny. Kristina Dent. Mark Denton. Jo Denton. Murray Denton-Giles. Erik Dermois. Sergio Deschamps
Deseymour. Andrew Desira. Maria Deutsch. Maurice Devane. Niranjan Devaraj. Tony Devcich. Sam Devere. Bruce Deverell. Bex Deverell. Richard Devine. Conor Devoy. Olga Devyatka. Doug Dew. David Dew. Keryn Dewar. Les Dewhurst. Jo Di Leva.
Leva. Lisa Diack. Adam Diamond. Trevor Dick. Shayne Dick. Brion Dickens. Maree Dickey. Russell Dickey. J Dickie. Kane Dickie. Tyler Dickison. Denis Dickov. Ross Dickson. Rod Dickson. Ryan Dickson. Jane Dickson. Rhonda Dickson. Guy Didsbur
Digby. Brendon Digby-Smith. Wayne Dil. Peter Dilks. Chris Dillon. Justine Dillon. Brian Dimbleby. Steven Dimitrakellis. Iain Dimmock. Ellen Dinatale. Brian Dineen. Rob Dines. Iain Dines. Mark Dingle. Hendrik Dinkelaar. Mark Dinniss. Carl Dinnisse
Dinnissen. Erin Discombe. Ross Ditmer. Darren Diver. Marion-Moana Dix. Peter Dix. Sue Dixon. Lawrence Dixon. Sherridan Dixon. Matthew Dixon. Nigel Dixon. Peter Dixon. Robyn Dixon. Bronwyn Dixon. Mbuyazwe Dlamini. Peter Dobbie. Gar
Dobbs. Hayden Dobbs. Allan Dobbs. Mark Dobson. Shane Docherty. David Dockerty. Brian Patrick Dockery. Mervyn Dodd. Hayden Dodds. Richard Dods. Mark Dods. Norm Doebel. Sean Doherty. David Doherty. Kevin and Alison Doig. Julia Doman
Maren Domke. Mike Don. Christopher Donahue. Simon Donald. Will Donald. Sam Donald. Sasha Donald. Andrew Donald. Ben Donaldson. Nigel Donaldson. Rebecca Dondertman. Michael Donehue. Andrew Donghi. Mark Donnelly. Dave Donnell
Donnelly. Kathryn Donoghue. Annabel Donovan. Matthew Doonan. Phil Dooney. David Dooney. Clinton Doran. Stephen Doran. Scott Dormer. Selwyn Dorward. Iona Double. Jay Dougherty. John Dougherty. Paul Doughty. Greg Douglas. Michael D
Malc Douglas. Ruth Douglas. Ron Douglas. Laura Douglas. Leonie Douglas. Dan Douglass. Ron Dow. Jonathon Dowd. Bryan Dowdle. Sean Dowdle. Rob Dowdle. John Dower. Kevin Down. Bruce Downes. Jenna Downes. Andrew Downey. Glen D

Downs. Colin Downs. Alan Doy. Rob Doyle. Rob Dragten. Robert Drain. Eugene Drake. Dawn Drake. Deidrye Drake. Richard Draper. Ryan Drew. David Dreyer. Paul Driver. Simon Drought. Carl Drumm. Aaron Drumm. Shirley Drummond. Debby
nd. Andrew Drummond. Nigel Drummond. Mark Drummond. Amy Drysdale. Elena Dubina. Anna Dubinina. Bronwyn Dudin. Craig Duff. Bernie Duff. Bernice Duff. Dylan Duffy. Natalie Duggan. Nick Duggan. Thomas Duggan. Andy Duligall. Andrew
Marie Duncan. Darryl Duncan. James Duncan. Kelley Duncan. Kaye Duncan. Bryan Duncan. Phil Duncan. Sam Duncan. Carolyn Dundass. Susan Dungey. Steven Dunham. Hamish Dunlop. Roger Dunn. Baz Dunne. James Dunning. Ian Dunning.
unsmore. Phil Durham. Mark Durkin. Andy Durling. Matt Durning. William Durning. Philippa Durrant. Stuart Dusevich. James Duthie. Louise Duthie. Roger Duxfield. Gwen Dwane. Julie Dwyer. James Dwyer. Robert Dyer. Kevin Dyke. Warren Dykes.
kzeul. Bryan Dynes. Jeremy Dyson. Josh Dyson. Steven E Joux. Hadyn Eade. Keith Eades. Geoff Eagle. Mike Eagle. Kirsty Eales. Hayden Eales. Lea Earl. Murray Earwaker. Ben Eason. Matt East. Paul East. Peter East. Brian Eastham. Kathryne Easton.
aston. Gayle Easton. Dave Eastwood. Dave Eaton. Matt Eaton. David Eaton. Lindsay Eaton. Benjamin Eatwell. Matt Ebbett. Adele Ebbett. Craig Ebbett. David Eckhoff. Phil Eddie. Craig Eddie. Julian Ede. Toby Eden. Tim Eden. Lynda Eden. Donna
a Eden. Frederick Eder. Felix Edgar. John Edgar. Keith Edgar. Steven Edkins. Paul Edkins. Selena Edlington. Chris Edmeades. Virunurm Edmond. Amber Edmonds. Jae Edmonds. Dave Edmonds. David Edmonds. Michael Edmondston. Ruth Margaret
. Phil Edwards. Jon Edwards. Bonnie Edwards. John Edwards. Caroline Edwards. Bevan Edwards. Gareth Edwards. Dale Edwards. Daniel Edwards. Rob Edwards. Stu (Festas) Edwards. Shane Edwards. Fletcher Edwards. Sergei Efremov. Carl Egan.
n. Margaret Egan. Barry Egerton. Bruce Eglinton. Alyona Egorovtseva. Debra Ehrlich. Alex Einam. Kerry Einam. Jason Eising. Bjorn Ekvall. Raed El Sarraf. Rodney Elder. Garry Ellem. Chris Ellicott. Lynne Ellingham. Mike Elliot. Rebecca Elliott.
iott. Jeremy Elliott. Brett Elliott. Mark Elliott. Craig Elliott. Ross Elliott. Jenny Elliott. David Elliott. John Ellis. Tim Ellis. Simon Ellis. Rhys Ellis. Kelly Ellis. Jared Ellis. Chris Ellwood. Paul Elstone. Phil Elworthy. Christer Emanuelsson. Kaye Emeny
rson. George Emmanouil. Stephen Emmerson. David Emmett. Chris Emmott. Joe Empson. Shane Emslie. Helen Emson. Edward Enersen. Fredrik Engqvist. Russell Ennis. John Ennis. Freddie Enslin. Terry Entwisle. Olga Eremenko. Conrad Ericksen.
ckson. Egan Erickson. Mikael Eriksson. Paul Erixon. Vitaliy Ermachkov. Darren Erni. Tim Errington. Guy Errington. Alex Ertl. Viktor Esadze. Neil Esler. Doug Espin. Joe Estermann. Walter Estermann. Mark Eston. Glen Etherington. Peter Evans.
vans. Daniel Evans. Dean Evans. Gertty Evans. Phil Evans. Sally Evans. Brock Evans. Kevin Evans. Janet Evans. Scott Evans. Diane Evans. Mathew Evans. Savannah Evans. Mandy Evans. Glen Evans. Cydne Evans. Mike Evans. Andrew John Evans.
est. Sam Everett. Neil Everett. Jakob Everiss. Scott Everitt. Zaitsev Evgenii. Valyansky Evgeny. Peter Evison. Marcus Ewart. Carole Ewen. Courtney & Katherine Ewen. Dave Ewen. Andrew Ewen. Nick Ewen. Simon Ewen. Trevor Ewens. Pip Ewing.
xcell. Ann Eyes. Max Eyre. Robin Eyre. Mesina Fabish. Kseniya Fadina. Mike Fagan. Laurence Fagen. Cameron Fahey. Graham Fairbrother. Tony Fairweather. Chris Falconer. Blair Falconer. Anthony Falconer. Glen Falconer. Donna Falconer. Andrew
Roger Fannin. Sandra Fannin. Andrew Faram. Louise Farley. Susan Farley. Trevor Farmen. David Farmer. Duncan Farmer. Amerillis Farmer. Michael Farmer. Annemieke Farmilo. Joanne Farquhar. David Farrar. Richard Farrell. Andrew Farrell. Mark
manda Farrell. Michael Farrell. Shirley Farrier. Brian Farrow. Benjamin Fath. Raewyn Fattorini. Hannah Faulkner. Sheryl Faulkner. Neil Faulknor. Ian Fear. Shaun Fearn. Kevin Fearn. Chris Fearn. Cameron Feather. Grant Febery. George Fechney.
Fedotoiv. Anne Feetham. Wayne Feisst. Michael Fell. Marcus Fellerhoff. Brett Felton. Ken Fensom. Ben Fentiman. Shady Fenton. Brett Fenton. Dani Fenwick. Melissa Fergus. Carley Fergus. Stuart Fergus. Alexander Fergus. Jan Ferguson. Logan
. Liz Ferguson. Paul Ferguson. Tim Ferguson. Mark Ferguson. Anthony Ferguson. Ben Ferguson. Caroline Fergusson. Godfrey Fernandez. Fiona Ferrar. Corne Ferreira. Graeme Ferrier. Michael Ferrier. Lisa Ferris. Lloyd Ferris. Sarah Kate Ferry. Keith
stair Fetch. Tristam Fetch. Mike Fetrow. Pierre-Marie Feuille. Paul Feyen. Robin Field. Mikee Field. Lawrence Field. Nathan Field. Chris Field. Fiona Field. Brigitt Fielder. Jake Fiennes. Bryce Fieten. Tyler Fifield. Guil Figgins. Pavel Filatov. David File.
. Symon Filet. Damo Filtness. Tracy Finch. Robyn Findlay. Dave Finegan. Heather Finer. Gemma Finlay. Carl Finlay. Graham Finlay. Dave Finlay. Jacob Finlayson. Don Finlayson. Bruce Finn. Kev Finnerty. Ed Finney. Andrew Firmedow. Natalie
v. Lena Fischbach. Gendy Fishburn. Ray Fisher. Andrew Fisher. Naomi Fisher. Dave Fisher. Mark Fisher. Chris Fisher. Wendy Fisken. Richard Fissenden. Robert (Bobby) Fithian. Pat Fitzell. Karyn Fitzgerald. Jim Fitzgerald. Tony Fitzgerald. Craig
l. Neil Fitzgerald. Pam Fitzgerald. Mark Fitzgerald. Zachary Fitzgibbon. Christine Fitzpatrick. Rebecca Fiveash. Tom Flaherty. Mike Flaherty. Rob Flannery. Gerhard Flatz. Sarah Flavell. Lex Flay. Juergen Fleissner. Andy Fleming. Martin Fleming.
etcher. Gordon Fletcher. Glen Fletcher. Mark Fletcher. Bruce Flett. Cameron Fleury. Charlie Fleury. Clayton Flight. Julie Flint. Vivianne Flintoff. Richard Flisher. Daniel Flood. Nickel Flux. James Flynn. Ben Flynn. Kristoffer Fodnes. Mihaly Foldvari.
ley. Derrick Foley. Lynne Fookes. Jason Foord. Chris Foote. Peter Foote. Steve Foote. Jeremy Forbes. William Forbes. Pete Forbes. Richard Ford. Andy Ford. Stuart Ford. Nathan Ford. Kevin Ford. Tanya Ford. Matt Ford. David Ford. Louise Forde.
Forde. Lindsay Forrest. Reid Forrest. Simon Forrest. James Forrester. James Gordon Forster. Nicky Forsyth. Dion Forsyth Forsyth. Neal Forsyth. Dominique Fortis. Joern E. W. Fortun. Murray Forward. Nicole Foster. Adam Foster. Josh Foster. Kevin
argie Foster. Neville Foster. William Foster. Emma Foster-Smith. Dennis Fouhy. Mark Fouhy. I Foulkes. John Fournier. Margaret Fowell. Pete Fowke. Benjamin Fowler. Joy Fowlie. Damian Fox. Jamie Foxley. Rachael Foy. Ben Foy. Edwina Fr. Mark
atthew Francis. Malcolm Francis. Mike Francis. Bruce Francis. Raymond Francis. Red Frank. Hamish Franklin. Simon Franklin. Alison Franklin. Nick Franks. Keith Frankum. Carl Fransen. Tim Fransen. Kelly Fraser. Robbie Fraser. Nigel Fraser.
aser. Clifford Fraser. Duncan Fraser. Ross Fraser. Kevin Fraser. David Fraser. Richard Fraser. Jason Fraser. Kim Fraser. Sandy Fraser. Lindsay Fraser. Nathan Gordon Fraser. John Fraser. Alf Frater. Michael Frayne. Wayne Frazer. Stephen Frazerhurst.
lerick. Bede Fredericks. Aaron Fredericksen. Micheal Free. Robert Free. Jason Free. John Freeland. Will Freeland. Trevor Freeman. Mark Freeman. Phil Freeman. Peter Freeman. Marc Freeman. John Freeman. Kevin Freeman. Lars Freeman. Jenny
tle. Shane Freemantle. Richard French. Ian French. Cole Frew. Paul Frewin. Turi Fricker. Daniel Friedman. Terry Frisby. Greg Frisken. Michael Frith. Nikita Frolov. .Dan Fromings. Tim Frost. Dennis Frost. Bevan Frost. Bill Frost. Dani Frost. Daimon
ke Frost. John Fry. Rod Fry. Karen Fry. John Frye. Chris Fryer. Robbie Fryer. Tahi Fu. Hayden Fugle. Steve Full. Linda Fuller. Andrew Fuller. Angela Fuller. Brendon Fuller. Craig Fulton. Qaz Fun. Penny Furjes. Andy Furminger. Michael Furness. Irina
Anna Fussell. Steve Fyfe. Roger Fyfe. Grant Gaby. Neville Gadd. Ian Gage-Brown. Peter Gagin. Alex Gale. Graeme Gallagher. George Gallop. Dave Galloway. Douglas Galloway. Bruno Galloway. Vic Galpin. Graeme Galyer. Tony Gan. Geoff Gannon.
pper. Clinton Gapper. Ian Gardiner. Mike Gardiner. Caleb Gardner. Rhodri Gardner. James Gardner. Rick Gardner. Israel Gardner. Robb Gardner. Melanie Gardyne. Donna Gardyne. Kelsey Gare. Thomas Garforth. Orlov Igor Garik. Barry Garland.
Garland. John Garland. Davy Garland. Dave Garlick. Jean Garman. Harriet Garmonsway. Dave Garner. Mike Garner. Fran Garnett. Steve Garnett. Simon Garrett. Troy Garrett. Sandra Garrett. Paul Garrett. Phillipa Garrett. Brett Garrett. Phil Garrett.
ick. Jessie Garrick. Bill Garrow. Jim Garry. David Garth. Kevin Garthwaite. Ardern Gary. Lesley Gaskell. Peter Gaskin. Heather Gaskin. Esmira Gasymova. Amy Gatenb. John Gates. Peter Gatley. Jason Gaukrodger. John Gaukrodger. David Gaunt. Ben
. Nigel Gavin. Sergey Gavrilov. Gwen Gaw. Sam Gawith. Stephen Gawn. Malcolm Gawn. Jose L Gay-Cano. Aaron Gaye. Emma Gaze. Matthew Gaze. Ben Geaney. Gail Geard. Richard Geary. Bede Geary. Brian Geck. Corey Geddes. Alan Geddes. Greg
Patrick Gedye. Adrian Gee. Allen Geerkens. Oliver Geisler. Mark Gellatly. Myles Gembitsky. Grant Gemmell. Martin Genet. Golov Gennady. Aidan Gent. Georgia Gentle. Alan George. Steven George. Blair George. Brendan Gepert. Bruno Geraghty.
Gerbich. Holger Gerding. Chris Gerken. Peter And Barbara Gerrard. Adam Gerritsen. Greg Gianino. Nicholas Gibb. Trev Gibb. Jonathan Gibbard. Tolly Gibbons. Brendan Gibbs. Daryl Gibbs. Harvey Gibbs. Karl Gibbs. Morrin John Gibney. Mike
Peter Gibson. Josh Gibson. Dave Gibson. Bryan Gibson. Angus Gibson. Campbell Gibson. Charles Gibson. Hamiora Gibson. Doug Gibson. Murray Gibson. Andy Gifford. Mark Gifford. Carl Gihon. Greg Gilbert. Wayne Gilbert. Grant Gilbert. Malcolm
ohn Gilbert. Michael Gilbert. Brian Gilbert. Ian Gilbert. Sarah Gilbertson. Tim Gilbertson. Ray Gilbertson. Gavin Gilder. Mark Gill. James Gill. Dave Gill. Richard Gill. Brendon Gill. Jessie Gill. Scott Gillam. Benjamin Gilles. Jason Gillespie. Katherine
Nathan Gillespie. Neil Gillespie. Ben Gillespie. Malcolm Gillice. Simon Gillice. Megan Gillies. Gary Gilligan. Heather Gillilgan. Shilise Gillingham. Andrew Gillingwater. Zoe Gilmer. Andy Gilmore. Stuart Gilmour. Bruce Gilmour. Louis Gilmour. Ben
Gary Gilpin. Liz Giltrap. Richard Gimpel. Eric Gin. Chase Ginders. Gordon Girvan. David Given. Guy Glasgow. Matthew Glass. Zane Glass. Rowan Glass. Gordon Glass. Roy Glass. Mike Glasson. Jason Gledhill. Warwick Glendenning. Dion Glenie.
enn. Synnove Glesnes. Lindsay Glover. Carl Glover. Paul Glover. Phil Glover. Phillipa Glubb. Russell Glue. Ben Goad. John Goble. Grant Goddard. Mary-Anne Goddard. Steve Goddard. Allan Goddard. Jim Goddin. Wayne Godfrey. Lance Godfrey. Peter
Maree Godsiff. Lyall Goggin. Ben Gold. Samuel Gold. John Gold. Allan Gold. Tim Goldfinch. Jason Goldie. Craig Golding. James Golding. Ross Goldsack. Linda Goldsmith. Bridget Goldsmith. Edward Goldwater. Jo Golightly. Wayne Golightly. Rachel
Richard Gollan. Vladimir Golovatsky. Franco Gomboso. Miguel Gomez. Warren Good. Derrick Goodall. Cameron Goodchap. Guy Goodeve. Paul Goodeve. David Goodger. Abbie Goodin. Nathan Goodsill. Linda Goodwin. Kyle Goodwin. Jenny
ght. James Goodyer. Jason Goodyer. Allan Goodyer. Tania Goodyer. Jake Goonan. Andrew Gordanier. Alex Gordon. Hayley Gordon. Laurence Gordon. Jeff Gordon. John Gordon. Duncan Gordon. Daniel Gordon. Kerry Gordon. Carey Gordon. Faye
Murray Gordon. Kristin Gordon. Garry Gordon. Ben Gordon. Ross Gornall. Darren Gorrie. Aaron Gorrie. Harry Gorringe. Sid Gorton. Scott Gosnell. Steve Goss. Daniel Goss. Mark Goss. Matthew Goudie. Susan Goudswaard. Tony Gould. Allwyn
Roan Gouws. Geoff Gover. Natalie Gow. Daniel Gow. Margaret Gowans. Ange Gower. George Gower. Andy Gowring. Tony Graam. Eric Grace. Jonathan Gracie. Jonathan Gradwell. David Grafton. Wayne Grafton. Joelle Gragilla. Ronald Graham. Blair
Steve Graham. David Graham. Andrew Graham. Bruce Graham. Pauline Graham. Kevin Graham. Sharon Graham. John Graham. Rick Graham. Jason Graham. Joseph Graham. David Grain. Thomas Grainger. William Grainger. Mark Grainger. Simon
Rodney Grant. Bruce Grant. Daniel Grant. Robert Grant. Trevor Grant. Neil Grant. Eain Grant. Robert S Grant. Latoya Grant. Robin Grant. Matt Grantham. Scott Grasse. Carolyn Gratton. Dave Gratton. Andre Gratzer. Jason Gray. Ian Gray. John Gray.
Gray. Paul Gray. Jonny Gray. Vicky Gray. Andy Gray. Chris Gray. Noel Gray. David Gray. Katherine Gray. Mark Grayling. Marilyn Greaney. Chris Greaney. Kent Greatbatch. Amy Greaves. Oxana Grecina. Andrew Green. Jono Green. Mark Green. Ross
oug Green. Cody Green. Garry Green. Paul Green. Cory Green. Joshua Green. Jane Green. Joy Green. Cameron Greene. Paul Greenfield. Simon Greenfield. Sheryl Greenhalgh. Rod Greening. Craig Greenslade. Paul Greenslade. Murray Greenwood.
reenwood. Hayden Greenwood. James Greer. Karen Greer. Richard Greer. Steven Greer. Ricky Gregory. Julie Gregson. Joanna Greig. Robert Vincent Greig. Bruce Greig. Michael Greig. Kathy Greville. Lindy Grey. Jaz Gribble. Dave Grice. Anne Griffin.
iffin. Nigel Griffith. Kay Griffiths. Dan Griffiths. Daniel Griffiths. Rob Griffiths. Kathy Griffiths. John Griffiths. Arthur Grigg. Caleb Grimshaw. David Grimwood. Ryan Grindrod. Brett Grindrod. Tony Grinstead-Jones. Tony Groome. Stephen Groot.
Groot. Piet Groot. Halei Groshinski. Daman Groshsinski. Michael Groters. David Grove. Mark Grover. Dan Groves. Brent Growcott. Hayden Growden. Hadlee Grubb. Dave Gruppelaar. Kathy Gruschow. Alexander Gryazev. Elena Gryaznova. Peter
ruce Gudsell. Brian Guerin. Richard Guest. Nicole Guilbert. Jenny Guild. James Guilford. Graeme Guise. Owen Gullery. John Gummer. David Gumn. Scotty Gundesen. John Gunn. Matthew Gunningham. Steve Gurney. Logan Gurney. Mark Gurr. Dale
Julie Guttery. Karl Guy. Adieva Guzel. David Gwerder. Phil Gwynn. Matt Gyde. Sybe Haakma. Jessie Haanen. Ken Habgood. Peter Habraken. David Hack. Travis Hackbarth. Jay Hackett. Lachlan Haddon. Mark Hadley. John Hadlow. Ian Hagan. Horst
n. Jim Hagen. Kyle Hagen. Mark Hahn. Nikita Haitana. Sam Halberg. Ben Haldane. Steve Halden. Max Hale. David Hale. Bill Hales. Peter Halford. Miles Haliburton. Nick Hall. Warren Hall. Lisa Hall. Tazmin Hall. Stephanie Hall. Gareth Hall. Simon
yne Hall. Richard Hall. Nikki Hall. Alan Hall. Michael Hall. Graeme Hall. Mike Hall. Eric Hall. Trevor Hall. Lindsay Hall. Shane Hall. Marilyn Hall. Lisa-Marie Hallam. Brett Hallberg. Anita Hallberg. Michael Halleron. Graham Hallett. Allan Halley.
lgarth. Pete Halliwell. Stewart Halliwell. Kirsty Halliwell. Michael Hallows. Jack Halstead. Malcolm Halstead. Svetlana Halzova. Mike Hamblin. John Hamill. Karen Hamilton. Craig Hamilton. Ion Hamilton. David Hamilton. Scott Hamilton. Louise
n. Mark Hamilton. Duncan & Cherryl Hamilton. Ross Hamilton. David B Hamilton. Innis Hamilton. Andrea Hamilton. Cruise Hamilton. Bruce Hamlin. Kerry Hammersley. Robert Hammerton. Deena Hammond. Craig Hammond. Gordon Forde
nd. Nick Hammond. Paul Hammond. Jeff Hammond. Fraser Hammond. Don Hammond. Ross Hampson-Tindale. Philip Hampton. Blair Hampton. Catherine Hampton. Rachel Hampton. Robert Hancock. Rodger Hancock. Clinton Hancock. Peter
Gavin Hancox. Sean Handley. Ian Hankin. James Hanley. Terry Graeme Hanlon. Steve Hanlon. Nomi Hannah. Georgina Hannah. Mathew Hannah. Stephen Hannam. Paul Hannibal. Marcel Hannon. Damian Hanrahan. Nicola Hansen. Cherie Hansen.
Hansen. Soren Hansen. Sarah Hansen. Ian Hansen. Bill Hansen. Joe Hansen. Corran Hansen. Mal Hansen. Hayley Hansen. Murray Hansen. Matt Hansen. Louise Hansen. Wendy Hansen. Tom Hapi. Syedtariq Haq. Helen Harbutt-Watson. Dan
. Carla Harcourt. Paul Hardaker. Simon Hardgrave. Robert Hardgrave. Timothy Hardie. George Hardie. Grant Hardie. Brian Harding. Rick Harding. Dallas Hardison. Jehanne Hardwick-Lee. Brent Hardy. James Hardy. Kelsey Hare. Jonathan Hare. Tina
pe. Martin Harkness. Stephen Harland. Reuben Harland. John Harland. Peter Harling. Clive Harman. Kurt Harmer. Matthew Harnett. Neal Harold. Terry Harpe. Robbie Harper. Lachie Harper. Robyn Harper. Kerry Harper. Sharee Harper. Deane Harper.
Harper. Andrew Harper. Ben Harricks. Grant Harrington. Allan Harris. Dave Harris. Regan Harris. John Harris. Jenny Harris. Lee Harris. Alan Harris. Cory Harris. Chris Harris. Tim Harris. Grant Harris. Blair Harris. Lesley Harris. Peter Harris. Wayne
Mark Harris. Ayson Harris. Jan Harris. Donald Harris. Jolyon Harris. Graeme Harrison. Kevin Harrison. Richard Harrison. Julie Harrison. Susan Harrison. Caroline Harrison. Dene Harrison. Mark Harrison. Kenneth Harrison. William Harrison. Mike
. Paula Harrison-Luff. Mike Harron. David Harrow. Patrick Harsveldt. Gary Hart. Brett Hart. Levi Hart. Glenn Hart. Rod Hart. Tammy Hart. Michael Hart. Paul Hart. Colin Hart. Tim Harting. Jason Hartle. Wayne Hartley. Pernell Hartley. Gantt Hartley.
rtley. Luke Hartnell. Martha Hartwell. Blake Harty-Isaac. Tim Harvey. Grant Harvey. Brett Harvey. Michael Harvey. Carolyn Harvey. Bruce Harvey. Ross Harvey. Brenda Harvey. Mike Harvey. Owen Harvey. Sam Harvey. Scott Harvey. Steven Harvey.
Harvey14. Nick Harwood. James Haselden. Phillip Hasler. William Hasley. Allan Hassall. Debbie Hastie. Murray Hastie. Tony Hastings. Wayde Hastings. Paul Hatch. Paula Hateley. Gerald Hateley. Tom Hatfull. Adam Hatton. Mark Hattrill. Christopher
ugh. Andrew Haultain. John Haultain. Jack Hauschild. Billy Havens. Sonda Havens. Bernadette Havill. Josh Hawes. Ralph Hawke. Hamish Hawker. Gail Hawkes. Kenn Hawkes. Mark Hawkins. Reece Hawkins. Sam Hawkins. Odelle Hawkins. Craig
n. Marjorie Hawthorne. John Hay. Grant Hay. Veronica Hay. Ross Hay. Andrew Hay. Sonja Hay. Alan Haycock. Gavin Haycock. Glenn Hayes. Greg Hayes. Neil Hayes. Rowan Hayes. Russell Hayes. Jeremy Hayes. Trevor Hayes. David Hayes. William
Dennis Hayfield. Chris Hayles. Pete Haynes. Aaron Haynes. Dean Hays. Johanna Hayward. Joe Hayward. Keith Hayward. Dylan Hayward. Tony Hayward. Lily Hayward. D.O.B. 28Th April 1963.. Digby Haywood. Brad Hazeldine. Ashley Hazlitt. Vicky
. Yibai He. Damien Head. Greg Head. Seb Head. Josie Heale. Nikki Heale. Matt Healey. William Healey. Peter Healey. Ron Healey. Mark Healy. Ed Heap. Justine Heaphy. Stu Heaps. Sonjya Heaps. Darryl Heaps. Veronica & Dan Hearn. Simon Hearsey.
Hearty. Scott Heasley. Robert Heathcote. Michael Heaven. Ruth Heaven. Kate Hebblethwaite. Simon Heerink. John Hefford. Craig Hegan. Andrea Hegan. John Heikoop. Erin Heine. Amanda Heine. Jan Heinen. Nick Hekkens. Sheryl Hellyer. Ralph Hemi.
emi. Tony Hemingway. Claire Hemsley. Tim Hence. Fiona Henchman. Sue Henderson. David Henderson. Nick Henderson. Matt Henderson. Chris Henderson. Ross Henderson. Megan Henderson. Midge Henderson. Rick Henderson. Dave Henderson.
nderson. Jamie Henderson. Des Henderson. Fraser Henderson. Pamela Henderson. Peter Henderson. Ian Henderson. Tony Henderson. Paul Henderson. Patrick Henderson. Greg Henderson. Suzanne Hendra. Ian Hendren. Chelsea Hendrickson. Barrie
Trevor Hendry. Andrew Hendy. Catherine Hennig. Chris Henriksen. Claus Henriksen. Corrina Henry. David Henry. Kim Henson. Wayne Henwood. Willie Hepburn. Mark Hepburn. Matt Herbert. Gardner Herbert. Renee Heremaia. Ben Herlihy. Graeme
. Stephen Hermens. Ryk Hermsen. Heather Heron-Speirs. Luis Herrera. Lewis Herrick. Karen Herrick. Bill Herrick. Billie Herries. Dan Herries. Graham Herries. Markus Hertweck. Ryan Herzog. Keith Heselwood. Ben Heslop. Annette Hewetson. Snow
n. Robert Hewett. Michael Hewison. Murray Hewitson. Robin Hewitt. Thomas Hewitt. Debbie Hewitt. Craig Heyward. Jack Heyward. Brendan Hiatt. Kelly-Anne Hibbard. David Hickey. Spencer Hickford. Dave Hickin. Kevin Hickland. Simon
n. Paul Hickman. Stephen Hicks. Kirsten Hicks. David Hide. Philip Higgan. Al Higgens. Johnny Higgins. Tom Higgins. Lester D Higgins. Tony Higgins. Russell Higham. Dean Hiini. Marcus Hildreth. Paul Hilhorst. Mike Hilhorst. M Hilhorst. Bev Hill.
. Nick Hill. Gordon Hill. Tim Hill. Phil Hill. Tony Hill. Gavin Hill. Roger Hill. Kevin Hill. Gerard Hill. Greg Hill. Graham Hill. David Hill. Paul Hill. Michelle Hill. Bob Hill. Matt Hill. Cam Hill. Graeme Hill. Kathryn Hill. Brian Hills. Vicki Hills. Garry
Tahinganui Hina. Keith Hinch. Thomas Hinchliffe. Ted Hindes. Mark Hindmarch. Jon Hinds. Kirk Hine. Paula Hingley. Maurice Hinton. Max Hinton. Peter Hinton. Tim Hinton. Amelia Hinton. Tony Hinz. Robert John Hirschberg. Wayne Hirst. Richard
ris Hishon. Kevin Hislop. Craig Hitchcock. Kate Hitchen. Chris Hitchings. Sarah Hitchman. Ron Hixon. Dave Hoare. Phillip Hoare. Andy Hobbs. Michael Hobbs. Mike Hobbs. Jill Hobden. Mark Hodder. Nigel Hodge. Gerry Hodges. Bryan Hodges.
odges. Emma Hodges. Craig Hodgetts. John Hodgkinson. Simon Hodgkinson. Paddi Hodgkiss. Julie Hodgson. Alan Hodgson. Jeff Hodgson. Bill Hodgson. David Hodgson. Deklan Hodsell. Jane Hoedemaeckers. Paul Hoekstra. Tony Hogarth. Gavin
. Frits Hogewoning. Stephen Hogg. Barry Hogg. Len Hogg. Fayln Hoggard. Damelza Hohepa. Stephanie Hole. Kevin Hollamby. Robyn Hollamby. Sarah Holland. Tim Holland. Justin Holland. Rachel` Holland. Shaun Hollander. Nigel Hollands. Cade
. Leanne Hollever. Stu Holley. Tom Hollingworth. Brian Hollis. Ingrid Hollis. Stephen Hollis. Craig Hollis. Colin Holloway. Ron Holme. Stewart Holmes. Lachlan Holmes. Linda Holmes. Peter Holmes. Jonathan Holmes. Dion Holmes. Murray Holmes.
olmes. Bev Holmes. Allister Holmes. Kelly Holmes. Graham Holmes. Glen Holmwood. Trevor Holmwood. Andrew Holt. Mike Holt. David Homer. Mark Homer. Kaydis Hona. Wayne Honey. Martin And Kerry Honey. Lisa Honey. Tessa Honeyfield. Alan
eville & Liz Hood. Ken Hood. Bev Hoogeveen. Mark Hook. Anne Hooker. Geoff Hooker. Lynton Hooker. Trevor Hookway. Craig Hoole. Mark Hooper. Kevin Hooper. Matthew Hooper. Marianne Hoosier. Shawn Hooton. Gayle Hopcroft. Debbie Hope.
ope. Phil Hope. Amelia Hopkins. Matthew Hopkins. Tracey Hopkins. John Hopkins. Tim Hopkins. Kel Hopkins. James Hopkins. Colin Hopkins. Warwick Hopkins. Diane Hopkinson. Daniel Hopkirk. Timothy Hopley. Sam Hopper. Lindsay Hopping.
oran. Jeremy Hore. Brad Hore. Gary Hore. Greg Horler. Quintin Horler. Trevor Horn. Neil Horn. Geoff Hornblow. Ken Horne. Mark Horne. Colin Horne. Robyn Horne. Mike Horne. Christine Horrocks. Damon Horrocks. Lulu Horrocks. Myron Horsford.
Horstman. Andrew Horton. Joanne Hosie. Clay Hoskin. Mark Hotson. Jamie Hotton. Ross Houghton. Daniel Houghton. Jane Houghton. Angie Houkamau. Garry Houlahan. Michaela Houliston. Sheree Hourston. Daniel Houweling. Stanley William
ovell. Daniel Hovell. Dylan Hovelle. David Howard. Brent Howard. Manins Howard. Jackie Howard. Daniel Howard. Jessica Howard. Shirley Howard. Stephanie Howard. Andrew Howard. Scott Howatson. Jamie Howe. Sherryl Howe. George Howells.
vey. Ross Howie. Regan Howley. Louise Howse. Wayne Howser. Hans J. Hoyer. Craig Hoyes. Ray Hoyle. Ekaterina Huang. Richard Hubbard. Richard Scott Hubbard. Kristen Hubbard. Sarah Hucker. Rowan Huckstep. David Hudson. Nigel Hudson. James
. Peter Hughan. Gareth Hughes. Susan Hughes. Matthew Hughes. Graeme Hughes. Davey Hughes. Maggie Hughes. Darryl Hughes. Erica Hughes. Sonya Hughes. Rae Hughes. Helen Hughes. Diana Hughes. Rob Hughes. Van Der Werff Hugo. Daniel
anne Huitema. Mark Hulena. Christopher Hull. Andrew Hull. Vinnie Hullah. Deb Hume. Julian Hume. Bob Hume. Graham Hume. Don Humphrey. Peter Humphreys. Kane Humphreys. John Humphreys. Graeme Humphries. Neil Humphries. Bruce
ris. Andrew Hunger. Gary Hunn. Bernard Hunsche. Stephen Hunt. Josh Hunt. Nigel Hunt. Nicholas Hunt. Brad Hunt. Michael Hunt. Zack Hunt. Tony Hunt. Garry Hunt. Tim Hunt. Brendon Hunt. Bill Hunt. Linda Hunt. Ben Hunt. Rae Hunter. Paul
Glen Hunter. Neil Hunter. Keith Hunter. Anna Hunter. Ian Hunter. Stephen Hunter. Bryce Hunter. Colin Hunter. Tahu Huriwai. Trev Hurley. Mark Hurley. Struan Hurley. Ross Hurly. Anastacia Hurndell. Richard Hurrell. Josh Hurrell. Graeme Hurren.
rring. Malcolm Hurst. Michael Hurst. Karl Hurst. Allan & Margaret Mitchell Husband & Wife --Ardent Users Of Swazi. Adrienne Hussey. Daivd Hussey. Bevan Hussey. Simon Hustler. Ernst-Jan Hut. Denise Hutchings. Grant Hutchings. Tim Hutchings.
utchins. Bruce Hutchins. Mike Hutchins. Andrew Hutchinson. Scott Hutchison. Brian Hutton. Hamish Hutton. David Hutton. John Huwatscheck. Rowan Huxford. Carl Huxford. Dale Hyde. Greg Hyde. Carole Hylton. Lyn Hymers. Jake Hynd. Mark
n. Robert Hyslop. Wayne Hyslop. Tania Iddon. Mike Ide. Vitaly Ijoshkin. Sergey Ilenkov. John Illingworth. Scott Illingworth. Jimmy Illinworth. Wayne Imms. Nicholas Imrie. Ryan Ingham. Jamie Ingham. Peter Ingle. Barry Ingle. Kristene Ingle. Mike
Malcolm Inglis. Gordon Inglis. Charles Henry Ingram. Hayden Inkster. Udalaya Inna. Becky Innes. Dean Innis. Carla Innis. Robert Inwards. Pablo Ipince. Campbell Irons. Antony Irons. Terry Irvine. Mark Irvine. Julian Irvine. Vanessa Irvine. Matt Irving.
ving. Cassie Irving. Susan Isaac. Irina Isaeva. Dan Isbister. Adam Isle. Vera Ivanchenko. Nikita Ivanov. Raoul Jaccard. Shane Warren Jack. Chrystall Jack. Aaron Jack. Janene Jackson. Tim Jackson. Alan Jackson. Ncr Jackson. Steven Jackson. Karina
. Darryl Jackson. David Jackson. Mark Jackson. Faith Jackson. Grant Jackson. Leslie Nigel Jackson. Paul Jackson. Debbie Jackson. Deb Jackson. Bryce Jackson. Evan Jackson. Murray Jacob. Tom Jacobs. Stephen Jacobs. Josh Jacobsen. Per Jacobsen. Karl
van Jakes. Ben Jakschik. Drazen Jaksic. Natali Jakusheva. Rick James. Samuel James. Nic James. Luca James. Keriann James. Bronwyn James. Daryl James. Karen James. Wilson James. Andrew Jamieson. Gillian Jamieson. Ian Jamieson. Bob Jamieson.
mieson. Dave Jamieson. Rodger Jamieson. Rosie Jamieson. Kegg Swazi Jamison. Jeff Janes. Lars Jansen. Janine Janssen. Irvin Janssen. Janek Januszkiewicz. Kathy Jaques. Rodney Jarman. Scott Jarvie. Jay Jay Jaslarz. Mark Jeffares. Kori Jeffcoat. Paul
Taylor. Kurt Jefferies. John Jefferson. Jean-Michel Jefferson. Chris Jefferson. Franklin Jefferson. Patrick Jefferson. Stuart Jeffrey. Paul Jeffries. Edward Jeffries. Doug Jelley. Lynne Jelley. Keith Jelleyman. Hugh Jellie. Warren Jellyman. Melanie Jenkins.
Jenkins. Wilson Jenkins. Ian Jenkins. Jack Jenkins. Kent Jenkinson. Robin Jenkinson. Tony Jenner. Nigel Jennings. Andrew Jennings. Gavin Jennings. Don Jennings. Graham Jennings. Tony Jennings. Scott Jennings. Kevin Jensen. H E Jensen. Gordon
Glenda Jensen-Schmidt. Chris Jermy. Hoki Jerry. Allan Jessep. Michael Jesson. Andy Jessop. Tony Jeurissen. Mark Jinkinson. Louise Jocelyn. Tracey Joe. Jono Joe. Gilbert Joe. Chloe Johansen. Alexandra Johansen. Damian Johansen. Henrik Johansen.
hansson. Gary John. Charlie Johns. David Johns. Mike Johnson. Aaron Johnson. Bonnie Johnson. Paul Johnson. Jannine Johnson. Ian Johnson. Trevor Johnson. Sam Johnson. Bridget Johnson. Russell Johnson. Mark Johnson. Brent Johnson. Kristian
. Daryl Johnson. Roger Johnson. Hayley Johnson. Nick Johnston. Steve Johnston. Kim Johnston. James Johnston. Robyn Johnston. Dean Johnston. Dick Johnston. Paul Johnston. Linda Johnston. Hartley Johnston. Anne Johnston. Bill Johnston. Rob
n. Mark Johnston. Mike Johnston. Mitchell Johnston. Mathew Johnstone. Paul Johnstone. Lindsay Johnstone. Lesley Johnstone. David Johnstone. Robert Johnstone. Owen Johnstone. Paula Johnstonp. Toni Jolliffe. David Jolly. Ben Jonasen. Sam Jones.
ones. Dillon Jones. David Jones. Gavin David Jones. Israel Jones. Don Jones. Michael Jones. Thomas Jones. Gareth Jones. Blair Jones. Royce Jones. John & Alison Jones. Neil Jones. Hayden Jones. Carol Jones. Aaron Jones. Ethan Jones. Kevin Jones. Mark
hys Jones. Craig Jones. Tania Jones. Edwin Jones. Phill Jones. Joce Jones. Lewis Jones. Robert Jones. Raymond Jones. Paul Jones. Alan Jones. Layne Jones. Philip Jones. Glenn Jones. Kat Jones. Geraint Jones. Wayne Jones. Andy Jones. Christine Jones.
es. Solveig Haugan Jonsen. Catherine Jopp. Blair Jopson. Amanda Jordan. David Jordan. Daniel Jordan. Garry Jordan. Brett Jordan. Bevan Jordan. Phil Josephs. Steve Joyce. Warren Joyce. Brodie Joyce. Theresa Joyce. Robyn Judd. Blair Judd. Charmaine
ennis Judd. Darryl Judd. Trevor Jupp. Tony Jurisich. Danielle Jury. Glen Jury. Jason K. Tira Kaa. Alister David Kaan. Sue Kaan. Tanisha Kahu. Samuel Kahui. Fred Kaiser. Yuriy Kalashnikov. Olga Kalinina. Marty Kampman. Marilyn Kan. Randall Kanter.
anuf. Wilson Karalus. Ksenia Kardashina. Dmitry Karpov. Vladimir Karpov. Wayne Kassian. Koben Katipa. Alexey Katrushenko. Phil Kavanagh. Warren Kawiti. Nick Kay. Gary Kaye. Adam Keane. Dave Keane. Hilary Kearns. Simon Keary. Peter Keary.
Keast. Chris Keefer. Robert Keegan. Gene Keelan. Rochelle Keeley. Todd Keen. David Keen. Debbie Keen. Mitchel Keene. Lawrence Kees. Alan Kees. Mandy Keesing. Ben Keet. Fiona Kehely. Johnny Keig. Wayne Keightley. Alastair Keiller. Andrew Keith.
eith. Karen Kell. Bernard Kellett. Shaun Kelliher. Colin Kells. Keith Kelly. Tony Kelly. Ron Kelly. Rachael Kelly. Lee-Anne Kelly. Brendan Kelly. Johanna Kelly. Ryan Kelly. Michael Kelly. Shaun Kelly. Grant Kelly. John Kelly. Swampy Kelly. Stuart Kelly. Isaac
Stuart Kelynack. Brad Kelynack. Shane Kemp. Brian Kemp. Jon Kemp. Shae Kemp. Chris Kempton. Richard Kendall. Mal Kendrew. Annmaria Kenneally. Laura Kennedy. Jed Kennedy. Mark Kennedy. Torquil Kennedy. John Kennedy. Cheryl Kennedy.
ennedy. Gary Kennedy. Oliver Kennedy. Andrew Kennett. Gerald Kennett. Samuel Kennett. Sam Kenniff. Bev Kenny. Tracey Kenny. Dean Kent. Marshall Kent. John Kenton. Peter Kenyon. John Kenyon. Tony Kenyon. Fintan Keogh. Warren Keoghan.
eown. Chris Kereopa. Sean Kerins. Don Kern. Ricky Kernohan. Hamish Kerr. Michael Kerr. Spud Kerr. Kieron Kerr. Heather Kerr. David Kerr. Dan Kerr. John Kerridge. Adam Kershaw. Julie Kersten. Braydan Kete. Ayren Kete. Marty Kett. Steven Ketter.
Kevin Riwai. Bruce Keys. Mikhaylo Khalchenya. Maksim Khudoleev. Saad Khurshid. Vitaliy Khutornoy. Shane Kibby. Aaron Kidd. Ian Kidd. Nick Kidd. Rob Kidd. John Kidd. Rochelle Kiddey. Al Kidner. Inia Kiel. Anthony Kiely. Michael Kiernan. Daniel
. David Kilford. Allanah Kilfoyle. Paul Kilgour. James Kilgour. Sam Kilpatrick. Rangi Kimura. Peter Kinane. Mike King. Joy King. Jim King. Shirley King. Reece King. Graham King. Matt King. Heath King. Sandy King. Chelsea King. Phil King. Ali King.
ng. Josh King. Reg King. Greg King. Heather King. Melissa King. George King. Sarah King. Nick King. Lisa King. David King. Andrew King. Gavin Kingan. Ari Kingan. Jason Kinghorn. Earl Kingi. Mark Kingsbury. Geoff Kingsford. Sam Kingston. Sam
ne. Michael Kingstone. Craig Kinney. Richard Kinsey. Jenny Kirby. Rosie Kirby. Allan Kircher. John Kiriakidis. Allan Kirk. Pat Kirk. Sam Kirk. Stefaan Kirk. Colin Kirkpatrick. Barry (Baz) Kirkwood. Brendon Kirkwood. Kristian Kirwin. Aaron Kitto.
Kittoe. Diana Kittow. Matt Kittow. Morten Kjaer. John Klaasen. Steve Klaus. Scott Kleeber. Dave Kleeber. Elena Klochko. Nathan Klohs. Chris Klosterman. Daniel Knauf. Stu Kneebone. Hadlee Knight. David Knight. Steve Knight. Nigel Knight. Jaimee
Russell Knight. Guy Knight. Jamie Knight. Steven Knight. Neil Knight. Denise Knight. Rod Knight. Ben Knight. Terry Knight. Cath Knight. Kieron Knight. Mike Knodel. Jason Knowles. Anthony Knowles. Bevan Knowles. Bruce Knowles. Ross Knowles.
e Knowles. Stuart Knox. John Knox. Jordan Knudsen. Warren Knudsen. Jenny Knuth. Philip Koch. Sergey Kochetov. John Kohm. Boris Kolpakov. Vaughan Komene. Natalia Konisheva. Ruslan Konovchenko. Neil Koot. Greg Koppel. Alexey Korchagin.
e Korevaar. Toni Korhonen. Alexander Korkin. Lucas Koroheke. Steve Kose. Kurt Kostyrko. Fester Kostyrko. Sergey Kostyuchenko. Jim Koustas. Anna Kovalchuk. Vlad Kovalenko. Paul Krans. Kyle Krause. Viacheslav Kraynikov. Jim Krcoski. Selina
Nick Kriletich. Peter Krippner. Patrick Krippner. Daniel Krivan. Olga Krivets. Wayne Krog. Christian Kropp. Tanya Krupinskaya. Viktoria Kucherenko. Robert Kuchlein. Andrey Kudriavsev. Charles Kuhr. Simon Kuiti. Eduard Kuklin. Elena Kulikova.
ulusheva. Tracey Kum Sing. Terry Kurvink. Colleen Kuypers. Dmitry Kuzmin. Ivan Kuznetsov. Fletcher Kydd. Dougie Kyle. Marie Labutina. Jeffrey Lachmund. Jacob Ladd. Kara Lagah. Mike Lagan. Craig Lahmert. Grant Laidlaw. Gordon Laing. Josef
ohnnie Laird. Gus Laird. Shaun Laird. Michael Lake. Heidi Lake. Sid Lake. Owen Laker. Paula Lalich. Marc Lalich. Craig Laloli. Stephen Laloli. Stephen Lamb. Shirley Lamb. Russell Lamb. Richard Lamb. Corey James Lambeth. Corey Lambeth. John
h. Russell Lambeth. John Lambly. Troy Lambly. Tony Lamborn. Miles Lambourn. Greg Lamont. Clyve Lamplough. Will Lampp. Harry Lanauze. Barry Lanauze. Levi Lanauze. Jamie Lanauze. Jacqui Land. Mikael Landqvist. Jim Landreth. Gary Lane.

Baz Lang. Peter Lang. Andy Lang. Jill Langdon. Sascha Langenbach. Vanessa Langford. Caroline Langford. Keith Langford. Malcolm Langley. Shannon Langley. Kharlos Langman. David Langridge. Zoe Lapping. Victor Laptev. Bob Lapthorne. Rob L
Sam Larabee. Dean Larkin. Tom Larsen. Simon Larsen. Col Larsen. Jenny Larson. Inga Lasavickaite. Nick Lascelles. Andrew Lasenby. William Lash. Danny Lassle. First Name Last Name. Paul Latta. Lianne Latta. Becky Latter. Nick Lattimore. Bar
Mark Laugesen. Kat Laugesen. Joel Laugesen. Rowan Laurence. Kirk Laurence. Jack Laurent. Rasmus Lauridsen. Hamish Laurie. Nicole Laurie. Paul Lavender. Ryan Laverock. Evgeniy Lavrinenko. David Law. Rob Lawler. David Lawler. David Lawn. Je
Hayden Lawrence. Matthew Lawrence. Adrian Lawrence. Oleg Lawrentyev. Patrick Lawry. Mike Lawry. Georgina Lawry. Michael Lawson. Shane Lawson. Harley Lawson. Scott Lawson. Jarrod Lawson. Shaun Lawson. Frank Lawton. Andy Lay. Loren
Wells Layton. Dave Layton. Sergey Lazarev. Daniel Le Brun. David Le Fevre. Peter Le Gros. Louis Le Lievre. David Le Page. Aaron Lealand. Matt Leamy. Daniel Leary. David Leary. Dave Leathwick. Gavin Lecky. Nancy Lee. Thomas Lee. Alice Lee. W
Tim Lee. Steven Lee. Hayden Lee. Polly Lee. Jill Lee. Richard Leece. Gabrielle Leech. Andre Leemeyer. Raymond Leemeyer. Mike Lees. Brian Lees. Des Legg. Daniel Leggett. Reece Legros. Oliver Leicester. Donna Leigh. Scott Leighton. Stu Leighto
Leighton Jones. Jeremy Leineweber. Michelle Leineweber. Mike Lembke. Phil Lemmon. Andrius Lenkovas. Simon Lennard. Pam Lennie. Andrew Lennox. Peter Lennox. Paul Lenz. Don Leonard. Jared Leonard. Greg Leonard. Cheryl Leonard. Pete
Greg Leonard-Jones. Dmitry Leontenko. Arkadiy Leontev. Sergey Leontev. Rai Leota. Craig Leov. Ian Leppard. Gill Lepper. Maria Lepper. Clynt Lereculey. Scott Leslie. Callum Leslie. Mike Leslie. Keith Leslie. Kayden Leslie. Keren Leslie. Tim Lesl
Leslie. Garth Leslie. Kevin Leveridge. Gareth Levers. Jamie Levien. Brent Levy. Henk Levy. Kelly Lewer. Neville Lewis. Monica Lewis. Brad Lewis. Wayne Lewis. John Lewis. Zane Lewis. Nick Lewis. Highland Adventures Company Limited Lewis. Andr
Amee Lewis. Guy Lewis. Murray Lewis. Bucky Lewis. Dylan Lewis. Phil Lewis. Dylan Leys. Phillip L'Huillier. Darren Liddicoat. David Liddle. Kenny Liddle. Callum Liefting. Daniel Lignã©. Graeme Dwayne Lile. Graeme Lile. Julia Lile. Scott Lillas. D
Lim. Wayne Lincoln. Matt Lind. Lowry Linda. Wayne Lindsay. Ian Lindsay. Hamish Lindsay. Darren Lindsay. Callum Lindsay. Jasper Lindsay-Arms. Neville Lines. Skinny Lingard. Hamish Linklater. Bevin Linnell. Peter Linnell. Daphne Linnell. Jaso
Allan Linton. Jonathan Linton. William (Bill) Linwood. Vova Lipartia. Ben Lissaman. Megan Lister. Maureen Lister. Olga Litovchenko. Robert Little. Gary Littler. Collin Littlewood. Ryan Littleworth. Stuart Littleworth. Anna Litvinova. Karina Live
Livesey. Lynne Livesey. Adrian Livesey. Mark Livingston. Martin Livingstone. David Llewelyn. Sean Lloyd. Blair Lloyd. Rita Lo. Warwick Loader. Duncan Lobb. James Lochead-Macmillam. Jordan Lock. Malcolm Lockl. Aaron Loder. Steve Lodge. S
Mark Loeffen. Walter Loesberg. Grant Loffhagen. Nicola Loft. Josiah Logan. Eileen Logan. Mark Logan. Philip Logue. Vladimir Logvinenko. Carl Lomas. Mary Lomas. Barbara Lomax. Richard Long. Carole Long. Rob Longley. Gary Longley. Mar
George Looney. Jim Loose. Dale Lopez. Janice Lopez. Rosemary Lord. Stephen Lord. Geoff Lord. Gary Lory. Tom Loughlin. Tim Loughnane. Shane Wilson Louie. Iain Lourie. Raelyn Lourie. Marshall Love. Robert Love. Grant Love. Don Love. Bruce
Love. Drew Love-Jones. Wayne Lovejoy. John Lovell. Ciara Lovelock. Scott David Lovelock. Samuel Steven Lovelock. Tony Lovelock. Kieran Loveridge. Warren Lovett. Dan Lovett. Jayne Lovett. Debra Lovie. Emma Lowe. Donna Lowe. Bryce Lowe. Sha
Damon Lowe. Bruce Lowe. Jake Lowe. Josh Lowe. Rebecca Lowe. Zeb Lowen. Grant Lower. Bruce Lowery. Brenda Lowry. Roger Lowry. Christy Lowry. John Lowther. Jake Lucas. Tony Lucas. Clayton Lucas. Rob Lucas. David Ludemann. Tony Lu
Luedke. Jess Luff. Tony Lumsden. John Lumsden. Thomas Lunt. Simon Lunt. Svetlana Lupanova. Robert & Maria Lupton. Wayne Lutton. Richard Luvsford. Bruce Luxford. Micah Luxford. Jocelyn Luxford. Andrew Luxon. Sheldon Lye. Tim Lyes. J
Simon Lyford. Dion Lynch. Matthew Lynch. Bernie Lynn. Iain Lynn. Stephen Lyons. Matthew Lyster. Heath Lyttle. Mat M. Kevin Maber. Za Maberly. Richard Mabin. Katie Macarthur. Phil Macaskill. Bruce Macaulay. Kirsty Macaulay. Iain Macau
(Gnome) Macbeth. Campbell Macdiarmid. Greg Macdonald. Maaka Macdonald. Steven Macdonald. Elise Macdonald. Liam Macdonald. Donald Macdonald. Wayne Macdonald. James Macdonald. Ewen Macdonald. Alan Macdonald. Menzies M
Sheryl Macdonald. Kerry Macdonald. Rongo Macdonald. Ryan Macdonald. Louisa Macdonald. Murray Macdonald. Donna Macdonell. Ben Macdonell. Dougal Macdougall. Malcolm Macfarlane. Nicki Macgibbon-Taylor. Kirk Macgregor. Liam M
Alexandr Machacha. Ado Machida. Colin Machray. Dave Mackay. Gareth Mackay. Steven Mackay. Scott Mackay. Hamish Mackay. Murray Mackenzie. Doug Mackenzie. Keith Mackenzie. Ged Mackenzie. Mark Mackie. Gus Mackie. Donald Mack
Mackie. Rebecca Mackie. Alastair Mackintosh. Al Mackinven. Alan Mackinven. Bill Mackrell. Renae Mackrell. Gareth Mackwood-Smith. Chris Maclean. Peter Maclean. Stephanie Maclennan. Kevin Macleod. Robert (Bob) Macleod. Quentin Macleo
Macleod. Dave Macmillan. Martin Macmillan. Duncan Macnab. James Macphee. Damien Macpherson. Grant Macpherson. James Macpherson. Glen Macpherson. Hamish Macpherson. Gerry Macpherson. Shona Macrae. Gareth Macrae. Wairata
Shane Maddison. Marty Madsen. Victoria Magazinovic. Tom Magill. Jerome Magisson. Jose Elmer Maglaqui. Ed Magor. Dave Mahar. Julie Maher. Julie Mahon. John Mahoney. Mike Mahoney. Terry Mahony. Tuhi Maihi. Norman Maikuku. Lisa Ma
Main. Milton Maindonald. Susan Mains. Paul Mair. Chris Maisey. Dean Maisey. Ron Maki. Kendall Malcolm. Maryanne Mallalieu. Tony Mallon. Sophie Malone. Andy Maloney. Kirsten Malpas. Roman Malygin. Troy Manderson. Buck Mangipane. Joh
Daniel Manley. Russell & Steph Mann. Phillip Mann. Russell Mann. George Mannering. Phil Manning. Brendon Manning. Philip Manning. Glen Manning. Rowena Manning. Alan Manning. Nathan Manning. Norm Mannix. Ray Mansell. Neil Man
Manson. Boyce Mantell-Harding. Paul Manuel. James Manusauloa. Peter Mapson. Drury Mapu. Bohdan Maramon. Nick Marasigan. Marc Marchal. Jan Marchant. Dean Marchetti. Ahmad Marda. John Mardell. Jared Mardle. Denise Mariu. Seth Ma
James Markel. Alan Marks. Richie Marlow. Kevin Marlow. Jaimee Marquet. Annette Marr. Toni Marr. Sue Marr. Colin Marriner. Chazz Marriott. Nigel Marriott. Ted Marris. Neville Marsh. Phil Marsh. Brian Marsh. Owen Marsh. Chris Marsh. Nick
Ian Marshall. Adam Marshall. Brad Marshall. Lex Marshall. Paul Marshall. Dawn Marshall. Evan Marshall. Murray Marshall. Donna Marshall. William Marshall. Alan Marshall. Colin Martin. Janine Martin. Dave Martin. Liam Martin. Brad Mar
Martin. Thomas Martin. Kristina Martin. Megan Martin. Gerald Martin. Sam Martin. Catherine Martin. Robyn Martin. Allan And Faye Martin. Barry Martin. Shirley Martin. Greg Martin. Lyn Martin-Clark. Phil Martinovich. Scott Martinsen
Martynova. Peter Marwood. Rowan Masey. Robert Maskell. Ian Maslin. Tim Maslin. Peter Mason. Fiona Mason. Paul Mason. Christine Mason. Steven Mason. Ryan Mason. Andrew Mason. Paul Massey. Jim Masson. Evgenia Masterova. Eugenia M
Steve Masters. Blair Masters. Pauline Masters. Andrew Masters. Brian Matchett. Paul Mather. Jethro Matheson. Bill Matheson. Donald Mathews. Joshua Mathews. Anne-Marie Mathiesen. Frano Matijasevich. Stefan Matravers. Roman Mats
Mattanen. Ellis Matthews. Kurt Matthews. Amanda Matthews. Shane Matthews. Willie Matthews. Paul Matthews. Hamish Matthews. Alison Matthews. Charlie Matthews. David Matti. Mark Mattison. Steven Mattock. Brent Mattsen. Irene Mattso
Mattson. Colin Mauchline. Erin Maule. Michael Mawhinney. Jill Maxwell. Rachel Maxwell. Jane Maxwell. Craig Maxwell. Steven May. Richard May. Timothy May. Glenn May. Cameron May. Locky May. Benjamin May. Rob Mayhead. Peter Mayna
Mayo. Dermot Mayock. Oscar Mwananyanda Mayumbelo. Allan Mc Donald. Jim Mc Dougall. Barry Thompson Mc Thompson. Elle Mcadam. Paul Mcaleese. Steve Mcalister. Geoff Mcalpine. Denise Mcalpine. Neil Mcalpine. James Mcanally. Ryan M
John Mcara. Paulette Mcarley. Matt Mcarley. Don Mcbeath. Grant Mcbeth. Connor Mcbreen. Ella Mcbreen. Murray Mcbride. Tom Mcbride. John Mcbride. Thea Mcburney. Nicola Mcburney. Steve Mccabe. Sean Mccaffrey. Charlie Mccaig. Ruarid
Adam Mccall. Bill Mccall. Jamie Mccall. Glen Mccall. Aaron Mccall. Gordon Mccallum. Matthew Mccallum. David Mccallum. John Mccarron. Grant Mccarron. Dean Mccarthny. Craig Mccarthy. Justin Mccarthy. Jaimee Mccarthy. Tara Mccar
Mccarthy. Amanda Mccaslin. Phil Mccaughan. Tony Mccleary. Rodney Mccleery. Roy Mccleery. Ian Mcclelland. Steven Mcclintock. David Mccloskey. Dean Mccloy. David Robert Mcclunie. Mike Mcclunie. Ian Mcclure. Vanessa Mccluskie. Graham Mc
Olivia Mccoll. Alister Mccoll. Abby Mccoll. Alan Mccollim. Matthew Mccombie. Mike Mcconchie. Evan Mcconchie. Campbell Mccone. Barry Mccone. Brendon Mccone. Elliot Mcconnell. Tara Mcconnell. Mark Mcconnell. Hamish Mcconno
Mccorkindale. Mary Mccormack. John Mccormick. Connor Mccormick. Ernie John Mccosh. Tom Mccoubrie. Craig Mccowan. Campbell Mccowan. Sandy Mccracken. Alan Mccraw. Tracy Mccready. Tom Mccready. Mike Mccready. Paul Mccullagh
Mccullough. Andrew Mccully. William Mccurdy. David Mccurdy. Peter Mccutcheon. Hayden Mcdermott. Jamie Mcdermott. Anne Mcdermott. John Mcdermott. Tony Mcdermott. Nanette Mcdonald. Rod Mcdonald. Clive Mcdonald. Peter John Mcdo
Mcdonald. Johno Mcdonald. Jason Mcdonald. Neil Mcdonald. Zac Mcdonald. Quintin Mcdonald. Steve Mcdonald. Linda Mcdonald. Shane Mcdonald. Robert Mcdonald. Carl Mcdonald. Louis Mcdonald. Leon Mcdonald. Shane Mcdonnell. Faye M
Gary Mcdougall. Raymond Mcdougall. Bernie Mcdowell. Sam Mcdowell. Jayne Mcdowell. Ross Mcduff. Francis Mcentee. Greg Mcewan. Geoff Mcfadden. Dave Mcfadzien. Fiona Mcfarland. Lyne Mcfarlane. Craig Mcfarlane. Tony Mcfarlane. Pat M
Donald Mcfedries. Keryn Mcfetridge. David Mcgahan. Patrick Mcgahan. Diane Mcgarvey. Andy Mcgaw. Flynn Mcgearey. Pete Mcghee. Steve Mcgill. Julie Mcgill. Warren Mcgillivray. Benjamin Mcgillivray. John Mcginlay. Graeme Mcginn. Andrew
Damian Mcglinchey. Shane Mcglynn. Pearse Mcgougan. Tony Mcgovern. Dean Mcgovern. Robert Mcgovern. John Mcgovern. Ross Mcgowan. Shane Mcgrath. Mathew Mcgrath. Simon Mcgrath. Bill Mcgregor. Philip Mcgregor. Margaret Mcgrego
Mcgregor. Troy Mcgregor. Evan F Mcgregor. Andrew Mcgregor. Eilish Mcgregor. Bruce Mcgregor. Theresa Mcgregor. Craig Mcguigan. Alan Mcguigan. James Mcguire. Kerry Mcguire. Graham Mchaffie. John Mchardy. Kevin Mchardy. Michael Mchug
Mcilraith. Tracy Mcilraith. Kelly Mcilwee. John Mcinnes. Greg Mcintosh. Trudy Mcintyre. Ryan Mcintyre. Peter & Sharon Mcintyre. Richard Mcintyre. Tim Mcintyre. David Mcintyre. Mark Mcintyre. Greg Mcintyre. Dean Mcivor. Clint Mcivor. Paul M
Dave Mckain. Nick Mckay. Richard Mckay. Andrew Mckay. Jas Mckay. Gregory Mckay. Bryan Mckay. Jason Mckay. David Mckay. Rachael Mckay. Andy Mckay. Cam Mckay. Mark Mckee. Duncan Mckee. James Mckee. Leo Mckeefry. Trent Mckenzie
Mckenzie. John Mckenzie. Richard Mckenzie. Duncan Mckenzie. Fraser Mckenzie. Lockie Mckenzie. Dave Mckenzie. Paul Mckenzie. Levi Mckenzie. Ross Mckenzie. Grant Mckenzie. Lyndon Mckenzie. Bruce Mckenzie. Andrew Mckenzie. Daniel M
Simon Mckenzie. Peter Mckenzie. Hayden Mckenzie. Shea Mckenzie. Mark Mckeown. Scott Mckie. Carol Mckie. Graeme Mckinlay. Alice Mckinley. Stuart Mckinney. Bruce Mckinnon. Blair Mckinnon. Rod Mckinnon. Scott Mckinstry. Daryl Mcki
Mclachlan. Linda Mclachlan. Kevin Mclaren. Fred Mclaren. Jennie Mclaren. Hamish Mclauchlan. Ben Mclauchlan. Arran Mclaughlin. Stewart Mclean. Ron Mclean. Richard Mclean. Alistair Mclean. Sandy Mclean. Aaron Mclean. Scott Mclean. Max
Terry Mclean. Susannah Mclean. Karl Mclean-Harvey. Melissa Mclean-Harvey. Grant Mcleay. Michael Mclees. James Mclees. Jessica Mclees. Brendon Mclellan. Steve Mclellan. Tracey Mclellan. Vaughan Mclellan. Matthew Mclelland. Colin Mclen
Mclennan. Andy Mcleod. Laurence Mcleod. Shane Mcleod. Don Mcleod. Morris Mcleod. Billy Mcleod. Peter Mcleod. Matt Mcleod. Keith Mcleod. Sam Mcleod. Geoff Mcleod. John Mcleod. Fraser Mcleod. Paul Mcleod. Greig Mcleod. Shane Mcle
Mclocklan. Jonathan Mcmahon. Eve Mcmahon. Gordon Mcmanus. Trevor Mcmaster. Alan Mcmaster. Garth Mcmaster. Don Mcmaster. Richard Mcmaster. Ryan Mcmaster. Dylan Mcmenamin. Craig Mcmillan. Ricky Mcmillan. Stuart Mcmill
Mcmillan. Mike Mcmillan. Ian Mcmillan. Jeremy Mcmillan. Peter Mcmillan. Julianne Mcmillan. Andrea Mcmillan. Sharon Mcmillin. Cherie Mcmullan. Douglas Mcmullin. Rod Mcmurdo. Daniel Mcmurtrie. Peter Mcnab. Susanne Mcnab. Dave Mcn
Mcnabb. Michael S Mcnabb. Derek Mcnabb. Glen Mcnabb. Robbie Mcnair. Scott Mcnair. Nathan Mcnally. Brian Mcnally. Micheal Mcnamara. Louise Mcnamara. Kim Mcnamara. Carl Mcnaught. Bevan Mcnaughton. Grant Mcnaughton. Ross Mcnaull.
Mcnear. Hector Mcneil. Jen Mcneill. Darryn Mcneill. Brian Mcneill. Jacob Mcneill. Nick Mcneill. Andrew Mcneill. Rick Mcneilly. Lana Mcnicholas. Jessica Mcnicol. Ryan Mcnicol. Jean Mcnutt. Lou Mcnutt. Rob Mcnutt. Daniel Mcnutt. Helen Mcnu
Mcphail. Shane Mcphee. Joshua Mcpherson. Michael Mcpherson. Darren Mcquilkin. George Mcquillan. Wade Mcquillin. Rory Mcquinn. Dianne Mcrae. Hamish Mcrae. Glenn Mcrae. Daryl Mcrae. Steph Mcrae. Sonny Mcroberts. Tim Mcveagh. Marcus
Malcolm Mcwhannell. Laghlan Mcwhannell. Hilary Mcwhinnie. Andrew Mcwilliam. Aidan Mcwilliams. Geoff Meacheam. Ivan Mead. Arthur Mead. Simon Mead. Haydon Meade. Steve Meadows. Sam Meadows. Pam Mearns. Hamish Mee. Matt
Andrew Meehan. Poyzer Megan. Hayden & Jacquie Megaw. Jenny Megaw. Barry Mehrtens. James Mehrtens. Mark Mehrtens. Aaron Meikle. Daryl Meikle. Jason Meikle. Gary Meiklejohn. Elias Meiklejohn. Lance Meiklejohn. Tommy Meldgaard. David
Hugh Melling. Lynda Mellor-Knight. Alexandr Melnikov. Braydon Melody. Dion Melville. Nic Menary. John Mendoza. Elfi Menpes. Damian Mens. Stu Mentor. Andrew Mentor. Caroline Mentz. Jason Menzies. Janelle Menzies. Jonny Menzies. Aaron
Andrew Mercer. Jono Merchant. James Merchant. Kelvin Meredith. Barbara Meredith. Ian Meredith. Rhys Meredith. John Meroiti. Wayne Merrie. Katrina Merrifield. Gary Merrin. Sam Merrin. Lee Merrin. Jackie Merritt. Henry Mestrom. Susan Mesz
Metcalfe. Simon Meuli. Karen Mexted. Don Meyer. Charlie Meyer. Alex Michael. Hans Michel. Clark Michelle. Jason Michie. Kent Mickleson. Raymond Mickleson. Steve & Marie Middleton. Derek Middleton. Stan Middleton. Nathan Middleton.
Middleton. Alan Midleditch. Artem Mihailov. Stacy Mihaka. Philippa Milburn. Nik Mildenhall. Clint Miles. Joe Milich. Peter Milich. Sarah Milicich. Craig Mill. Cameron Mill. Dennis Millan. Hayden Millar. Shaun Millar. Shane Millar. Louise Millar. Chr
Graeme Millar. Josh Millard. Tracey Millard. Mike Millen. Penny Millen. Diane Miller. Corey Sam Miller. Ed Miller. Tyler Miller. Dave Miller. Paul Miller. Shane Miller. Mark Miller. Tony Miller. Scott Miller. Ian Miller. Karen Miller. Iain Miller. Bruce M
Miller. Craig Miller. Lance Millett. Paul Millin. Wayne Millington. Ian Millman. Theo Mills. Brian Mills. Dave Mills. Michael Mills. Daryl Mills. Jeff Mills. Vincent Mills. Sam Mills. Tess Mills. Ian Milne. Glen Milne. Darryl Milne. Wendy Milne. John Mil
Milne. Percy Milner. Elizabeth Milsom. Dave Minty. Jarrod Minty. Cojocari Miroslav. Graham Mist. Dmitriy Misuira. Tim Mitchell. Gail Mitchell. Tony Mitchell. Christina Mitchell. Grant Mitchell. Charles Mitchell. Andrew Mitchell. Donna Mitche
Mitchell. Jody Mitchell. Nathan Mitchell. Humphrey Mitchell. Rachael Mitchell. Dennis Mitchell. Craig Mitchell. Judy Mitchell. Heather Mitchell. Kazumasa Mizuno. Tamati Moana-Orupe. Bjorn Moe. Stuart Moeller. Mike Moffat. Russell Moffat. Pete
Ralph Moffatt. Emma Moffett. Trav Moffitt. Roger Mogford. Charlotte Mogg. Kerri Moir. Arkadiy Moiseev. Roger Mole. Neil Molina. James Molloy. James Moloney. Simon Moloney. Martin Moloney. Liz Molony. Diane Moloughney. Neville Monah
Monahan. Scott Monahan. Dom Monard. Vince Monk. Dougal Monk. Kevin & Gillian Monks. Steve Monks. Gary Monson. Robert Monteith. Jon Moodie. Tony Moody. Adrian Moody. Anaru Moon. Julie Moor. Jake Moore. Malcolm Moore. Kevin Moor
Moore. Pataka Moore. Jeff Moore. Ashley Moore. Neil Moore. Mary Moore. Cecelia Moore. Steve Moore. Nicholas Moore. Stevo Moore. Jannine Moore. Chris Moore. John Moore. Holly Moore. Rory Moore. Vanessa Moore. Kelly Moore. Dominic Moore. C
Moore. Warren Moorfield. Brian Moorhead. Simon Moorhouse. Gary Moran. Patrick Moran. Troy Moran. Jo Moran. Rhys Mordecai. Mark Mordovtsev. Darya Mordvinceva. Bradd Morelli. Craig Morey. Jono Morgan. Lichelle Morgan. Bruce Morg
Glyn Morgan. Glyn Morgan. Bryce Morgan. Lynette Morgan. Wayne Morgan. Jake Morgan. Dudley Morgan. Jane Morgan. Mathew Morley. Jarred Moroney. Kay Moroney. Chris Morrin. David Morris. Reg & Carrol Morris. Kyle Morris. Tim Morris. Tony Morr
Morris. Keith Morris. Lisa Morris. Wayne Morris. Roy Morris. Wain Morris. Chas Morris. Dave Morris. Bret Morris. Jonathan Morris. Kurstie Morris. Anna-Marie Morris. Katherine Morris. Hamish Morrison. Gordon Morrison. Gary Morrison
Morrison. Peter Morrison. Chris Morrison. Brent & Caralyn Morrison. Pete Morrison. Jeremy Morrison. Kevin Morriss. Des Morriss. Jemma Morrissey. Kent Morrissey. Andrew Morritt. Chris Morrow. John Morrow. Janelle Morrow. Peter Morse. Jame
Colin Mortensen. Murray Mortimer. Oliver Mortimer. Mark Mortimer. Tony Mortimore. Dean Morton. Glen Morton. Richard Morton. Brad Morton. John (Mort) Morton. Jenna Morton. Troy Morzelewski. Andrew Moseley. Philip Moses. Angela Mosle
Moss. David Moss. Jordan Moss. Gary Moss. James Mossman. Ruslan Motko. Marina Motozuk. Darryl Mouat. Tim Mouat. Kevin Mountford. Joel Mountney. David Mowbray. Peter Moy. Jacob Moyle. David Moynahan. Ivan Moynan. Bridget Moynih
Mudgway. Karen Mudgway. Kent Mudgway. Neil Mudie. Peter Muir. Murray Muir. Willie Muir. Jan Muir. Ross Muir. Patricia Muir Bullard. Brett Muirson. Ray Mulder. Geoff Mulder. Sinead Mulhern. Trina Mullan. David Mullen. Jan Mullooly. Brooke M
David Mumberson. Jonathan Mumford. Michelle Munn. Dean Munn. Amy Munns. Blair Munro. David Munro. Colleen Munro. Clem Munro. Grant Munro. Chris Munro. Clayton Munro. Hamish Munro. Reece Munro. Michael Munsey. Elena Muravye
Murdoch. Chris Murdoch. Bain Murdoch. Troy Murley. Finn Murphy. Bruce Murphy. Eddie Murphy. Christopher Murphy. Peter Murphy. Mark Murphy. Mark Daniel Murphy. Scott Murphy. Camron Murphy. Richard Murray. Pat Murray. Bryce Murray.
Murray. Owen Murray. Bob Murray. George Murray. Nathan Murray. Teraika Murray. Jim Murray. Chris Murray. Scott Murray. Donna Murray. Jonathan Murrow. Tom Murton. Sam Musgrove. Tyson Musil. Ross Mutton. Vlad Myasoedov. Tim Myco
Myers. Sergey Nabokin. Bev Nairn. Parisa Najd. Rachel Nally. Nicholas Nametyshev. Paul Napier. Grant Nash. Peter Nash. Brett Nasmith. Lyudmila Nasonova. John Nation. Simon Natterer. Travis Naylor. Ken Naylor. Mike Naylor. Edwin Naylor-William
Nazarov. Murray Neal. David Neal. Phil Neame. Zeev Nederman. Jeanette Elaine Nee. Nigel Neehoff. Jim Negus. Kevin Neil. Mark Neill. David Neilson. Tony Neilson. Nicky Neiman. Alan Neioti. Denise Nelson. Matt Nelson. Ricki Nelson. Mathew Ne
Nelson. Brett Nelson. Anthony Nelson. Shirley Nelson. James Nelson. Les Nelson. Jesse Nepia. Indira Neuendorff. Chris Nevins. Bruce Newbury. Allen Newby. Wayne Newcombe. Sandy Newcombe. Bryce Newlove. Jenny Newman. Keith Newman.
Newman. Matthew Newman. Megan Newman. David Newport. Merrin Newport. Shelley Newson. Chris Newson. Paul Newth. Chuck Newton. Sam Newton. Grant Newton. Alaistair Newton. Lyn Newton. Dan Newton. Glen Newton. Mark Newton. Kar
Chuck Ngaira. Dean Ngarotata. Ross Niccol. Kere Nichol. Vanella Nicholas. Mike Nicholas. Chris Nicholls. Alan Nicholls. Dale Nicholls. David Nicholls. Travis Nicholls. Scott Nicholls. Amy Nicholls. Lyn Nicholls. Adam Nicholson. Nigel Nicholso
Nicholson. Aaron Nicholson. Neil Nicholson. Dave Nicholson. Steve Nickson. Russell Nicol. Campbell Nicol. Wade Nicol. Calvin Nicoll. Nick Nicolson. Doug Nicolson. Dennis Nielsen. Guy Nielsen. Brad Nieuwkoop. Wendy Nieuwland. Tawera Nikau. J
Nikkels. William Nikoia. Jenn Nikora. Paul Niles. Dereck Nilsen. Erik Nilsson. Scott Nimmo. Gary Nimmo. Kath Nimo. Pam Nind. Colin Nisbet. Malcolm Nitschke. Dan Nixon. Matiu Noakes. Brad Nobilo. Heather Noble. Carl Nock. Russell S. Noga. Pe
Irene Norbis. Leif Henning Nordahl. Col Nordstrom. Jon Norfolk. Ross Norman. Alexander (Ally) Norman. Lyndon Norman. Paul Norrish. Matthew Norris-Hill. Robyn North. Julia Northcote Northcote. Simon Northcote. George Northcote. Tony No
Sammie Northcott. Michelle Northcott. Bevan Northcott. Kirsty Northcroft. Matthew Norton. Charles Norwood. Vanessa Norwood. Mark Nossiter. Katelyn Notman. Charlie Nott. David Novelle. Sergej Novikov. Dina Novikova. Ira Novikova. Ben Now
Nunn. Alan Nunn. Ainaz Nuretdinov. Karl Nuttall. Shale Nyberg. Bill O'Leary. Martin O'Malley. Les. O'Brien. Chris O'Meeghan. Rick O'Shea. Rupert Oakley. Greg Oates. Michael Oberdries. Matthew Oberlin-Brown. Meighan O'Brien. Geoff O'Brien. Rory
Matt O'Brien. Peter O'Byrne. Dave O'Callaghan. Kevin O'Callaghan. Pat Oconnor. Ben O'Connor. Peter Oden. Carl Odonnell. Warren O'Donnell. Manaia O'Donnell. Lawrence Odonoghue. Erich Oettli. Lara Offutt. Richard Ogden. Jonathan Ogg. Darre
Kieran Ogle. Alexandr Ogurtsov. Ross Ohagan. John O'Hagan. Jude O'Hagan. Paul O'Halloran. Dan O'Halloran. Brian O'Hare. Mike Oldfield. Peter Oldham. Scott Olds. Phil O'Leary. Patrick O'Leary. Darryl Oliver. Roz Oliver. Shane Oliver. Kirsten Ol
Oliver. John Oliver. Paul Oliver. Alex Oliver. Philip Oliver. Nick Oliver. Craig Oliver. Charlie Ollerenshaw. Brad Olsen. Kelly Olsen. Burke Olsen. Peter Olsen. Emily Olsen. Jon Olson. Simon Omalley. Colin Onaka. Trevor O'Neil. Pru O'Neill. Kevin
Charmaine O'Neill. Jacqui Oogan. Irvin Openshaw. Jemma Opie. Mike Opie. Arne Martin Oppegaard. Kerwyn Oppert. Jason Orchard. Mike O'Reilly. Simon Orlowski. James Ormond. Daniel Ormond. John Ormsby. Nigel Orpwood. Owen Orr. Quentin
Orr. Richard Orsulich. Trevor Osbaldiston. Andrew Osborn. Hannah Osborne. Charlotte Osborne. Hamish Osborne. Geordie Osborne. Gavin Osborne. Tony Osborne. Rex Osborne. Matt Osburn. Grant Oshanassy. Brent O'Shea. Wayne Osmond. Rodrigo
Terry Ostrom. Tim O'Sullivan. Michael O'Sullivan. Geoff Oswald. Nicki Ottaway. Judith Otto. Roger Oughton. Ari Overmars. Andrew Overton. Tom Overton. Mark Overton. Laura Overton. Sam Owen. Robert Owen. Geoff Owen. Mike Owens. Ian Ow
Oxborrow. Steve Oxnam. Geoff Pacey. Andrew Packer. Kerry Packer. Steve Paddiosn. Hugh Paddison. Andrew Padula. Cynthia Page. Geoff Page. Terry Pahl. Elliot Paice. Brad Pailthorpe. Richard Paine. Tony Painter. Jon Palenski. Andy Palles-Clark. Ric
Robert Palmer. Aaron Palmer. Svitlana Panchenko. Steven Panganis. Ross Paniora. Rihi Paora. Doug Papps. Karen Parker. Stephen Parker. Neville Parker. Dayne Parker. Maree Parker. Kyle Parker. Craig Parker. Geordie Parker. Cate Parker. Trudi Parker
Parker. Baz Parker. Rochelle Parker. Brent Parker. Bevan Parker. Trina Parker. Bruce Parker. Edward Parker. Harold Parker. Kerry Parker. Shannon Parkes. Thomas Parkes. Pip Parkin. Jon Parkins. Eric Parkins. Cameron Parkinson. Carolyn Parkinso
Parmenter. Wayne Parr. Nathan Parris. Shayne Parry. Andrew Parry. Walter Parry. Jeremy Parsons. Chris Parsons. Bruce Parsons. Tom Edward Parsons. Rebecca Parsons. Kerry Pascoe. Stephen Pask. Vincent Passarelli. James Passmore. Francesco
Frank Patanio. Kate Patchett. Sue Pate. Shayne Pateman. Murray Paterson. Bruce Paterson. Jeremy Paterson. Fiona Paterson. Abbey Paterson. Don Paterson. Grant Paterson. Fergus Paterson. Barry Paterson. Clive Paterson. Scott Paterson. Chris P
Neil Pates. Arne Patetterson. Nick Patmore. Dean Paton. Ben Paton. Croydon Paton. Brendon Patrick. Kirill Patsenko. Leon Patten. Graham Patterson. Ian Patterson. Kate Patterson. Matthew Patterson-Green. Jeremy Patterson-Green. Landey Patton
Pattullo. Brent Paulsen. Derek Pawley. Ken Pawson. Daniel Pay. Owen Payne. Kristopher Payne. Vince Payne. Sandra Payne. Phil Payne. Matt Payne. Grant Payton. Trevor Payton. Bryan Peach. Brett Peachey. Jock Peacock. Alistair Peacock. Carl Peaco
Peacock. Joshua Peacock. Dave Peacocke. Jarred Pead. Tony Peak. Andrew Pealing. Stephen Pearce. Graham Pearce. Regan Pearce. Sue Pearce. Jannine Pearce. Rod Pearce. Noel Pearce. Bruce Pearce. Steve Pearce. Tony Pearce. John Pearcy. Richard
Henry Pearse. Robert Pearson. Chris Pearson. John Pearson. Tony Pearson. Dylan Pearson. Maria Pearson. Sarah Pearson-Coats. Virginia Peck. Heather Pedersen. Megan Pedersen. Stewart Pedersen. Rud Pedersen. Tony Peebles. Marianne Peebles.
Peek. Ian Peel. Pim Peeters. Paul Peetoom. Barrie Peez. Jim Peffers. Grant Pegden. Adrian Pehi. Barbara Pemberton. Don Pemberton. Vanessa Pendergrast. Wilson Penman. Spencer Penney. Bob Penter. Megan Penzig. William Pepper. Curt Perano. Troy
Paul Perano. Joseph Perano. Doug Percival. Daryl Percy. Matthew Percy. Ashley Perfect. John Perkins. Frank Perkins. Michael Perman. Mark Perren. Dean Perrett. Alex Perring. Larry Perrott. Kelly Perry. Emma Perry. Tyler Perry. Shaun Perry. James Per
Perry. Layton Perry. Ian Perryman. Rick Persse. David Peryer. Donald Pescini. Mark Pescini. Graeme Peter. Roy Peters. Neville Peters. Lorne Peters. Tracy Peters. Gary Peters. Bruce Peters. Shane Peters. Annie Petersen. Troy Petersen. Colin Petersen.
Petersen. Soeren Petersen. Shaun Peterson. Heather Peterson. Des Peterson. Rick Peterson. Barry Petherick. Nataliya Petlina. Oleg Petrov. Natasha Petrove. James Pettengell. Ronnie Pettersen. Joakim Pettersson. James Pettley Iii. Tim Pevreal. Chris
Chris Peychers. Dion Peyroux. Axel Pforter. John Phibbs. Dean Phibbs. Terry Philburn. Robbie Philip. Bryce Philip. Bryan Edward Phillips. Jacqui Phillips. Gerard Phillips. Mike Phillips. Dave Phillips. Nicola Phillips. Murray Phillips. Deborah Phil
Phillips. George Phillips. Roger Phillips. Budd Phillips. Leeanne Phillips. Aaron Phillips. Jamie Philp. Tom Philpot. George Pickel. Andy Pickering. Craig Pickering. Cody Pickles. Ashley Pickworth. Riemper Piemper. Kyran Pierce. Kramer Pierce. Dennis
Reice Piggott. Shanan Pihema. Steve Pike. Warren Pike. Jadon Pike. Hamish Pilbrow. Graeme Pile. Gabrielle Pile. Josie Pile. Zion Pilgrim. Matt Pilkington. Deborah Pilkington. Julie Pilkington. Mark Pincock. Jonny Pinfold. Roger Pink. Mark Piper. Gra
David Pitchford. Eduard Pitsentiy. Kate Pittard. Lou Pitts-Brown. Mike Plant. Ollie Platt. Oleg Plautin. Pete Plaza. Emma Pleasants. Des Pledger. Mike Plivelich. Clive Plucknett. Warren Plum. John Plunkett. Campbell Pocock. Travis Pocock. Henryk
Alexandr Podyachev. Igor Podzolko. Devon Polaschek. Grant Pollock. David Pollock. Lesley Pollock. Deb Polyblank. Tess Pomana. Graham Pomeroy. Ivan Ponomerev. Chris Pont. Natasha Ann-Marie Pont. Andrew Poon. Lawrence Pope. Zeljko Popovic.
Popplewell. Andrew Porritt. Justin Port. Christopher Porteous. Andy Porteous. Kim Porteous. Jessica Porteous. Denise Porter. Joselyn Porter. Joanne Porter. Dean Posthuma. Amy Posthuma. George Potaka. Mark Potter. Christine Potter. Robyn Pott
Potts. Blair Poulter. Louise Poulton. Andrew Poulton. John Poulton. Bev Poulton. Christine Pounsford. Ewan Powdrell. John Powdrill. Kelly Powell. Doug Powell. Mike Powell. Larry Powell. Zac Powell. Tara Power. Michelle Power. Ben Powley. Barry
Don Poy. Mark Poynter. Eric Pragnell. Grant Pram. Peter Prangley. Wendy Prankerd. Owen Pratt. Derrick Pratt. Andrew Pratt. Trish Pratt. Lindsay Prattley. Charity Preece. Keith Prendergast. Bede Prendergast. Leon Prendeville. Jim Presly. Hannah Pre
Zac Prestidge. Guy Prestney. Shane Preston. Murray Preston. Mark Preston. Ryan Preston. Jane Preston. Campbell Preston. Dion Pretty. Warwick Prewer. Daniel Price. Aj Price. Mike & Gillian Price. Warrick Price. James Price. Norman Price. Garet
Warren Price. Kieran Priddle. Daryl Priest. Sally Priest. Gordon Priest. Aidan Priestley. Maurice Priestley. Natasha Priestley. Jevon Priestley. Anna Priestley. Sam Priestley. Hamish Prins. Clive Prinsloo. Lynne Prior. Josh Pritchard. Kate Pritchard.
Pritchard. Greg Pritchard. Don Procter. Allen Procter. Angela Procter-Rofe. Christine Proffit. Ivan Prokopenko. Charmaine Proudman. Brian Prtichard. Gordon Pryor. Benjamin Pryor. Bruce Pryor. Fa'I Pudney. Lillyanne Pugh. Bleddyn Pugh. Brendo
Tara Puke. Tim Pukeiti. Neil Puleston. Derek Pulham. Adrienne Pulham. Mike Pullen. Jane Pullen. Andy Pummell. Joss Purbrick. Elizabeth Purcell. Clinton Purches. Chris Purdie. Evan Purdie. Tangi Purea. Len & Jenny Purser. Darryn Purser. Fraser
Alexey Pushkin. Hunter Puterangi. Christopher Putt. Darin Pytlik. Li Ying Qin. Mike Quarrie. Les Quartermaine. James Quartley. Brandon Quick. Ian Quinlivan-Potts. Grant Quist. Mike Rabarts. Adam Rabbidge. Jim Rackley. Leslie Arthur Rack
Radford. Dion Rae. Paul Rae. Malcolm Rae. Josh Rafin. Henry Raikes. Darren Raikes. Rebekah Raine. Jim Rainey. William Rainey. Rodney Ralph. Robbie Ramlose. Bill Ramsay. Gordon Ramsay. Lloyd Ramsay. Graeme Ramsay. Leon Ramsey. Tony Ra
Colleen Randell. Scott Randrup. Nicole Ranger. Stuart Ranger. Grant Rangi. Matewai Rangiuia. Glen Rankin. Ed Rapley. Chris Rapsey. Frank Rasing. Malcolm Rasmusen. John Rasmussen. Cliff Rasmussen. Theresa Rasmussen. Glenn Rastrick. Daniel R
Yogi Rausch. Mario Rautner. Justin Rawcliffe. Scott Rawlinson. Vicky Rawnsley. Tom Rawnsley. Neil Rawson. Jb Ray. Keith Raymond. Nick Rayner. Alex Rayson. Shannon Rea. Dave Read. Shane Read. Leanne Read. Alan Read. Roz Read. Dean Re
Reardon. Bruce Reddington. Graham Redington. Gary Redmond. Paul Redmond. Keith Redmond. Murray Redmond. Dale Redpath. David Redvers. Alan Redwin. Scott Redwood. Henry Reed. Keith Reed. Kelven Reed. Tony Reed. Stacey Jane Reedy. Da
Kim Rees. Gareth Rees. Lorraine Rees. Simon Rees. Dave Reese. Bruce Reeve. Euan Reeve. Aarron Reeves. Ted Reeves. Kelvin Reeves. Philip Reeves. Brandon Rehm. Sonny Rehua. Wayne Reichel. Bryce Reichel. Jimmy Reid. Logan Reid. Mark Reid.
Reid. Pete Reid. David Reid. Ian Reid. Richard Reid. Sally Reid. Eleanor Reid. Martin Reid. Gary Reid. Woody Reid. Robert Reid. Don Reid. Linda Reid. Charmane Reid-Spicer. Ann Reidy. Paul Reilly. Chris Reilly. Carl Reisima. Matthew Thomas Remme
Justin Remnant. Nic Renall. Paul Renall. John Rendall. Marty Rendall. Bill Rendle. David Renfrey. William Renkert. Alan Renowden. Deborah Renton-Green. Lance Retemeyer. Joanna Retemeyer. Quentin Rewi. Paul Rewiri. Karl Reyland. Paul Reynold
Reynolds. Dean Reynolds. Brian Reynolds. Petra Reynolds. Tina Reynolds. Hunter Reynolds. Mathew Reynolds. Craig Rhind. Jayson C T Rhind. Charles Rhodes. Philip Rhodes. Simon Rice. Steve Rice. Harvey Rice. Karen Richards. Matty Richards. Jill R
Alex Richards. Mike Richards. Scott Richards. David Richards. Linda Richards. Allan Richards. Andy Richards. Marty Richards. Sam Richards. Shannon Richardson. Gerry Richardson. Mark Richardson. Neil Richardson. Hamish Richardson.
Richardson. Gary Richardson. Aaron Richardson. Colin Richardson. Jude Richardson. Dean Richardson. Andrew Riches. Ashley Richmond. Ben Richterjork. Mitchell Rickard. Steve Rickards. Brian Rickey. Lisinda Rickman. Charlie Riddell. Matthew
Denise Ridley. Marlene Ridley. Chris Riedel. Wilfred Riepen. Nathan Rietveld. Leon Rietveld. Mike Rigarlsford. Dion Rigby. Nathan Riini. Wayne Riini. Lukas Riklin. Carol Riley. Elliot Riley. Stuart Ringer. Trev Rippon. Rosemary Rippon. Wayne Ritch
Ritchie. Jan Ritchie. George Ritchie. Kevin Ritter. Jeremy Roach. Tony Roache. Dianne Roadley. Jason Robb. Bradley Robb. Maureen Robb. Doug Robbie. Cameron Robbie. Ann Robbie. Lindsey Robbins. Scott Robbins. Kylie Robbins. Peter Robbins. Zach

Robert. Roy Robert. Arden Roberts. Gary Roberts. Kevin Roberts. Raymond Roberts. Andy Roberts. Karl Roberts. Sue Roberts. Cameron Roberts. Aaron Roberts. Mark Roberts. Linda Roberts. Clive Roberts. Geraint Roberts. Bruce Roberts. Anna
Drew Robertson. Andrew Robertson. Albie Robertson. Ross Robertson. Anne Robertson. James Robertson. Ian Robertson. Wayne Robertson. Maree Robertson. Debbie Robertson. Katrina Robertson. Julie Robertson. Paul Robertson. Craig
n. Nick Robertson. Julie & Ian Robertson. Sally Robertson. Struan Robertson. Brett Robertson. Daniel Robertson. Alex Robertson. Aaron Robertson. Anastasia Robin. Marie Robinson. Stefan Robinson. Cathy Robinson. Jamie Robinson. David
n. George Robinson. Paul Robinson. Fiona Robinson. Mike Robinson. Pam Robinson. Lee Robinson. Patricia Robinson. Tim Robinson. Peter Robinson. Anna Robinson. Lucy Robinson. Simon Robinson. Brent Robinson. Clayton Robinson. Aaron
n. Shaun Robinson. Quentin Robinson. Bill Robinson. Chris Robinson. Steven Robinson. Mark Robinson. Stanley Robinson. Nigel Robinson. Robert Roborgh. Paul Robottom. James Robson. Stephen Robson. Mike Robson. Colin Robson. Rick Robson.
son. Pete Robson. Pratt Rochelle. Steve Rod. Warren Rodger. Iain Rodger. Carl Rodgers. Tony Rodgers. Keith Rodgers. Wb Rodgers. Dmitry Rodionov. Gavin Rodley. James Rodwell. Luc Rodwell. Ben Rodwell. Katrina Roebuck. Sharn Roebuck. Cornelia
artin Roest. Steve Rogal. James Rogatski. Matt Rogers. Noel Rogers. Blair Rogers. Peter Rogers. Neil Rogers. Bim Rogers. Chris Rogers. Ramari Rogers. Alan Rogers. Preston Rogers-Brown. James Rogerson. Karen Rohloff. Jonathon Rohloff. Ben
. Andrew Roke. Blair Rolinson. Lynette Rolston. Mark Spencer Rolston. Levin Roman. Brian Romer. Pascal Romy. Troy Ronald. John Ronaldson. Brian Ronke. Mike Rooney. Rachel Rooney. David Rooney. Kevin Rooney. Gary Roper. Neale Rosanoski.
Rose. Darrell Rose. Caleb Rose. Vaughan Rose. David Rosie. Paul Rosier. Jolene Roskam. Shirley Rosman. Kelvin Ross. Adam Ross. Murray Ross. Matthew Ross. Peter David Ross. Greg Ross. Craig Ross. Duncan Ross. Stu Ross. Olivia Ross. Steve Ross.
ss. Cliff Ross. Carl Ross. Steve Rosser. Summer Rossiter. Dan Rotar. Graham Rotch. Yvonne Rothery. Chris Rotzel. Malcolm Rough. Sean Roughan. Patrick Roughan. Neil Roughton. Nigel Roulston. Daniel Round. Bill Roundhill. Russell Rountree. Tom
Mark Rouse. Michael Rouse. Randal Routledge. Rob Rowan. Aj Rowan. Julie Rowan. Scott Rowden. Wendy Rowe. Simon Rowe. Kim Rowe. Keith Rowe. Peter Rowe. John Rowe. David Rowell. Andrew Rowland. John Rowland. Allan Rowland. Tom
s. Bob Rowley. Joanne Rowley. Michael Rowntree. C.W. "Butch" Rowse. Colin Rowse. Clifford Brian Rowsell. Jeff Rowsell. Allan Rowsell. Geoffery Rowson. Jason Roxburgh. Penny Roy. Ashley Roy. Nathan Roy. Justin Roy. Colin Roycroft. Wade Roycroft.
oydhouse. Mark Royds. Peter Rubischon. John Rudd. Iris Ruddell. Ken Ruddenklau. Paul Ruddenklau. Steve Rudsdale. Suzanne Ruebe. Felix Rueppell. Anita Ruiterman. John Rumbal. Bryan Rusden. Tony Rush. Paul Rushbrooke. James Rusk. Marie
leb Russ. Cameron Russ. Nigel Russell. Graham Russell. Brendon Russell. Kelly Russell. Jafa Russell. Dene Russell. Steve Russell. Craig Russell. Jon Russell. Isaac Russell. Geoffrey Russell. Helen Russell. Bob Russell. Lionel Russell. Duncan Ruthe.
utherford. Bruce & Maxine Rutherford. Margaret Rutherford. Boyd Rutherford. Liam Rutherfurd. Chris Rutherfurd. Ian Ruthven. Amy Rutledge. Ann Rutter. Jeffry Ryall. Nigel Ryan. Fred Ryan. Matt Ryan. Benjamin Ryan. Suzy Ryan. Ivory Ryan. Kelly
aun Ryan. Maksim Ryazanov. Viktor Rybakov. Sam Ryburn. Danny Ryder. Nathan Ryder. Chris Ryder. Tom Ryder. Josh Ryder. Bob Rye. Dmitry Ryzkov. Margaret S. AgustãN Sá¡Nchez. John Sabin. Sara Sabin. Nadezhda Saburova. Julie Sadler. Andrew
Mihail Safonov. John Sager. Fabien Salles. Hamish Salmond. Malcolm Salmond. Kevin Salt. Jarad Salt. Angela Salter. Justin Salter. Forsyth Sam. Rinat Samigullin. Svetlana Samozhenova. Jeff Samuels. Eric Samuli. Benjamin Sanders. Helen Sanders.
anderson. Rex Sandford. Quentin Sands. Roydon Sands. Jason Sanford. Olga Sankova. David Sanson. Blair Sanson. Robert. Sanson. Matt Sanson. Kevin Sapsworth. Wayne & Brigitte Sargent. Julius Sargent. Ray Sarjeant. Ben Satherley. Yuki Sato. Dale
e Saunders. Carl Saunders. Peter Desmond Saunders. Alan Saunders. Stewart Saunders. David Saunders. Nick Saunders. Patrick Sauni. Roy Savage. Rebecca Savage. Steve Savage. Allister Saville. Marina Savshenko. Denis Sax. Dave Saxton. Michael
mothy Sayer. Rob Sayers. Grant Scaife. Craig Scaman. Maria Scammell. Mike Scanlan. Annette Scanlan. Peter Scarborough. Alistair Scarfe. Alastar Scarle. Roger Scarlett. B Schaay. Karl Schaefer. Suzanne Schaw. Marcelo Scheihing. Dennis C.
el. Andrew Schepetiuk. Olesya Schevchenko. Tom Schicker. Cameron Schinkel. Mike Schionning. Jacquie Schlaepfer-Wyn. Michael Schmidt. Guy Schmidt M.D.. Sigi Schmitt. Veronika Schneider. James Schoenne. Royston Scholes. Simon Schollum.
cholz. Anna Schouten. Brent Schouten. Dave Schrader. Peter C Schram. Barry Schroder. Alexander Schroeder. Tom Schubert. Frank Schuler. Sam Schumacher. Eric Schusser. Andrew Scobie. Roddy Scoles. Alan Scoltock. Ho Scorgie. Waren Scot. Blair
. Jack Scott. Wayne Scott. Patrick Scott. Brendon Scott. Shaun Scott. James Scott. Michael Scott. Margaret Scott. Kate Scott. Jim Scott. David Scott. Tom Scott. Chris Scott. Graeme Scott. Bill Scott. Christine Scott. Paul Scott. Cory Scott. Robert Scott.
Scott. Jason Scott. Gary Scott. Owen Scott. Josh Scott. Paddy Scott. Ian Scott. John Scott. Jeremy Scott. Joss Scott. James Scott-Harden. Blair Scoullar. Diane Scown. Ray Scrimgeour. Matthew Scrimshaw. Glen Scrivener. Jimmy Scully. Matt Scully.
urr. William (Bill) Seal. Brad Seaman. Susan Searancke. Steve Searle. Jason Searle. John Searle. Amber Searle. Colin Searle. Tony Sears. Craig Sears. Mark Sears. Matthew Seavill. Gary Sedcole. Dave Seelye. Dave Sekles. Bruce Selbie. Jack Selby. Katarina
ecil Sell. Mark Sellers. Richard Sellick. John Selwood. Evi Semling. Aaron Senior. Maria Sennikova. Alexey Sergeev. Cuzimin Serghei. Julia Sergiichuk. Peter Setz. Neil Seville. Ken Seville. Grant Sewell. Adam Sewell. John Sextie. Richard Seymour. Jason
r. Jane Seymour. Bodie Seymour. Robin Seymour. Grigoriy Shaad. Stephen Shailer. Wayne Shailer. Owen Shailer. Kirill Shalashow. Andrew Shallard. Chris Shallard. Mohammed Shameer. Jimmy Shand. Ian Shanks. Bradley Shanks. Ronie Shanks. Glen
Daniel Shannon. Nina Shapowalowa. Darren Sharland. Dave Sharland. Yana Sharobaeva. Neville Sharp. Chris Sharpe. Natalia Shatrova. Yuriy Shavkunov. Jen Shaw. William Shaw. Andrew Shaw. Trevor Shaw. Mark Shaw. Ben Shaw. Gerry Shaw. Kevin
arl Shaw. Cameron Shaw. Tim Shaw. Janet Shaw. Janne Shaw. Robbie Shaw. Simon Shaw. Sam Shaw. Kent Shaw. Durham Shaw. Danny Shaw. David Shaw. Andrew Shearer. Judith Shearer. Tim Shearer. Sam Shearer. Hannah Shearer. Blair Shearer. Ang
gahuia Sheedy. Ben Sheehan. Craig Sheehy. Bob Sheely. Martin Sheffield. Vladimir Shegay. Natalia Shekhovtsova. Gail Shellard. Miles Shelley. James Shelliker. Matt Shelton. Nikolai Shepelev. Robert Shephard. Karl Shepherd. Allistair Shepherd. Scott
d. Israel Sherratt. Andrew Sherriff. Sam Sherriff. Glenn Sherson. Arthur Glenn Sherson. John Shewan. Michael Shewan. Richard Sheward. Brian Shields. Samuel Shields. Andrey Shilin. Barry Shine. Sergei Shiparev. Gregory Shiraeff. Brenda Shirer.
irley. Peter Shirley. Alexey Shirokikh. Elena Shiryaeva. William Shoemaker. David Shoosmith. Tony Shores. Flick Short. Sam Short. Susan Shorten. Alexander Shutov. Gail Shuttleworth. Chris Sicely. Barry Sidon. Nikolai Sidorenko. Jeff Siems. Jamie
d. William Signal. Scott Signal. Ksenia Silaeva. Chris Silk. Nick Sim. Joanna Sim. Jeffrey Sim. Murray Sim. Philippa Sim. Rob Simcic. Kathy Simcox. Richard Sime. Ivica Simic. Greg Simmonds. Warrick Simmonds. Debbie Simmons. John Simmons.
Simmons. Matthew Simmons. Barbara Simmons. Heber Simmons, Jr. Deb Simon. Debby Simoneau. Kevin Simons. Paul Simons. Les Simons. Beau Simonsen. Mike Simonsen. Jonathon Simpson. Martin Simpson. Warwick Simpson. Rob Simpson.
impson. Jo-Anne Simpson. Brent Simpson. Maahi Simpson. Leny Simpson. Neil Simpson. Niall Simpson. Delwyn Simpson. Kerrian Simpson. Craig Simpson. Dean Simpson. Jim Simpson. Shane Simpson. Mike Sinai. Dave Sinclair. Mandy Sinclair.
Sinclair. Rob Sinclair. Peter Sinclair. Nick Sinclair. Joe Sinclair. Glen Sinclair. Ian Sinclair. Cameron Sinclair. Duncan Sinclair. Iain Sinclair-Black. Dan Sincock. Ray Singer. Craig Singer. Philip Singer. Andrew Singers. Mohan Singh. Harpal Singh-Sandhu.
h Singh-Thandi. Mantez Singh-Thandi. Adele Singleton. Tracy Sinton. Calum Sinton. Grant Sirl. Ian Sirrell. Kasey Sisson. George Skeet. Peter Skelton. Jan Skelton. Jess Skepper. Sam Skerman. Joe Skerman. Mike Skinner. Jarred Skinner. Derek Slatter.
attery. Trevor Slattery. Callum Slavin. Nicholas Sleeman. Roman Slinkin. Gemma Sliz. Stephan Sloane. Paul Sloane. Sheree & Matt Sloane. Lee Slomp. Vladislav Slovo. Matt Smail. Ed Smales. Kelvin Small. Lisa Small. Michael Small. Stephen Small.
Small. Pete Small. Sean Small. Brian Small. Brook Smallfield. Rex Smart. Ian Smart. Adrian Smart. Duncan Smillie. Scott Malcolm Noel Smillie. Jim Smith. Darryl Smith. Phil Smith. Eli Smith. Robbie Smith. Jake Smith. Iain Smith. Gillian Smith. Ben
Andrew Smith. Kelly Smith. Josh Smith. Philip Smith. Wayne Smith. Lynette Smith. Peter Smith. Graham Smith. Jamie Smith. Ashley Smith. Mark & Vanessa Smith. Paul Smith. David Smith. Tamati Smith. Lorraine Smith. Mitchell Smith. Blaine Smith.
Smith. Kerry Smith. Martyn Smith. Gavin Smith. Brad Smith. Arvid Smith. Neil Smith. Rose-Anne Smith. Alister Smith. Conrad Smith. Lloyd Smith. Sarah Smith. Frank Smith. Lachlan Smith. Charlie Smith. Trevor Smith. Maureen Smith. Murray
Alex Smith. John Smith. Glynn Smith. Bruce Smith. Warrick Smith. Aaron Smith. Craig Smith. Dave Smith. Amy Smith. Kevin Smith. Alan Smith. Robert Smith. Al Smith. Charles Smith. Rodney Smith. Ian Smith. James Smith. Warren Smith. Vanessa
Brent Smith. Michael Smith. Tess Smith. Hayden Smith. Marty Smith. Katrina Smith. Russell Smith. Karen Smith. Sharon Smith. Nigel Smith. Lachie Smith. Jo Anne Smith-Flueck. Ernest Smolej. Luke Smyth. Steve Smyth. Tracy Smyth. John Smythe.
Snadden. Talon Sneddon. Mark Snell. Don Snell. Simon Snelson. Barry Snook. Brian Snooks. Gary Snooks. Lynda Snoxell. Kevin So. Natalia Sokolova. Barbara Soler. Dwayne Solly. Kirk Solomon. Arild-Bjã¸Rn Solvang. Marilyn Somerville. Belinda
r. Ryan Songhurst. Grant Soper. Tony Soper. Martin Sorensen. Peter Sorensen. Rob Soulsby. Sid Soulsby. Neil Soundy. Andy Souter. Nathan South. Haydon South. David Southall. Mike Southam. Malcolm Southee. Gillian Southgate. Jack Sowerby.
n Sowman. Rob Sowman. Jaap Spaans. Thornton Spackman. Ron Spanton. Jude Sparks. Andrew Sparks. Frank Sparks. Petra Specht. Walter Speck. Jason Spedding. David Speedy. Kim Speedy. Ian Speirs. Gary Spelman. Ann Spence. Craig Spence. Cory
Heather Spence. Tim Spencer. Dylan Spencer. Howard Spener. Kirsten Spierling. Romon Spiers. Paul Spiers. Craig Spittle. Allan Spooner. Dave Spring. Thomas Ross [Spring] Springford. Marjan Sprock. Peter Spry. Royce Squire. Barrett Squire. Paul
Kerry Squire. Steffan St Clair-Newman. Chris Stacey. Dave Stackhouse. Bethney Stafford. Jae Staite. Brad Stalker. Ben Stallworthy. Robert Alistair Stammers. Ian Standen. Ian Stanford. Diana Staniland. Dave Stanley. Andrew Stanley. Andrew Stannett.
Staples. Lois & Bear Stapleton. Mike Stapp. Gavin Stark. James Stark. Mic Stavar. David Stead. Jens Stedeler. Peter Steedman. Paul Steegh. Peter Steele. Chris Steele. Tony Steele. Jan Stella. Andrej Stelmashok. James Stenton. Kylie Stenton. Michael
sov. El Stepanuk. Elena Stepanuyk. Malcolm Stephen. Maria Stephens. Ben Stephens. Sam Stephens. Nisan Stephens. Robyn Stephens. Kristy Stephens. Lorraine Stephenson. Annie Stephenson. Brent Stephenson. Sandy Steven. Brendon Stevens.
tevens. Toby Stevens. Adam Stevens. Linda Stevens. Gary Stevens. Shane Stevens. Michelle Stevens. Wayne Stevens. Mike Stevens. Michael Stevenson. Nick Stevenson. Paul Stevenson. Daniel Stevenson. Carole Stevenson. Simon Stevenson. Darren
on. Bruce Stevenson. Brent Stevenson. Aaron Stevenson. Margaret Stevenson. Todd Stevenson. Gary Steward. Kane Steward. Lynne Stewardson. Kelby Stewart. Megan Stewart. Stretch Stewart. Chris Stewart. Dale Stewart. Clayton Stewart. Doug
. David Stewart. Raymond Stewart. Lockie Stewart. William Stewart. Ferg Stewart. Sambo Stewart. Angus Stewart. Andrew Stewart. Susan Stewart. Warwick Stewart. Mark Stewart. Bradley Stewart. Paul Stewart. Sid Stewart. Kelvin Stewart. Sarah
. Robert Stewart. Ken Stewart. Fraser Stewart. Ashleigh Stewart. Kareena Stewart. Todd Stewart. Sue & Alan Stewart. Neil Stewart. Margaret Stewart. Dennis Stewart. Mark Stichbury. Wendy Stichbury. Wayne Stiff. Craig Still. Danny Still. Wendy
Rebecca Stirnemann. Sarah Stirrup. Shaun Stock. Simon Stock. Storm Stock. Shane Stocker. Sue Stoddart. Mark Stokes. Mark Stokman. Cameron Stokman. Simon Stokoe. Moira Stolp. Brian Stone. Rob Stone. William Stonecypher. Blair Stones. Greg
Kevin Storey. Bob Storey. Will Stovell. Lindsay Stowell. Debbie Stowell. Tony Stowers. Alexander Strachan. Hamish Strachan. Bruce Strahan. Paul Straight. Steve Strand. John Strang. Jill Strang. Mike Strang. Jonathon Strange. Kate Strange. Andre
d. Nathan Stratford. Jason Strawbridge. Diane Street. Richard Street. Greg Street. Maree Street. Artem Streltsov. Kira Streltsova. Bill Strickland. Bridgette Strid. John Stringer. Nathaniel Stringer. Johan Strom. Scott Strong. Lindsay Strong. Dave
man. Sean Struthers. Andrej Stselmashok. Raman Stsiatsenka. Gray Stuart. Richard Stuart. John Stuart. Nathan Stuart. Nairn Stuart. Kris Stubbington. Ben Stubbs. Tony Stubbs. John Stubbs. Peter Stubbs. Murray Studholme. Andrew Stupples. Jarrett
n. Hayden Sturgeon. Chris Sturgeon. Janeen Sturm. Debbie Sturme. Jessica Sturme. Andrew Sturt. Max Sturt. Peter Stutsbury. Andrew Styche. Lea Styles. Bryan Styles. June Styles. Vikki Subritzky. Mitchell Suckling. Nigel Sue. Ekaterina Suetina.
na Suhotskaja. Viktor Suhotski. Mihails Suhovs. Rob Suisted. Graham Sullivan. Paul Sullivan. Glenn Sullivan. Robert Patrick Sullivan. Carol Summerfield. Emma Summers. Tara Summers. Bob Summers. Todd Summers. James Sunde. Linda
and. Bulat Sungatullin. Bridgett Surridge. Nigel Surtees. Stephen Surtees. David Sutcliffe. Lyndon Sutherland. Mathew Sutherland. Mark Sutherland. Hamish Sutherland. Sue Sutherland. Wade Sutherland. Malcolm Sutherland. Pam Sutherland. Julie
and. Ross Sutherland. Konrad Sutter. Leah Sutton. Carl Sutton. Joanne Sutton. Hamish Sutton. Alan Sutton. Grant Sutton. Malcolm Sutton. Bruce Sutton. Ben Sutton-Davis. Jan Robert Sveen. Hakan Svensson. Roman Sviderskyy. Matt Swailes. Ken
on. Craig Swan. Leighton Swan. Rick (Or Richard Ancestral = Rijkent) Swan (Ancestral = Zwaan). Pieter Swanepoel. Bob Swann. Glenn Swanson. Jonathan Swanston. John Swarbrick. Richard Swarbrick. Levin Shop Peeps Swazi. Swazi Swazi. Mark
y. Leanne Sweeney. Phil Sweet. Allan Swenson. Hayden Swetman. Mark Swinburne. Shane Swinehart. Brynley Swinson. Nathan Swney. Chris Symes. James Symes. Geoff Symes. Blair Symon. Craig Symons. Leonard Symons. Sandra Symons. Natalia T.
Robyne Taafe. Cynthia Fregwelj Tabaco. Geoffrey Taggart. Quinten Tahuri. Joe Taipeti. Bryce Tait. Pip Tait. Hamiora Taite. Marilyn Tamakehu. Andrea Tamasese. Joel Tamblyn. Kristie Tammeryn. George Tan. Chrissie Tandy. Ian Tanner. Nathan Tapp.
Tapper. Michael Tapper. Chris Tapsell. Hans Tapsell. Barry Tarbotton. Andre Tarplett. Darryl Tatana. Ryan Tate. Alan Tate. Robyn Tate. John Tatham. Greg Tattersfield. Hemi Taurima. Alex Tawhara. Eileen Taylor. Tash Taylor. Irene Taylor. Wayne Taylor.
or. Jason Joseph Taylor. Shaun Taylor. Matthew Taylor. Dean Taylor. Sarah Taylor. Rachel Taylor. Jean Taylor. Robert Taylor. Hayden Taylor. Justin Taylor. James Taylor. Kevin Taylor. Chris Taylor. Burgen Taylor. Dave Taylor. Barry Taylor. Kirsty Taylor.
Taylor. Ben Taylor. Sharon Taylor. Warren Taylor. Rebekah Taylor. Rick Taylor. Clark Taylor. Doug Taylor. Andy Taylor. David Taylor. Josh Taylor. Ryan (Rocky) Northland Mobile Crushing Ltd Taylor. Tammy Taylor. Kylie Taylor. Richard Taylor. Rikki
Cornelius F Taylor. Murray Taylor. Scott Taylor. Blair Taylor. Lochie Taylor. Nik Taylor. Moar Taylor Ian. Avril Taylor-Crozier. Rachel Te Brake. Marcel Te Brake. Kelly Te Huia. Eddie Te Kahika. Raanie Te Purei. Duane Te Wheoro. Simon Teague. Kath
Katrina Teichelman. Taylor Teixeira. Colin Telfar. Wayne Telfar. Joyce Telfar. Pascal Tellenbach. Jasen Teller. Michael Temme. Bruce Temple. Wayne Temple. Brian Temple. Andrew Teplov. Neil Ternouth. Nick Terpstra. Sam Terrell. Latham Terry. Mary-
erry. Louise Terry. Bill Terry. Joeroa Terupe. Simon Tessier. Sergey Teterin. Janice Tetley-Jones. Wayne Tewnion. Chris Tews. Spring Thacker. Kellie Thain. David Thatcher. Chris Thelin. Andrew Theobald. Nigel Theobald. Lee-Ann Third. Holly Thomas.
mas. Nicky Thomas. Earle Thomas. Max Thomas. Simon Thomas. Hayden Thomas. Gavin Thomas. Brad Thomas. Riss Thomas. Martin Thomas. Noel Thomas. Trev Thomas. Roger Thomas. Daniel Thomas. Murray Thomas. Allan Thomas. Carole
s. Adrian Thomas. Dietrich Thomas. Ray Thomas. Janine Thomas. Robyn Thomas. Donald Thomas. Brian Thomas. Angela Thomasen. Steve Thomason. Cameron Thomassen. Karl Thompson. Louis Thompson. Kyle Thompson. Matthew Thompson.
Thompson. Glen Thompson. John Thompson. Nigel Thompson. Justin Thompson. Gary Thompson. Patrick Thompson. Jim Thompson. Josh Thompson. Gareth Thompson. Alan Thompson. Wayne Thompson. Ben Thompson. Dan Thompson. Grant
son. Kerry Thompson. Belinda Thompson. Jason Thompson. Liz Thompson. Jeremy Thompson. Mark Thompson. Sam Thompson. Joe Thompson. Steve Thompson. Chris Thompson. Kayne Thompson. Ian Thompson. Sara Thompson. Patrick Thoms.
omsen. Kayne Thomson. Nick Thomson. Henry Ian Thomson. Mitchell Thomson. Gary Thomson. Chris Thomson. Dave Thomson. Calvin Thomson. Shaun Thomson. Barry Thomson. Brian Thomson. Frank Thomson. Grenville Thomson. Marty
on. Stephen C Thomson. Ruth Thomson. Lincoln Thomson. Paul Thomson. Shane Thorburn. Petra Thorn. Lindsay Thorpe. Grant Thorpe. Sam Thorpe. Dave+Alison Threadgill. Garry Threnoworth. Julian Throp. Mike Thrupp. Albert Thundercliffe.
Thurlow. Glen Thurston. Philip Thurstun. Callum Thwaites. Allan Tibble. John Tickner. Rex & Heather-Anne Tidey. Trev Tidey. Thomas Tietjen. Josie Tietjen. Kit Till. Martin Tiller. Doug Timanus. Grant Timlin. Craig Timms. Dmitry Timofeev. Lane
ff Tindale. Tony Tipper. Nigel Tippet. Lisa Tippett. Morag Tippett. Jamie Tippins. Kent Tisdall. Nat Tisdall. Keryn Titchmarsh. Katherine Titmuss. Sandy Titterton. Jay Tkac. Tania Todd. Bevan Todd. Gregg Todd. Jason Todd. Simon Todhunter. Maurice
aul Toivonen. Jocelyn Tolley. Bill Tometich. Carl Tomich. Steve Tompkins. Hamish And Maree Tong. Lynn Tong. Lisa Tong. Ian Tonge. Gerry Tonkin. Geoff Topp. Annette Topping. Kenneth Torckler. Jenni Torrens. Nigel Torrens. Daniel Torresan. Andrew
ton. Lynette Torstonson. Natalia Toshina. Villi Tosi. Karen Toulmin. Lance Tovey. Jared Towler. Warren Town. Simon Townsend. Ben Towse. Glenn Trafford. Tim Trafford. Mark Trafford. Stewart Train. Rob Trainor. Emma Transom. Dayne Travers.
ayes. Glen Trayner. Margarette Treacher. Hayden Treagus. Chris Tregilgas. David Treloar. Grant Tremewan. Stephen Trethowen. Viktor Tretjakov. Heather Trevathan. Susie Trewavas. Deb Treweek. Basil Treymane. Cody Keri Trezise. Dennis Tribe. Vera
ova. Zoya Troitskaya. Wladimir Troitsky. Graeme Trotman. Pam Trotter. Ed Trotter. John Trotter. Ross Troughton. Richard Trousdale. Salmo Trout. James Truebridge. Scott Trusler. Dmitry Tsarev. Adrian Tseberg. Jimmy Tsokos. Zhenya Tsybizov. Joss
aron Tucker. Anne Tudor. Mike Tuffin. Matt Tuffin. Quentin Tuite. Bernard Tuite. Martin Tukiri. Ben Tumata. Keri Tuna. Stanley Tung. Sally Tunnage. Andrew Tunnicliffe. Wayne Turei. Jason Turkilsen. Jane Turnbull. Brad Turner. Southern Turner.
rner. Peter Stuart James Turner. Justin Turner. Tim Turner. Mark Turner. Matthew Turner. John-Paul Turner. Craig Turner. Gregory Turner. Brian Turner. Aaron Turner. Keith (Shrek) Turner. James Turner. Stuart Turner. John Turner. Russell Turner.
Turner. Gareth Turner. Greg Turner. Jack Turner. Don Turner. Marilyn Turney. Jacob Turnhout. Kevin Turnhout. Craig Turpie. Brett Tutty. Mark Tutty. Dave Twaddle. John Tweedale. George Tweedy. Simon Twigg. Chris Tyerman. Claire Tylee. Rowena
unga Tyler. Colin Tyler. Rae Udy. Michael Udy. Vince Udy. Danielle Unahi. Jo Uncles. Kevin Underhay. Thomas Underhill. Dean Underwood. Sharn Unka. Stewart Unmack. Allan Upson. Karen Upton. Michael Urban. Brian Uren. Jacqui Uridge. Dan
Tim Urquhart. Michelle Urquhart. John Paul Urwin. Jeremy Ussher. Simon Ussher. Craig Vaile. Vjacheslav Vakulenko. Simon Vale. Ngareta Valentine. Peter Valentine. Matthew Valentine. Guy Vallance. Micheal Vallance. Basil Vallender. Liz Van Beek.
-Lee Van Biljon. John Van Bysterveldt. Carl Van Dam. Lewis Van Dam. Andy Van De Vyver. Ivan Van De Water. Kerrie Van Den Anker. Monica Van Der Aa. Michael Van Der Aa. Maria Van Der Geest. Tony Van Der Heyde. Ben Van Der Hoeven. Paul Van
ag. Greg Van Der Lee. Susan Van Der Pol. Jonas Van Der Pol. Teunis Van Der Put. Nicholas Van Der Sande. Nick Van Der Spek. Josh Van Der Valk. Shan Van Dooren. John Van Duin. Paul Van Echten. Bianca Van Emmerik. Leo Van Es. Peter Van Essen.
Van Gaalen. Laurelle Van Gaalen. Richard Van Gaalen. Frits Van Geldorp. Harry Van Gog. Anthony Van Heuven. John Van Heuven. Martin Van Heuven. Paul Van Klink. Marieke Van Kooten. Gary Van Lankveld. John Van Leeuwen. Hans Van Lieshout.
Van Loon. Aaron Van Orden. Fritz Van Rooden. Anthony Van Son. Paul Van Veen. Herbert Van Veen. Elisabet Van Velsen. Wayne Van Vuuren. Roy Van Wely. Justin Vande Sandt. Marita Vandenberg. Arne Vanderburg. Serena Vanderslik. Mark Vanmeter.
annisselroy. Shannon Vanstone. Andrew Varcoe. Nikita Vasenin. Vladislav Vasilev. John Vassilimis. Jason Vaughan. Stuart Vaughan. Luke Vaughan. Jono Vaughan. Angela Vegar. Brian Veitch. Andrew Vena. Joan Vendrell Marce. Roger Venimore. Hendrik
Janis Vercoe. Marguerite Verheul. Joseph Verhey. Reuben Vermeer. Elaine Vermeer. Bill Vermy. Colin Vernon. Stu Verrall. Paul Verry. Marina Vershinina. Elena Veselkina. Trish Vessey. Graeme Vial. Janine Vicars. Jennifer Vick. Sheree Vickers. Hazel
. Reon Viles. Deb Vince. Leon Vincent. Joe Vincent. Chris Vine. Sergey Vinogradov. Edmond Virunurm. Irena Vishnevska. Justin Visser. Bryce Visser. Prazetski Vitali. Mark Vogel. Andrew Voigt. Joe Voigt. Paul Voigt. Christine Von Geldern. Dean Von
omby Vonelders. John Voorend. Valeriy Voroshko. Evgenija Voskobojnikova. Roger Voss. Betty Voss. Nathan Vowell. Randy Voyles. Sergey Vykhovanets. Kim Waddell. Linda Waddell. Ann Waddell. Sarah Wade. Carey Wade. Samantha Wadsworth.
Wadworth. Aaron Wafer. Rowan Waghorn. Roslyn Waho. Charlie Waide. Maria Wainohu. Duncan Wait. David Waite. Sharon Waite. Bryan Waitoa. Nathan Waitoa. Thomas Waka. Tim Wakefield. Aaron Wakeford. Tony Wakelin. Andy Wakelin. Paul
n. Jo Wakelin. Stuart Wakeman. Peter Wald. Aaron Walden. Ross Walden. Dirk Waldin. Josey Wales. Don Walker. David Walker. Kaye Walker. Derrell Walker. Shane Walker. Warren Walker. Reg Walker. Corey Walker. Hamish Walker. Pierce Walker. Kevin
. Jason Walker. Julie Walker. George Walker. Lance Walker. Paul Walker. Diane Walker. Katie Walker. Stuart Walker. Vanessa Walker. Richard Walker. Matt Walker. Dale Walker. Mike Walker. Adam Walker. Yvonne Walker. Javan Walker. Brian Walker.
e Walker. Rueben Walker. Leanne Walker-Berry. Jeff Walkington. Dave Walklin. Simon Wall. Mitch Wallace. Brayden Wallace. Justin Wallace. William Wallace. Melissa Wallace. Annie Wallace. Paul Wallace. Bill Wallace. Nicky Wallace. Mark Wallace.
Wallace. Nola Waller. Phil Wallington. John Wallis. Simon Wallis. Ethan Walmsley. Kent Walmsley. Valerie Walpot. Joseph Walsh. Wayne Walsh. Sean Walsh. Paul Walsh. Mark Walsh. Les And Debbie Walsh. Tony Walsh. Chris Walsh. Patrick Walsh.
Walter. Jody Koro Walters. Tony Walters. Darrin Walton. Anders Wanstrup. Simon Warbrick-Smith. Warwick Ward. Eileen Ward. Chris Ward. Shane Ward. Jamie Ward. Angela Ward. Phillip Ward. Lionel Ward. Lucy Ward. Ricky Ward. Christine Ward.
Ward. Charlie Ward. Bryan Ward. Bob Ward. Terry Ward. Lynette Ward. Jim Ward. Rob Ward. David Wards. Andrew Wards. Hayley Wards. Craig Wards. Matt Ware. Ben Warren. Jayson Warren. Mark Warren-Smith. Geoff Warriner. Lorraine Washington.
ason. Jonny Wassink. Les Wasson. Ken Watchorn. George Waters. John Waters. Mandy Waterson. John Waterworth. Andrew Waterworth. Kate Watkins. Jeanette Watkins. Renn Watkins. Alastair Watkins. Nathan Watson. Maxine Watson. Ken Watson.
Watson. Leea Watson. John Watson. George Watson. Kenny Watson. Damien Watson. Craig Watson. Darcy Watson. Chris Watson. Scott Watson. Robbie Watson. Paul Watson. Stephen Watson. Travis Watson. Robert Watson. Hayden Watson. Mark
. Grant Watson. Jarrod Watt. Craig Watters. Neil Watts. Amy Watts. Chris Watts. John Watts. Eddie Watts. David Watts. Kieran Watts. Carolyn Waugh. Mark Way. Scott Weatherall. Nic Weatherhead. Andrew Weatherley. Sean Weatherley. Gary Weaver.
Weaver. Nicola Weaver. Shannon Webb. Bryan Webb. Caleb Webb. Campbell Webb. Dale Webb. Roge Webb. Wayne Webb. Natasha Webb. Graham Webber. Anne Webber. Nick Webby. Lawton Weber. Alan Webster. Bjorn Wedeen. Lyndon Wedge. Merinda
ag. Chrissy Weeks. Jay Weeks. Darrell Wayne Wehi. Jake Weklch. Tare (Dolly) Welch. Murray Welch. Pam Welch-Cropp. Roger Weldon. Brian And Jacqui Wellington. Shanan Wellman. Tom Wells. Mandy Wells. Hamish Wells. Craig Wells. Tony Wells.
And Joy Wells. Scotty Wells. Sherryl Wells. Benn Wells. Mike Wellwood. Nicholas Wellwood. Brigid Wellwood. James Wellwood. Kieran Welsby. Jonathan Welsh. Isaac Welsh. Kate Welten. Paul Welten. Jonny Wemyss. Hartmut Wendt. Craig Wenn. Barry
Hayley Were. Pete Wesselink. Nick West. Andrew West. Allen West. Graham West. Todd West. Dean West. Stephen West. Chris West. Don West. Dave Westbury. Graham Patrick Westcott. David Westerby. Allan Westerman. Susan Westgarth. Carl
ate. Dave Westlake. Keith Weston. Stefan Weston. Danielle Whakarau. Phil Whakataka-Tutauha. Sonia Whakatihi. Richard Whale. Bobbie Whale. Basil Wharehoka. Tracey Wharehoka. James Wharerau. Emily Wharerimu. Gary Wharton. Rona
don. Stephen Wheeler. Chris Wheeler. Todd Wheeler. Kenneth Wheeler. Martyn Wheeler. Shane Whitaker. David Whitaker. Ben Whitcher. Rod Whitcombe. Chris White. Martin White. Richard White. Brendan White. Matt White. Ken White. Geoff
Jason White. David White. Warren White. Jon White. Gregory White. Margaret White. Nathan White. James White. Conor White. Tom White. Ross White. Don Whitehair. Jared Whitehead. Sam Whitehead. Rob Whitehead. Belinda Whitehead. Benn
head. Murray Whitehead. Sam James Whitehead. Peter Whitelaw. Owen Whiteman. Kent Whiteman. Pete Whiteman. Allan Whitfield. Jori Whitfield-Topp. Aaron Whitford. Rob Whitford. Andy Whitham. Ed Whiting. Gavin Whiting. Kerry Whiting.
Whitney. Howard Whitteker. John Whittle. Tierre Whiu. Cairo Tyson Whiunui. Greg Whyte. Sam Whyte. Colm Whyte. Nick Whyte. Sharyn Whyte. Lindsay James Whyte. Refael Whyte. David Whyte. Sam Wickett. Ieuan Wickham. Terehia Wickliffe.
cks. Dave Widdowson. Agnieszka Wieczorek. John & Carolyn Wielinga. Travis Wier. Sam Wiffen. Logan James Wiggins. Derek Wiggins. Craige Wiggins. Aaron Wigglesworth. Grant Wightman. Chris Wightman. Phillip Wilce. Richard Wilcock. Shaun
Ashley Wildbore. Alice Wilde. Chris Wildermoth. Maurice Wilke. Daniel Wilkes. Steve Wilkes. Kath Wilkie. James Wilkie. Yvonne Christine Wilkins. Richard Wilkins. Brad Wilkins. Scott Wilkinson. Bruce Wilkinson. Pip Wilkinson. Shane Wilkinson.
Wilkinson. Ryan Wilkinson. Cameron Wilks. Junior Wilks. Steve Wilks. Heather Wilks. Donna Willacy. Brunton Williams. Richard Willer. Jesse Willetts. Jacob Willetts. Maitland William. Wayne Williams. Roger Williams. Takirau Williams. Gene
ns. Graeme Williams. Jamie Williams. Mathew Williams. Marcelle Williams. Benjamin Grant Williams. George Williams. Jenni Williams. Ashley Williams. Brian Williams. Anita And Alan Williams. Clive Williams. Susan Williams. John Williams.
Williams. Dafydd Williams. Brigid Williams. Howard Williams. Mark Williams. Gary Williams. Gavin Williams. Owen Williams. Trevor Williams. Justin Williams. Selwyn (Kiwi) Williams. Glyn Williams. Virginia Williams. Tony Williams. Carl
ns. Peter Williams. Richard Williams. Ross Williams. Jeremy Williams. Kay Williamson. Mike Williamson. Craig Williamson. Steve Williamson. Jamie Williamson. Tim Williamson. Fyfe Williamson. Colin Willis. Pablo Willmann. Warren Willmot. Debby
ks. Thomas Willocks. Michael Willoughby. Ross Wills. Kyle Wills. Meredith Wills. Barrie Wills. Robyn Wills. R Wils. Sandy Wilson. Alana Wilson. Carol Wilson. Anne Wilson. Jim Wilson. Andrew Wilson. Jarred Wilson. Iain Wilson. Peter Wilson. Murray
. Gordon Wilson. Anna Wilson. Megan Wilson. Phil Wilson. Colin Wilson. Duncan Wilson. Chris Wilson. Gavin Wilson. Grant Wilson. Noel Wilson. Craig Wilson. Shane Wilson. Mark Wilson. Dave Wilson. Kevin Wilson. Jonty Wilson. Daniel Wilson.
Wilson. Vergne Wilson. Dean Wilson. Nicky Wilson. Steve Wilson. James Wilson. Harrison Wilson. Allan Wilson. Greg Wilson. Wayne Wilson. Steven Wilson. Michael Wilson. Lynda Wilson. James Wilson-Bishop. Ian Wilton. Cameron Wilton. Bianca
. Dean Wilton. Steve Wilton. John Wiltshire. Sam Wiltshire. Mike Winchester. Brian Windham. Craig Wing. Don Wingert. Paul Winspear. Dave Winterburn. Graham Winterburn. Melissa Winters. Murray Winters. Robbie Winterson. Tony Winyard.
Wirihana. Geoff Wise. Simon Wishnowsky. Ray Wisnewski. Dave Wistrand. Rodger Withell. Judith Withers. Michael Ian Withers. Dan Withers. Lindsay Withington. Mary Witsey. Fred Witton. John Wolff. Maurice Wolland. Sebastian Wollschlã¤Ger.
Wong. Alex Woo. Liselle Wood. Chris Wood. Mark Wood. Larry Wood. Kerry Wood. Sally Wood. Richard Wood. Dale Wood. Ryan Wood. John Wood. Angus Wood. Ineke Wood. Grant Wood. Keith Wood. Malcolm Wood. John Woodard. Chris Woodcock.
Woodcock. Andrew Woodford. Wayne Woodford. Pete Woodham. Stewart Woodhead. Steve Woodhead. Christine Woodhouse. Denys Woodroffe. Leeann Woods. Bruce Woods. Mike Woods. Peter Woods. Maria Woods. Oliver Woodward. Kevin
ward. Dennis Woodward. Peter Woodward. Dave Wooldridge. Susan Woolerton. John Woolf. Ian Woolford. Kent Woolford. Michael Woolley. Reuben Woolliams. Chris Woolmore. Carl Woolright. Karl Woolsey. Mike Woolsey. Seth Woolston. Trevor
on. Ross Woon. Matt Wooster. Maurice Wooster. James Worner. Alan Worsfold. Rajivini Worsley. John Worthington. Bruce Worthington. Biddy Worthington. Greg Wos. Bob Wotherspoon. David Wregglesworth. Steve Wright. John Wright. Regan
. Kane Wright. Stuart Wright. Reg Wright. Jonathan Wright. Jared Wright. Anna Wright. Jack Wright. Glen,Christine Wright. Lindsay Wright. Fiona Ann Wright. Peter Wright. Graham And Alex Wright. Kylie Wright. Josh Wright. Paul Wright. Jennifer
. Nigel Wright. Dylan Wright. Michael Wright. Todd Wright. Bill Wrigley. Steve Wyatt. Andrew Wylie. Mark Wylie. Heather Wylie. Trent Wylie. Brennan Wyllie. Don Wyllie. Mark Wynands. Colin Wynn. Dave Wynn. Rob Wynn. Tim Wynne-Lewis. Valery
ovets. Alexey Yakubovich. Rupert Yates. Aaron Yealands. Mike Yeates. Oscar Yee. Christy Yeo. Paul Yeoman. Tony Yetton. James Young. Matt Young. Dorothy Young. Brendan Young. Andrew Young. Quinton Young. John Young. Bev Young. Kerry Young.
in Young. Paul Young. Jolene Young. Quinn Youngman. Michael Youngman. Johny Yuile. Jason Yukich. Birch Yuknis. Sergey Yun. Yura Yura. Yuri Denisov Yuri Denisov. Mike Zachan. Mike Zacharuk. Sviatlana Zaichyk. Bob Zajakovski. John Zander.
mina Zandvoort. Julie Zapoli. Alexandr Zaporozhets. Olga Zarubina. Konstantin Zavyyalov. Jim Zepaltas. Svetlana Zhigaleva. Ilya Zhuzhelski. Sam Zieltjes. Peter Zimmerman. Roman Zinenko. Vladimir Zubritskii. Meek Zuiderwyk. Lisa Zwaans.
Zykov. Olga Zykova. Tatyana Zykova.

Acknowledgements

From the outset I imagined this book as a long-awaited platform to share my ideas, philosophies and, of course, photos from the field. Along the way the idea developed of adding line drawings that the reader would appreciate, plus some of my favourite images from selected photographers. Over the years there have been plenty of outdoor books peppered with illustrations. I believe the calibre of the illustrations crafted by Rob Coats and Lou McNutt in this book far surpass all others.

I've borrowed photos from some fantastic artists, including Rob Suisted, who in my opinion, is a national treasure. Whenever I'm in need of inspiration I sneak onto his website, www.naturespic.com and drift through the thousands of inspiring images there. Steve Lawrie made the painting of me on page 8. David Hamilton took great shots of hunting scenes as did Dave Abbott, my amazing producer, cameraman and confidant, with whom I have shared some gobsmacking — and totally terrifying — moments as we travel the world making our TV series *Adventures in Wild Places*. My dear friend Danny Ellis allowed me use of the image Lover's Cove on page 214. This image says so much. It is the south-east Alaska I have come to love, and Dan has captured it so incredibly well.

Thanks to John Bougen and Chrissie Fernyhough, high-country sheep farmers (and much more) from Castle Hill Station, for their support in getting this project off the ground. John would sit with me on the porch for hours schooling me in the how to's of book writing.

Justin Brown, who would always bring his laughter and enormous wit to our sessions, helped to pen this book. I am forever in his debt.

To the super team at Random House, thank you guys. Rebecca Lal edited the manuscript. Damn, she did a fine job! Stu Lipshaw pushed me all the way and Megan van Staden, along with Rob Coats of Coats Design, has done such a beautiful job in putting the whole thing together. Jennifer Balle, my publicist, is a woman of so much energy and so many ideas. Thanks to my wonderful publisher, Nicola Legat, who has been a rock, skilfully steering the project and guiding me through all the processes, from inception to the finished book.

Thank you to all the friends I have shared many a great adventure with. People who have taught me much about the wilderness and, indeed, about life, I am beholden to you.

Lastly, thank you to my family for putting up with a husband and father who is away so often. I cannot tell you the number of times I have been on a trip that the physical pain of longing to be home with you has sat me down on my arse. I simply could not do it without you. I love you all so dearly.

Aroha.